CASPIAN SEA

Nineveh

TIGRIS RIVER

MESOPOTAMIA

EUPHRATES RIVER

Babylon

Susa

Ur

I R A N

Persepolis

INDUS RIVER

PERSIAN GULF

INDIAN OCEAN

NT WORLD

LIFE IN THE ANCIENT WORLD

ILLUSTRATED BY STEELE SAVAGE

A CHANTICLEER PRESS EDITION

LIFE
IN THE
ANCIENT
WORLD

BART WINER

2057

RANDOM HOUSE

Planned and produced by Chanticleer Press, Inc., New York.

Acknowledgments

The publishers would like to thank Professor Morton Smith
of Columbia University for reading the chapters on Mesopotamia,
Palestine, Iran, Crete, Greece, and Rome, and also Mr. Eric Young
of the Metropolitan Museum of Art for reading the chapter on Egypt.

For their courtesy in furnishing photographs, and for their
patient answering of questions concerning the original art work,
the publishers are grateful to the following:
the Metropolitan Museum of Art; the University Museum
of the University of Pennsylvania;
the American Museum of Natural History; the Brooklyn Museum of
Art; the Oriental Institute of the University of Chicago; the Boston
Museum of Fine Arts; the Jewish Museum of New York;
the British Museum, and the Louvre.

2057

Library of Congress Catalog Card Number: 61—7876
Manufactured in the United States of America

Contents

DATES B.C.	MESOPOTAMIA	EGYPT	PALESTINE
5000	Earliest known farming village (4750) Sumerians develop cities (3500–3000)	Kingdoms of Upper and Lower Egypt formed	
3000	Cuneiform writing Death pits of Ur (2450) Sargon, a Semite, rules Sumer (2350) Sumerians rule again (2060–1955)	Hieroglyphic writing Old Kingdom, 2700–2200, the Pyramid Age, with capital at Memphis Middle Kingdom (2050–1800): capital at Thebes	
2000	Old Babylonian Kingdom (1890–1595) Hammurabi issues law code (1726)	Hyksos, invaders from east, bring horse and chariot, and rule (1700–1570)	Abraham, father of Hebrews, leaves Ur for Canaan At Sinai Canaanites use alphabetic writing
1500	Kassites on horseback invade and rule Babylonia for 500 years Assyrians in north rise as a power	Egyptians drive out Hyksos and establish New Kingdom or Empire (1570–1100) Hatshepsut (1486–1469) sets up obelisks Thutmose III, "Napoleon of Egypt" (died 1436) Akhnaton (1380–1362) worships "one god" Tutankhamun buried (1352) Ramses II, builder of monuments (1301–1234)	Israelite exodus from Egypt into Cana (sometime between 1385 and 1250)
1200	Beginning of Assyrian empire (1100)	Sea Peoples attack at mouth of Nile Priests rule Libyans rule (950–710)	First real alphabet is developed Philistines settle on coast Age of "Judges", Israelite heroes Saul chosen king (1025) Solomon (971–931) builds Temple
900	Height of Assyrian power (750) Ashurbanipal (668–663), warrior king Medes and Chaldeans take Nineveh (612) New Babylonian empire (612–539), ruled by Chaldeans Nebuchadrezzar II (605–562) builds Hanging Gardens Cyrus of Persia takes Babylon (539); ends captivity of Israelites Part of Persian empire (539–331)	Ethiopians rule (710–663) Pharaohs from Saïs revive Egyptian rule (663–525) Persians conquer and rule (525–332)	Kingdoms of Israel and Judah Sennacherib of Assyria invades Jud Jerusalem falls and inhabitants sent captivity at Babylon (587)
500	Alexander takes Babylon (331) Alexander dies at Babylon (323) Seleucus, Alexander's general, founds ruling house (312–63)	Alexander conquers (332) Ptolemy, Alexander's general, founds ruling house (323–30)	Temple rebuilt Ruled by Ptolemies (until 198)
300			Ruled by Seleucids Judas Maccabeus frees Jerusalem (Hebrew kingdom (143–63)
100	Ruled by Parthia (63)	Cleopatra VII, last Ptolemaic ruler (51–30) Roman province (30)	Roman occupation (63) Birth of Christ (5)

NCIENT   WORLD

Dates are approximate. Unless otherwise
indicated, only a king's reigning dates are given.

RAN	CRETE AND GREECE	ROME
miths working copper bbably earliest civilization at Susa 2700) gdom of Elam (from 2350)	Minoan civilization begins on Crete (2800) Palace (called House of Double Ax) built at Knossos	
	Greek-speaking people invade land that became Greece Mycenaean civilization on Greek coast	
	House of Double Ax falls; Cretan power ends (1450) Mycenaean cities rule northern Mediterranean	
mites carry off stone with Hammurabi's laws written on it	Troy besieged and burned by Greeks Dorians invade Greece and Crete	
do-Europeans or Iranians arrive des in north; Persians in southwest rus the Great (559–530) founds Persian mpire rius the Great (521–486)	Greeks adapt Phoenician alphabet First Olympic Games held (776) First coins minted (in Asiatic Greece)	Etruscans in Italy Rome founded (753) Greeks found colonies in Italy and Sicily Rome expels kings and becomes republic (510)

laces of Persepolis begun
 	
rxes (486–465) invades Europe by boat
ridge
 	
exander defeats Darius III at
Gaugamela (331)
 	
led by Seleucids (until 250)
	Greeks defeat Persians at Marathon (490) and
	   Salamis (480)
	Great age of tragic drama (484–406)
	
	Age of Pericles, golden age of Athens (460–429)
	Peloponnesian War between Athens and
	   Sparta (431–404)
	
	Philip of Macedon wins Greece (338)
	Alexander the Great rules Greece (336) and
	   sets out to conquer world
		Twelve Tables, the Roman law code,
		   published (451–450)
		Gauls invade Rome (390)
		
		First aqueduct and Appian Way built (312)

thridates II (124–88) rules Parthian mpire	Taken by Rome (146)	Punic Wars (264–146) Hannibal crosses Alps with elephants (218) Carthage destroyed (146)

		Last years of republic (70–43), the Age of Cicero
		Caesar conquers Gaul (58–51)
		Caesar assassinated (44); Mark Antony rules
		   eastern Roman world (42); Antony and
		   Cleopatra defeated at Actium (31)

Piecing Together the Past

NOT TOO LONG AGO, among many bricks dug out of the ruins of an ancient city, one brick told a story. On it were two sets of animal footprints. After being examined, they turned out to be the footprints of a cat and a dog. Four thousand years ago, in that city, a dog chased a cat across some wet bricks drying in the sun. No written records told us anything about the city's inhabitants, but the brick told us that they kept pet dogs and cats.

From such scraps of evidence, we piece together the story of how people once lived. In a royal grave, for example, four harps or lyres were found buried. Musicians had therefore played—and perhaps sung—for their king and queen. On tomb walls we see paintings of men pressing out grapes for wine and baking loaves of bread. We can almost taste the grape juice and smell the bread baking. On other walls are scenes of women spinning linen thread or dancing in delight. We have found small, lifelike wooden models of girls grinding grain or milking cattle. Sometimes, a picture on a wall of thousands of years ago shows a curious invention still used today. For example, on the wall of an ancient palace, an artist had shown men paddling a round-bottomed boat. Nearby, shipwrights still turn out the same design for river travel. From the modern boat we learn the probable size of the ancient one and how much cargo it carried.

A bouquet of withered flowers and a dancing doll, a copper-headed battle-ax and an iron-tipped plowshare, a make-up kit and a piece of cloth

8

stuck inside a silver jar—all help us to see the ancient peoples as flesh-and-blood creatures. They tell us of gardens and games, of battles and farms, of cosmetics and clothes.

Besides these relics, the ancient peoples have left us their actual words. An Egyptian king tells the story of his war campaigns in carvings on a temple wall. A Mesopotamian king stamps his deeds on bricks or writes them on clay tablets. From them we learn that he planted a magnificent garden—or dyed the mountains red with the blood of his enemies. On an old law code, engraved on a stone shaft, we read that housebreaking and kidnaping were sometimes punished by death, that married women could own property, that a surgeon whose patient died might have his hand cut off. These laws give us a glimpse of ancient customs.

From inscriptions on stones, papyrus paper, and clay tablets, we discover ancient poems, maps of estates, and even problems in arithmetic. A businessman signs a contract with a farmer, leasing his field for so many bushels of grain. Down the centuries, the field turns to desert dust, but the clay contract endures. An Egyptian boy learning his lessons throws away his paper. Thousands of years later, it is found and, with it, several others like it. All begin with the same story—the lesson the teacher assigned. And all are full of mistakes and have the teacher's corrections in the margins.

Not all the ancient records are trustworthy. Like modern laws, some ancient laws were merely "on the books" but weren't enforced. In their inscriptions, kings exaggerated, even lied about, their achievements. Where we have no contemporary documents, we often have traditions that have been handed down from father to son for generations. Eventually these traditions are written down. A Greek astronomer and geographer in Egypt in the second century, for example, located the source of the Nile in the "mountains of the moon." In the twentieth century, explorers discovered that the river did indeed rise from snow-clad mountains on the equator.

The early writers of history freely mixed fact with fiction. The Greek historian Herodotus, who visited Babylon in the fifth century B.C., described climbing to the top of what the Bible calls the Tower of Babel. From the ruins of other such towers, we can verify much of what he relates. However, in other parts of his "history" he tells stories of miraculous births and of gods descending to earth. Five hundred or so years later, the Roman scholar Pliny describes, fairly accurately, how papyrus paper was made. But he also gives detailed descriptions of plants and beasts that existed nowhere on earth.

Today, we try to separate fact from fiction in the ancient histories, traditions, and inscriptions. We examine the words against relics that can be measured, placed under a microscope, and otherwise examined. New finds constantly come to light that corroborate, or prove false, long-held beliefs. Finally, we fill in the picture of ancient man as he looked and lived in his everyday life.

MESOPOTAMIA
The Cradle of Civilization

"And they said ... let us build us a city and a tower, whose top may reach unto heaven."

So begins the Bible's story of the Tower of Babel. This tower wasn't just a legend. Once upon a time the temple-tower of Babylon, jutted 300 feet into the air. It was as tall as a modern twenty-two-story building. Babylon was then the largest and mightiest city in the world. A caravan of donkeys from Syria could sight the tower from ten miles away. It glittered in the bright sun like a lighthouse across a sea of yellowbrown sand. To the caravan merchant and his drivers, the heat waves dancing in the air were demons who could harm them. Even so, they relaxed for the first time since their journey from the west had begun. They no longer had to fear desert bandits and the lions that lurked in thickets. Soon they could refill their empty goatskins with water. They would be in Babylon, the scorching sun would set, and a new day would begin. For these people, the new day began at sunset, with the pleasant coolness of evening.

Nearing Babylon, they reached fields of ripe barley and wheat that stretched out for miles. They traveled alongside an irrigation canal where farmers were piling up the harvested grain, covering each stack with a reed mat for protection. The caravan passed a grove of tall date palms, then fruit orchards growing in the shade of the palms.

The caravan trudged through the suburbs of Babylon, past cowsheds and

Babylon's Ishtar Gate. Within, a walled road led past the Hanging Gardens to the "Tower of Babel."

sheepfolds, barns and granaries and whitewashed mud-brick houses. Before them loomed the stout brick walls of Babylon—ninety feet tall where the towers rose at regular spaces on the top. The king's archers, on guard in these towers, kept their bows ready for action. The walls were so thick that two chariots could pass each other on the road that ran on top. Below the wall, a deep moat had been dug from the Euphrates River. It ran completely around the city walls.

The caravan crossed a floating bridge of rafts over the moat and entered a double building that served as the gateway into the city. Here soldiers stood guard at the bronze door that clanged shut at night. Past the gateway, the caravan soon reached a broad muddy river spanned by a wooden bridge resting on stone piers. It was one of the earliest permanent bridges in the world. On the other side of the bridge, longshoremen unloaded cargoes of cedar and copper from the boats tied to the wharves. Some of the boats were huge wooden rafts buoyed up with inflated goatskins tied on the bottom of the planks. Two men, with bags of grain stacked between them, rowed to shore in a round wickerwork boat shaped like a basket.

The road into the city was flanked by walls. Within the white walls on the left side of the road was the temple-tower that had guided the caravan home. It had seven terraces, each painted a different color. To the right stood the temple of Marduk, the patron god of Babylon, its walls covered with blue enameled bricks with rows of golden bulls and dragons carved on them. Passing between tower and temple walls, the caravan turned into a stone-paved highway. Down this road the priests and priestesses carried the gilded and jeweled statue of Marduk during the New Year celebrations. Then Babylonians lined the road, and sang hymns to the music of drum and flute, tambourine and harp.

At the end of the road, the caravan merchant could see the walled palace where the king and his court lived. Alongside towered a mountain of plants that the king had built for his queen, who had been lonesome for the mountains of her homeland. A series of stone terraces had been covered with soil, then planted with trees, shrubs, and flowers. The trees and shrubs spread their leaves and trailed their vines from terrace to terrace. Flowers from the top terraces raised their blooms over the lower terraces. Branches of trees on the lowest terrace hung over the palace walls. The Greeks would later call these Hanging Gardens of Babylon one of the Seven Wonders of the World.

The caravan turned right through a gateway leading to a large group of buildings the fronts of which were regularly indented like the teeth of a saw. These were the city's market buildings. The caravans passed the stalls where potters molded clay bowls on a wheel. Further on, coppersmiths were casting statuettes. Down an alley, basketmakers were weaving baskets and reed coffins. Across the alley, weavers operated their looms, turning out fine woolen cloth. Finally, the caravan stopped, and the drivers unloaded the bales of Syrian cloth and the jars of Syrian wine that were slung over the donkeys' backs. The merchant would sell his products, pay his drivers, and go home.

This Babylon the Great of over 2500 years ago is a group of dusty mounds today.

But before its walls crumbled and dust blew over it, it had had a long history. In the time of our caravan it was the capital of the new Babylonian empire. Earlier, the Assyrians from the northern plain had ruled it for five hundred years. Before then, it had been the capital of the old Babylonian empire. In its earliest period, it had been an unimportant village on the frontier of the first civilized state. Ten thousand years ago, it had been a spit of land on the sea.

A gufa, a craft in use since ancient times, moves down the Tigris today. The wooden framework was once covered with animal hides; now pitch is used. The large ones, over seven feet deep, carry heavy cargoes.

12

MESOPOTAMIA—LAND BETWEEN THE RIVERS

Babylon had been built on the banks of the Euphrates River. The Euphrates and the Tigris rivers rush down from the mountains of Armenia. They carry a load of silt that piles up in the Persian Gulf, where the rivers run out to sea. In ancient times, they created all the land from Babylon to the southern cities of Eridu, Ur, and Lagash. These first cities in the world were once on the sea. Today, their ruins lie far inland, for the river goes on creating land at the rate of seventy-two feet a year, or a mile and a half a century.

The land between the rivers has been called Mesopotamia, from Greek words meaning "between rivers." A great plain stretched over about 350 miles from Ashur in the north to the mouth of the rivers. On the east and the north lay mountains, to the south the sea, to the west a vast desert. Roughly, modern Iraq covers ancient Mesopotamia.

To this great plain, probably from the northeastern mountains, came the Sumerians. They conquered the villagers farming the land and living in reed huts. They dug canals to make the soil more fertile. Out of clay they made bricks and with them built permanent houses. And from drawing pictures they discovered the art of writing. In about 3000 B.C. history begins. The villages of huts had turned into cities with industry and government and man had become civilized. In Mesopotamia, the Sumerians created the earliest civilization in the world. And that's why Mesopotamia has been called the cradle of civilization.

FAMILY LIFE

From earliest times, there were slaves in Mesopotamia. But a man didn't look down on his slave as an inferior person. Everyone ran the risk of becoming a slave. Prisoners captured in battle became slaves. So today's master could become tomorrow's slave. A father could sell his wife and children into slavery to pay off a debt. Or he could rent them out as slaves for a period of years. If an adopted son didn't like his new home he could say to his father, "You're not my father," and would no longer be a member of the family. The only trouble

Common on the ancient Tigris and Euphrates were the gufa and the kelek, a wooden or reed raft buoyed up with inflated animal skins.

with this, however, was that his former foster father could then sell him as a slave. A father could also disinherit one of his own sons merely by saying, "You're not my son."

In early times, a slave was branded or tattooed. Later, he wore a clay tag around his neck or had his head shaved. Though a slave was the master's personal property like a cow, he had certain legal rights. He could own property, trade in business, and save up enough money to buy back his freedom. If a slave married a free woman, their children were free from birth. And if a free man married a slave woman, she and their children became free when he died. Of course, he could also grant them freedom during his lifetime.

The father was head of the house. Though he had signed a marriage contract, he could divorce his wife simply by saying, "You're not my wife." He arranged his sons' futures and his daughters' marriages. If he was devout, he gave his daughters to the temple as priestesses. Brides always brought their husbands a dowry, and the groom gave his betrothed wedding gifts. In Assyrian times, a man became engaged by giving his future bride gifts, then pouring perfumed oil over her head. He signed the marriage contract with his future father-in-law, spoke the words "She is my wife" before witnesses, placed a veil on her head, and was married for life. A man could take a second wife, but she was usually a slave who also served his first wife.

Only a free woman could wear the veil. If a slave was caught wearing a veil, she might have her ears cut off. The old Moslem custom of veiling women thus came from the ancient way of distinguishing a free woman. A Mesopotamian woman didn't always cover her face with the veil as Moslem women did. She sometimes wore it on the top of her head or let it fall in folds beside her face.

A 5000-year-old clay "teapot" from a town near Ur. The baked clay is almost indestructible.

Women didn't always stay at home. They bought and sold land and slaves, ran businesses, and kept taverns. One reason for divorce was the wife's gadding about at business when her husband thought she ought to be home looking after the household. Priestesses didn't merely perform their temple duties. They, too, could carry on businesses. Like other women, they married and had children.

Families were large, for the father wanted as many workers as he could get. Also, children had to support their aged parents. For these reasons, too, Mesopotamians were fond of adopting children. A craftsman adopted a son and taught him his trade. A priestess adopted a girl and taught her a suitable profession or pledged her to the temple.

In one period of history, poor men actually adopted rich men. The state had passed a law prohibiting a man from selling his land. He could only leave it to his sons, who inherited it when he died. To get around this law, a man who wanted to sell his small plot adopted the man who wanted to buy it. According to the laws of adoption, the father and adopted son exchanged presents. So the poor father gave his rich son a token gift, and in return the "son" would pay him what the land was really worth. A rich man had himself adopted by as many as a hundred poor "fathers." When they died, all their land went to him.

HOUSES OF CLAY

Houses in the city were made of mud brick. Mesopotamia has little building stone, but plenty of clay. The brickmaker piled his clay on a reed mat, poured water on it, scattered straw or dung on top, then trod the mixture underfoot. He poured the mixture into rectangular wooden molds open at top and bottom.

Sumerian temple compound, where religion was mixed with business. In the foreground is a potter's shop; to the right are the steps leading up to a shrine in the temple-tower or "ziggurat."

Typical Sumerian, shaven and shorn, with hands clasped and wearing the usual flounced skirt.

Some molds made two bricks at one time. The top of the brick was dried in the sun, then the mold was turned over so the bottom dried. The hotter the sun, the faster the bricks could be made. Since sun-dried mud brick absorbs water, swells, and crumbles, bricks were also baked in kilns or ovens. Baked bricks were used to line palace and temple roads and to strengthen the outside of important buildings like the temple, the palace, and the city walls. They were so well made that modern Iraqis dug up these 2500-year-old bricks and used them to repair their houses.

In building a house, a man first built up a mound of mud and let it dry. This raised the foundation of his house and protected it from flood and damp earth. Then he cemented his bricks with a mortar made of liquid clay. Palm trunks and leaves were laid over the brick walls for a roof, then plastered with mud. If wind or rainstorms washed off the mud, the house owner repaired the leaky roof with more mud. This happened so often that some men kept a heavy roller on the roof, ready to flatten out the new-laid mud.

Rich men, the priests, and the king cemented their brick buildings with bitumen, or pitch. The bitumen industry near Hit is said to be the oldest continuously operated industry in the world.

When the walls of his house crumbled, a man repaired them until it was cheaper to knock the walls down and build a new house. He leveled off the rubble, throwing the extra bricks into the street, and built on top of this new foundation. As a result, the cities rose higher and higher with the passing years. Old bricks, clam shells, broken pots, and all garbage were thrown into the streets. So the street level rose, too. Houses and streets became a jumble of different levels. When they were deserted, and sand covered them, they became the mounds we recognize today as the sites of ancient cities.

The average house was a group of rooms built around a courtyard. One small door led to the street, and there were no windows on the outside walls. This arrangement kept out the stench of the streets and the larger insects and rodents. Light and air came from the courtyard and from air vents sometimes made through the outer walls. The floors were usually bare earth, though the better houses had brick or flagstone paving. The roof doubled as a terrace. The family climbed up a courtyard or inside stairway and slept there in summer.

Houses of the rich and the palaces were like clusters of the poorer houses. They had several courtyards with many rooms branching off and were three and four stories high. They even had bathrooms and toilets that flushed out onto the street through a sewer system of brick drainpipes.

None of the houses had much furniture. The poor slept on reed mats or wool rugs, while the rich slept in a high bed raised at the head. The poor sat on cushions or palm-wood stools, while the rich had cane-backed armchairs. At night, the house was lit by oil lamps burning crude oil or sesame oil. Early lamps looked like saucers with a spout out of which the wick came. Later ones were shaped like a shoe. Houses of the poor had no separate kitchen. A clay stove or a stone or metal brazier served to cook the food and helped heat the house in winter.

BREAD, DATES, AND BEER

At dinnertime, the poor family squatted on cushions on the floor. The food was piled into a large bowl and set on a small stand. Everyone stuck his fingers

Using reed "straws," three drinkers share a pot of beer. In early Mesopotamia almost half of the cereal crop went into beermaking.

16

into the bowl and ate. The rich man, however, dined at a high table, sitting on an armchair or reclining on a couch.

Because they ate with their fingers, Mesopotamians washed their hands before dining. But cleanliness wasn't one of their virtues. Bathing was mainly a religious rite, and they washed when they went to pray.

Most of the people lived on a vegetarian diet. Cereals were roasted or cooked into a mush and eaten with milk and honey. The shepherd usually ate goat's milk and dates, just as he does today in Iraq. Those who lived near the rivers caught fish, which they ate raw, dried, or salted. Prosperous farmers who bred cattle and raised sheep dined on roasted or boiled beef and mutton. Game birds were a favorite delicacy, and in late times chickens were cooped in the yards. Barley bread and onions was the poor man's dinner. Cakes were made from bread dough mixed with dates and honey. Locusts, which devoured the grain crops, were caught, spitted on skewers, roasted, and eaten.

Every house had its clay pot filled with drinking water. It stood on a stand with a strainer underneath to filter out weeds and pebbles. Goat's and mare's milk was a food rather than a drink. But *the* drink of Mesopotamia was beer. In later times, the Greeks used to insult the Mesopotamians by calling them beer drinkers. The Greeks, of course, drank wine. Even the gods, the Mesopotamians thought, liked beer. They believed that there were cripples because the gods were drunk from beer when they made men.

Women not only brewed beer from barley for their menfolk. They also sold it outside the home and opened the first "beer parlors." If a man could prove that a woman tavernkeeper sold watered beer, she would be tossed into the river. If she let outlaws congregate in her tavern and didn't have them arrested, she could be killed. The tavern was about the only place where a priestess wasn't allowed to be seen. She could be killed if caught going inside.

Life in Mesopotamia was hard. The religion of the land recognized this and set aside certain days in the month as unlucky—days when it was best to do nothing. Since these days occurred every seven days, the people had a day of rest once a week. We inherited this tradition, and the unlucky day became our sabbath or Sunday.

Ancient penthouses. The housewife picks up an oil lamp made from a seashell and will climb to the roof to sleep in the cool night air. During the day, the windowless outside walls and the narrow streets keep out the sun.

LIFE ON THE FARM

The houses that huddled together in the city belonged to merchants, laborers, and craftsmen or were rented by them by the year. Outside the city gates and along the canals and rivers were the farmhouses with their cattle stalls and sheepfolds, poultry yards and vegetable gardens. Beyond the plowed fields lay the desert. But even here plants grew after the spring rains. Cattle grazed on these plants, and shepherds and farmers plucked them to use as fuel for their fires.

Poor farmers hoed, planted, and watered small plots of land. Rich farmers owned vast acres and employed many workers. Often men went into partnership and rented fields. These large farms used what was probably the world's earliest farm machine—a combination plow and seeder.

Wheat, sesame, and flax were grown, but the main crop was barley. Barley was used as a form of money. A man borrowed so many bushels of barley and paid back the loan with interest in the form of extra bushels of barley. The barley could be exchanged for the goods he wanted. In later times, silver was used as a standard for pricing articles of trade. The city merchants used weights called shekels and minas in trading. One mina was worth sixty shekels. Let us say a date picker wanted to sell two bushels of dates. A merchant would offer him one shekel for his dates. Now, the date picker didn't pocket the shekel and go home. He took what one shekel was worth in barley. Eventually, however, men bought and sold with the weights themselves. They were using money.

Near the canals, farmers kept vegetable gardens. Over sixty varieties of vegetables were grown—onions, leeks, garlic, cucumbers, radishes, beets, beans, lettuce, squash, and flavoring herbs. Fruit trees shaded the vegetable gardens—lemon, quince, pomegranate, fig, apricot, and mulberry. And the fruit trees grew in the shade of the date palms. The date palm was almost as important a crop as barley. Farmers sang a song that praised the date palm because it had 360 uses. The trunk was fashioned into boats, doors, and wagons. The ribs of the tree made beds and chairs. The leaves were bound into brooms to sweep the dust away. The fibers were woven into baskets, ropes, and fish-nets. The young shoots at the top of the tree made a tasty salad, while the date itself was a nourishing food. The date could be made into honey, vinegar, and wine. The date pits were dried and burned like charcoal, or ground and mixed with fodder to feed the cattle.

RICHES FROM WATER

Little rain falls on Mesopotamia. The temperature rises to 120 degrees in the shade in summer. The hot sun burns the soil and turns it to dust—unless there is water. But there was water. The god of water is said to have dug the first canal, and every governor of a city and every king in Mesopotamia followed the god's example. With canals, the farmers could reap two or three harvests a year. They could support their government and king by paying taxes out of their crops. They could offer part of their grain and livestock to the gods in thanks for the gods' blessing. With these riches, the kings built palaces and the priests built temples. They fed men who didn't grow their own food—brickmakers, boat builders, jewelers, sculptors, toolmakers, weavers. Merchants took the products the people couldn't use and traveled to distant lands. Here they exchanged them

Servants carrying fruit, fowl (above), and locusts on skewers, as well as pomegranates and hares.

18

for things not found in the land between the rivers—gold and silver, ivory and copper, lead and marble, cedar and spices.

Mesopotamia's network of canals was like the arteries and veins in the human body—it fed the people and kept them alive. The rivers were the highways of Mesopotamia, the canals the roads. Boats and barges sailed up and down the waters, while caravans and wagons traveled along the banks.

The main canals led water from the Euphrates into the Tigris and away from both rivers. In spring, when the rivers rose over their banks, the canals carried off the excess water and helped prevent floods. These canals were huge engineering projects. One of the largest was over 400 feet wide and over 200 miles long. Canal gates regulated the water. For if too much water flowed through, the embankments would be washed away and the fields flooded. If too little water flowed, weeds and silt would choke up the canals and the precious water wouldn't reach the fields.

Each farmer had to keep his section of the dikes and ditches in repair. If he caused the water to flood a neighbor's field, he had to pay his neighbor for the crops destroyed. As long as there was peace, there was prosperity, for men could operate the canals. When war broke out and men had to fight, the canals were neglected. Then there was famine. Today, Iraq still suffers because the canals were destroyed. Once fertile land has become sterile sand.

The farms were surrounded by irrigation ditches leading from the canals. To water his crop, a farmer knocked a hole in the mud bank of the ditch with

An Assyrian king dining in his palace garden at Nineveh in the 7th century B.C. He reclines on a couch, his queen sits in a chair nearby, and servants with whisks keep off the flies.

19

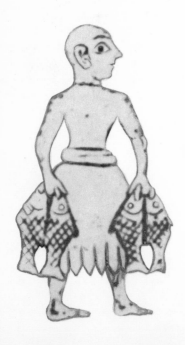

his hoe. When his field was flooded, he plugged up the hole. To water his fruit trees and vegetable garden, he used a *shaduf*. A stick with a bucket on one end and a weight of clay on the other was balanced like a seesaw. The farmer dipped the bucket into the water, let go, and the counterweight automatically pulled it up. He then emptied the bucket of water into a trough leading to his trees and vegetables. The Hanging Gardens of Babylon were probably watered by a chain of these shadufs on each terrace. These worked like an automatic bucket brigade.

In northern Mesopotamia, a king of Assyria had his engineers construct a canal to bring water from the hills to his city of Nineveh, more than thirty miles away. The canal had to cross a valley with a river flowing through. So here the engineers built the earliest known aqueduct. Two million blocks of limestone paved an elevated canal about 1000 feet long and eighty feet wide. The aqueduct walls were nine feet thick. It took a year and three months to build.

The Mesopotamians believed that the gods sent floods because the people had sinned. They lived in constant terror of floods. Sometimes the floods were made by men rather than by gods. An attacking army dug a new bed for a canal

20

or a river, sending the water through the city and drowning its inhabitants. After severe winters, the spring floods swept over the land with such violence that water and mud buried even the city walls. Archeologists digging at Ur discovered signs of a gigantic flood that sank the city beneath twenty-five feet of water. So deep a flood must have engulfed an area three hundred miles long and a hundred miles wide.

The Mesopotamians retold the story of these catastrophic floods in a legend. It seems that the gods intend to unloose a flood that will wipe out mankind. Only one man and his family will be saved. He is told to build an ark and take on board "the seed of all living things." So he builds a ship seven stories tall and puts on board all his gold and silver, his family and kin, "the beasts of the field, the wild creatures of the field." A violent storm erupts, and a mighty flood sweeps over the earth. Even the gods are frightened. After seven days the ark comes to rest on a mountain, and the captain sends out a dove, a swallow, and a raven. When the raven doesn't return, he knows there is dry land. He comes out of the ship and offers a sacrifice to the gods. It is similar to the story that the Bible would later tell of Noah's Ark.

Mosaic panels, made of shell and lapis lazuli, showing servants and farmers bringing gifts to their king in Ur 4500 years ago. (On opposite page) Sumerian fisherman from panel shown above.

21

A Mesopotamian signature. When a cylinder seal was rolled over clay, it left a raised impression like this one, which shows a hero chasing an ostrich.

HOW TO WRITE CUNEIFORM

We know about the Mesopotamian Noah and his ark because his story was told on the broken bits of a clay tablet found in the ruined city of Nineveh. It was one of many tablets that brought the dead land back to life.

Writing seems so natural to us that we can't imagine a time when men couldn't write. The art of writing was first developed in Mesopotamia. Farmers brought the first fruits of their crops to their gods. The priests accepted these gifts in the god's name. When a disaster struck the people, the priests interpreted that as failure on the people's part to give the gods what they wanted. So the priests figured out a scheme of heavenly taxation. Everyone had to pay the gods so many head of cattle, so many lambs, so many bushels of grain, so many fish. This way, the gods would be content and not strike out at men.

Now, when a farmer brought in, let us say, ten bushels of barley as his gift, the priest had to find a way to keep the god's accounts. He took a reed and drew a picture of an ear of barley on a small flat piece of wet clay. Beside it, he drew a circle to indicate the number 10. If a farmer brought in cattle, he drew a cow. If a fisherman brought in a string of fish, he drew a fish.

Since the gods were in heaven, they couldn't really use all the products the temple accepted. Soon the temples had to build granaries, sheepfolds, and cattle stalls. They became centers of wealth, bought lands and slaves, and lent money at interest. The priests needed to write down accounts of all their business dealings. Simple pictures were not good enough to indicate what they meant. For example, to write "plow," the priest drew the picture of a plow. But this could also mean plowman. To tell the difference between such words, he now used word signs. When the word sign for wood was written before the plow, the word obviously meant "plow." With the word sign for man before it, it meant "plowman." Eventually, the priest used word signs to indicate syllables.

22

If our civilization were to perish, our written records would soon turn to dust. Luckily for us, Mesopotamians wrote on clay. Baked clay, in the shape of a pot or a tablet, lasts for thousands of years. It was easy to scoop up clay along the river and canal banks, mix it with water, stir it, pick out the pebbles and weeds, and flatten it into a tablet for writing. The early tablets were about the size of our playing cards, but thicker. The writer, or scribe, held it in his left palm, while in his right hand he held a reed or wooden pen. As the accounts became longer, the tablets were made larger and had to be rested on the scribe's knees or on a table.

At first the scribe wrote in vertical columns from right to left. Then, possibly because his hand smudged the first column when he wrote the second, he shifted the position of the tablet. Instead of being right side up, the pictures were on their backs. In the drawing of a head, for example, the nose faced upward and not to the right. The scribe now wrote from left to right in horizontal lines as we do.

To draw a picture on moist clay, you need a sharp pen. It takes time and patience and artistic ability. To speed up his work, the scribe cut the tip of his pen in the shape of a wedge rather than a point. Instead of slowly drawing pictures, he jabbed the pen into the clay with quick strokes. He tried to imitate the pictures with his wedge marks. The result was writing. The word for "head" didn't look like a head any more. It was a design of seven wedge marks. We

A public stenographer. A scribe in the market place presses his reed pen into a moist clay tablet to write a letter for a customer.

call this kind of wedge writing cuneiform (from the Latin word for "wedge," *cuneus*). The men who first rediscovered this ancient writing thought that cuneiform looked like nail heads. To us it looks more like golf tees.

Cuneiform spread from Mesopotamia throughout the ancient world. Princes of the Near Eastern countries and even pharaohs of Egypt wrote their treaties and diplomatic letters in it. Cuneiform was written right up to Christian times.

SCHOOLS AND "BOOKS"

Boys who wanted to learn to write were sent to schools run by the temples. Only sons of rich men could spend the years it took to be able to write cuneiform. Poor boys went to work in the fields or learned a trade. The student first memorized a list of word signs—almost six hundred. The alphabet had not yet been invented. The teacher wrote a sample line of cuneiform on the top or the back of a clean tablet. The student then copied it, and the teacher corrected it. If a boy made a mistake, he balled up his clay, flattened it out, and started over again. Or he took a wooden ruler and pressed it over the moist surface of the clay, erasing the mistakes. If the clay became too dry, he dipped it into the trough of water beside his bench.

The ancient classrooms were rooms off the temple courtyard with rows of brick benches. When archeologists dug them out of the ruins, they found clay tablets with the same stories written on them. For the students had copied the same opening lines of a legend and never seemed to get past the beginning. And their writing was full of mistakes.

When the student was graduated, he worked as a scribe for the temple, the government, the palace, the army, or went into a business office. Sometimes he set up in business for himself as a public writer—like our public stenographers who have offices in hotel lobbies.

Scribes stacked their large clay tablets in earthenware jars or woven baskets. They piled up the smaller tablets, one on top of the other. This was their filing system. If the writing on one tablet continued onto another, they numbered the tablets just as we number the pages of a book. Often they wrote the first few words of tablet No. 2 on the bottom or edge of tablet No. 1. Then, if the tablets got mixed up, the scribe knew in what order to read the "pages" of his "book."

Businessmen filed their business records in their offices. The priests, who wrote long hymns and stories, kept their clay books in a temple library. Some of the kings who loved learning sent their scribes all over the country to copy down well-known legends preserved on the temple tablets. They had their scribes make copies of the laws and decisions the courts had handed down. They had the histories of their reigns written on other tablets. All these tablets were placed in the king's library. Like our library books, they were stamped with the name of the library to which they belonged.

HOW TO SIGN YOUR NAME

Today, near the gates of a city in Iraq, a public writer sometimes sits in the shade with his pen and paper, waiting for business. In ancient Mesopotamia, the public scribes did the same. Most of the people couldn't read or write, and the

A sculptured head, possibly of Hammurabi, a great ruler who left us one of our oldest law codes.

scribe wrote their letters for them. Often, the scribe enclosed the clay letter in a thin clay envelope with the name and address written on the outside. To open it, you broke open the envelope.

As in the modern world, all legal agreements in Mesopotamia had to be put into writing and signed by witnesses. Let us say a man wanted to lease a plot of land from his neighbor. If the neighbor was rich enough to have a scribe working for him, he dictated the terms of the lease to him. Otherwise both parties went to a public scribe. He wrote down the terms they had agreed upon and read the document to them and the witnesses they had brought with them. None of them could read or write—they couldn't even spell their names. The scribe wrote their names for them at the bottom of the lease. Then each person put his signature next to his name.

These signatures were made with a seal. Every man or woman who could afford one had his own personal seal. Because they were shaped like a small cylinder—a kind of miniature rolling pin—they are called cylinder seals. Seal cutters carved scenes from everyday life or from legends on the seals. The seal might show a man watering a tree with a shaduf or a hero fighting a monster. When rolled across wet clay, the seal left a raised picture in the clay—a seal impression. This was the Mesopotamian's signature. He wore his seal on a string around his neck or pinned it like a brooch to his clothes.

Seals had been invented even before writing. Probably, they had originally been magic charms or amulets to keep away evil spirits. The earliest seals were cut from common stones, but later ones were cut from semiprecious stones like red jasper or translucent crystal. Since seal cutters used hand tools and different sizes and shapes of stones, no two seals were ever exactly alike.

Clay seal impressions were the Mesopotamian's lock and key. A farmer leaving his house to go to market pressed a lump of wet clay across the edge of his door, then rolled his cylinder seal over it. When he returned and found the seal damaged, he knew somebody had broken in. A housewife suspicious of her servants tied a cloth over the mouth of her oil jar, then covered the string with a thick layer of clay. Before the clay hardened, she rolled her seal over the clay. Now she'd know if anyone was helping himself to her oil.

Top part of six-foot stone on which Hammurabi's law code was engraved. It shows the ruler receiving the laws from Shamash, god of justice.

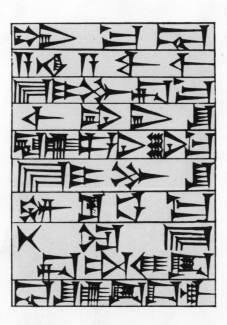

Two of Hammurabi's laws: (At left) If a man knocks out the tooth of a man of his own rank, one of his teeth shall be knocked out.

(At right) If a builder builds a house for a man and the house collapses and causes the death of the owner, the builder shall be put to death.

Alas, not all Mesopotamians could afford to own seals. How did they sign a marriage contract or a deed of sale? They almost anticipated our system of fingerprinting. They rolled a fingernail over the wet clay document. Perhaps no two fingernails are alike, either.

GODS AND GHOSTS

Many seals portrayed the gods of Mesopotamia. For the people felt close to them. They believed that man had been created out of clay and blood to serve the gods—to feed, house, and clothe them. Priests washed and dressed the statues that represented the gods. On the altars built to them, the priests placed their food and drink. The gods were like men—they quarreled with each other, they made mistakes, and they loved to eat and drink.

During festival time, the people dined with their gods. A bull or sheep was led to the god's altar, killed and butchered, then burnt in fire. The part that went up in smoke reached the god in heaven. The rest of the meat was shared by the worshipers and the priests. In case the god was thirsty, a priest spilled a jug of milk or beer at the base of the god's statue, where there were holes for the liquid to run out. Or he poured the drink into a large jar set before the statue.

Each city worshiped its own god, who kept the city happy and prosperous. But just in case the other gods might grow jealous, they, too, were worshiped. Families also had their household gods, who looked out for them. Men prayed to their gods when they were sick or in trouble. In fact, our attitude of prayer, with hands clasped in front, originated in Mesopotamia.

The Mesopotamians didn't pray for peace in the other world. They asked for help in this world. To them, life after death was a miserable state. The spirits

Procession into a ziggurat shrine. Every Mesopotamian city had a ziggurat where priests performed religious rites by day and watched the planets and stars by night.

A royal lion hunt. "I learned
to shoot the bow, to ride,
to drive, and to seize the
reins," boasted Ashurbanipal, the Assyrian king. Here
he draws his bow while
his charioteer drives.

of the dead lived in dust and mud in an underworld. Here the ghosts flew around
like bats. When a mother or father died, the children brought food and drink
to the grave several times a year. Otherwise, the ghost would have to eat mud.
Often, Mesopotamians dug their graves beneath the house. This made it easier
to feed the departed spirits. If a man wasn't properly buried, they believed that
his ghost roamed the streets, grabbing food from the gutters. Or, like a vam-
pire, the ghost bit an unwary traveler.

TEMPLES AND ZIGGURATS

Mesopotamians had private chapels in their houses. Along the streets, chapels
were built into the walls. A city like Babylon the Great had fifty-three temples
of the great gods, fifty-five shrines to Marduk, three hundred shrines to earth
gods, six hundred to heavenly gods, and hundreds and hundreds of altars. In
every city the main temple and shrines were in a separate walled section known
as the sacred area.

The earliest temples were built with recessed walls to give them an illusion
of height. To increase this impression, the temples were often built on platforms
of solid brick. The platforms also kept the temples from crumbling when the
rivers flooded. A ramp or stairway led up to the temple from the plain.

The early temples were painted with frescoes. In other words, the artist painted the walls while the plaster on them was still wet. Later temples were covered with enameled or glazed bricks. Life-size lion heads in copper, with mother-of-pearl teeth and lapis-lazuli eyes, guarded the temple entrance. Inside the temples were the sacred shrines, the statues of the gods, and, around an inner courtyard, the rooms of the priests.

The temple-tower was erected on a separate terrace near the main temple. This ziggurat, or "mountaintop," was supposed to be a link between earth and heaven, between man and his gods. Every city had its ziggurat, but the best remaining one stands in ruins in the mounds of Ur. Two hundred feet long and 150 feet wide, it rose in three receding terraces seventy feet high. Two side stairways led to a lower shrine, while the central stairway led through this shrine up to the top, where there was a second shrine. The terraces were solid brick and were probably covered with soil and planted with trees and shrubs.

Mesopotamia was a land of bright colors. The woolen clothes the people wore were dyed bright red, purple, yellow, and green. The shrine at the top of the ziggurat of Ur was made of enameled blue bricks. The bottom terrace was black, and the one above red. In the north, as in Babylon, the towers were usually seven stories high, each story painted a different color. The ziggurat at Khorsabad began with a bottom terrace painted white, the succeeding terraces being black, red, white, orange, silver, and gold.

What a colorful spectacle the New Year's festival must have been! Then long lines of priests and priestesses climbed the three ziggurat stairways to the sound of drums and sacred songs. Only the high priest and a special priest and priestess entered the holy shrine on top. Here they performed rites that they thought would make the soil fertile and the city prosperous.

The ziggurats were also used as observatories. Priests stationed on the terraces watched the moon as it changed its phases, charted the position of the planets and stars, and watched for signs from the gods. The Mesopotamians believed that the gods sent down signs from heaven of events to come. These signs could be read in the motions of the heavenly bodies.

Kings were proud of the temples they built to the gods. So they wrote down their achievements on large clay nails and buried them in the temple walls. Or they boasted of their deeds on clay barrels and tablets, deposited them in a box, and buried the box in the temple foundations. Today, our builders do much the same thing, burying a "time capsule" in the cornerstone of a skyscraper.

OMENS IN LIVERS

The temple staff was vast. The temple employed scribes, bakers, brewers, butchers, shepherds, boatmen, musicians, and dancers. Besides the various orders of priests and priestesses who conducted religious services, there were seers or diviners who foretold the future and exorcists who cast demons out of the body.

The diviners studied omens and dreams and then interpreted the meaning. If a king had a dream, he sent for a priest to "divine" its meaning. For dreams also came from the gods. The diviner studied other omens—a flock of birds in flight, the sudden eruption of an earthquake, a comet zooming across the sky, an eclipse of the moon or sun. The will of the gods was in these strange happenings—if only a man could read the meaning.

Giant winged bull. This protective spirit guarded the doorway to the palace of Ashurnasipal II in Assyria.

Ram caught in a thicket.
This statuette, from an Ur
"death pit," has fleece of
shell and lapis and a body
of gold and electrum over
a wooden core.

If the king wanted a question answered about the future, a priest wrote it down on a tablet and placed it at the feet of the image of the city god. Then a sheep was sacrificed and its liver cut out. In Mesopotamia, the liver was thought to be the main organ of life. The diviner now examined the lines and discolorations of the liver, its lumps and bumps. For years priests had studied sheep livers and written texts on what each line and spot meant. They had also fashioned clay models of the liver indicating the danger zones. The diviner compared the liver with the model and consulted his texts. For example, if the liver had a long lobe, it indicated a long life for the king. When the diviner reached a diagnosis, he then answered the king's question.

When the omens were unfavorable to the king, he sometimes put the royal robes on a statue. This way the god's vengeance struck the statue instead of the king. If the omens predicted a death in court, the king sometimes chose a substitute from temple or palace to rule as a puppet king. Though the substitute lived in the palace and gave the royal orders, actually the real king managed affairs of state behind the scenes. If the expected death occurred, the substitute returned where he came from. If the omens grew worse and no death occurred, the substitute was put to death and buried with royal honors.

HOW TO CURE A TOOTHACHE

Demons and angry gods inflicted diseases on men, according to the Mesopotamians. Sickness was a punishment for sins. If a man had a toothache, he called in the exorcist-priest. The priest could drive out the demon or calm the god's anger. The priest recited the Incantation Against the Toothache in front of the suffering man. This was a magic text telling how toothaches began. First the heavens, then earth, rivers, canals, and marshes had been created. Then the marsh created the worm. The hungry worm begged one of the gods for food. When he was offered a fig and a apricot, the worm turned them down. "Lift me up and let me live in the gums and the teeth!" he begged. "I'll suck the blood of the tooth and gnaw the roots of the gum!" Because the worm spoke so rashly to a god, the god would strike him down and thus cure the toothache. The priest had to recite the verses three times to cure the man's toothache. If the ache was still there, the priest applied sunflower root or pulled the tooth.

A man suffering from a high fever had his family send for the exorcist-priest. Dressed in his dark robes, the priest walked to his patient's bedside, swinging a pot of burning incense. The fumes might drive away the demons. He said prayers over the sick man, put a string with a magic row of knots in his hands, or perhaps applied a magic poultice of oil and ground bones. Sometimes the priest made clay or dough figures. Then he intoned magic prayers to drive the demons of sickness out of the man and into the clay figure. The clay figure was then burned or buried and the demon destroyed.

Sometimes the priest used a live animal to exorcise demons or drive away ghosts. If a girl had an earache, the priest might hold a dog or a pig to her ear. Then the hand of the ghost that was tugging at her ear and causing the earache might let go and grab the animal's ear instead. If the earache continued, he burned juniper berries and blew the smoke into her ear.

In time, the exorcist turned into a doctor. He learned the magic properties of drugs and prescribed them for his patients. As for the diviner, with his liver examinations, he paved the way for the science of anatomy.

THE KING—HUNTER AND WARRIOR

The Sumerians, who brought civilization to southern Mesopotamia, believed that kingship came down from heaven. Throughout Mesopotamian history, kings claimed to rule because the gods had chosen them. In the early Sumerian

Procession entering a death pit. At a royal funeral in early Ur, men and women of the court, as well as soldiers and musicians, went into the grave as human sacrifices.

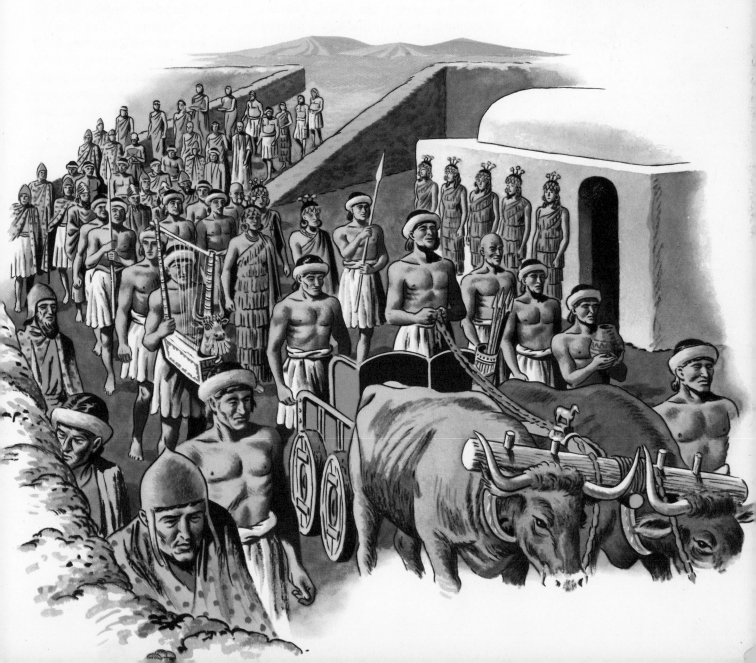

period, kings must have expected to rule with the gods after death, for archeologists discovered royal tombs in Ur where the whole court was buried with the king and queen. Some of these "death pits" held as many as sixty-two corpses—soldiers wearing copper helmets, grooms standing beside oxcarts, a harpist with his mother-of-pearl harp, and court ladies wearing headdresses of lapis lazuli and carnelian beads from which hung golden leaf pendants. They had apparently walked alive into the pits, drunk poison or a drug, and

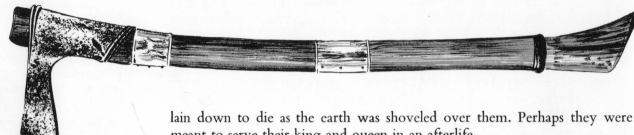

lain down to die as the earth was shoveled over them. Perhaps they were meant to serve their king and queen in an afterlife.

The first kings ruled small city-states. Then one king would conquer his neighboring kingdoms and rule over a larger territory. History's first known conqueror, Sargon the Great, founded the world's earliest empire. Like all Mesopotamian kings, he was a mighty hunter. In fact, lion hunting was the sport of kings. In later Assyrian times, Ashurbanipal even imported lions from Africa and kept them caged until the royal hunt took place. The animals were released, beaters and dogs drove them out of the thickets, and the king pursued them by chariot. If a lion leaped near the chariot, the king drove a long spear into it. Otherwise, he shot them with arrows until the ground was littered with slain lions.

The chariots of the early kings and soldiers were drawn by onagers, or wild asses. A mountain people from the east brought the horse into Mesopotamia, where it was called the "ass of the east." The horse revolutionized warfare, for chariots and horsemen could now speed into attack.

Early wars were like raids. The men had to sow the crops in the spring. In summer it was too hot to fight and in winter too muddy. After the harvest and date-picking time, the men were free to go to war. Then the king led his men on raids into enemy territory to settle disputes over land and water rights. But as the population grew and cities became larger and richer, war became a part of state policy. For in war the king and his men captured slaves and took rich prizes home with them.

Of all the Mesopotamians the Assyrians of the north, perfected the art of war. The government was run as a military state. Every male citizen had to bear arms, which were regularly inspected. The richer the man, the more weapons and animals he had to supply to the state. Every city had its arsenal where spears, daggers, bows and arrows, shields, and axes were stored. The king organized a spy system—today we would call it army intelligence—so that he would know where and when to attack.

Ancient water wings. An Assyrian soldier on an inflated goatskin swims across a river.

The Assyrians were especially skilled in besieging a city. First, the commanders set up a fortified camp. Inside the camp walls, grooms tended the horses, soldiers prepared their meals, the king and his staff planned their strategy, and engineers built scaling ladders, earth mounds, and battering rams.

The battering ram was like a vertical tank. A platform on wheels, it had a tower on top sometimes as high as a city wall. Inside, in the lower part of the machine, soldiers worked the beam that rammed a hole through the city's gates or walls. In the upper part of the machine, archers fired volleys of arrows through an arrow-proof brick turret.

The Assyrian army moved to attack in vast numbers, pulling their earth mounds and battering rams with them. If a river had to be crossed, the siege machines were ferried across on rafts. The foot soldiers swam across on inflated goatskins. At the city walls, the soldiers pushed their earth mounds and battering rams close, protected by archers on foot and mounted. Soldiers on top of the earth mounds fought to climb on the walls, while the battering rams hammered away at the gates and the scaling ladders went up. Once the gates or part of the wall gave way, the foot soldiers poured through, followed by charioteers and horsemen. The enemy leaders were impaled on stakes, the bodies of enemy soldiers were piled into mounds, temples and palace were looted, slaves were taken, camels and oxen were laden with silver and gold, and the city was set afire. The enemy princes were beheaded, and the high government officials had to march on foot to Assyria with the heads strung round their necks.

WHAT MESOPOTAMIA GAVE US

The Persians put an end to Mesopotamian political power in 539 B.C. The famous ancient cities eventually were swallowed up in sand. But the Mesopotamians passed on their ideas to us through the ancient Greeks and the Bible of the Hebrews. The signs of the zodiac, the twelve-month year, the seven-day week, the day of rest, the pound weight, the sixty-minute hour—all come from Mesopotamia. Even words we use today come from the ancient languages they spoke—words like crocus, sesame, naphtha, and camel. Our doctors treat scalp conditions with sulphur ointments as theirs did. The shaduf seems nothing more than a simple device to raise water. Actually, it is the first step on the path of invention that led to the electric pump. The ancient law codes of Mesopotamia guided the Near Eastern world and reached us by way of the Bible. Even some Mesopotamian superstitions are alive with us today—we too fear a black cat crossing our path.

Assyrians storming a town. They pounded the walls with siege machines and threw up scaling ladders. Their kings boasted of capturing 200,000 people and dyeing the mountains red with the blood of their enemies.

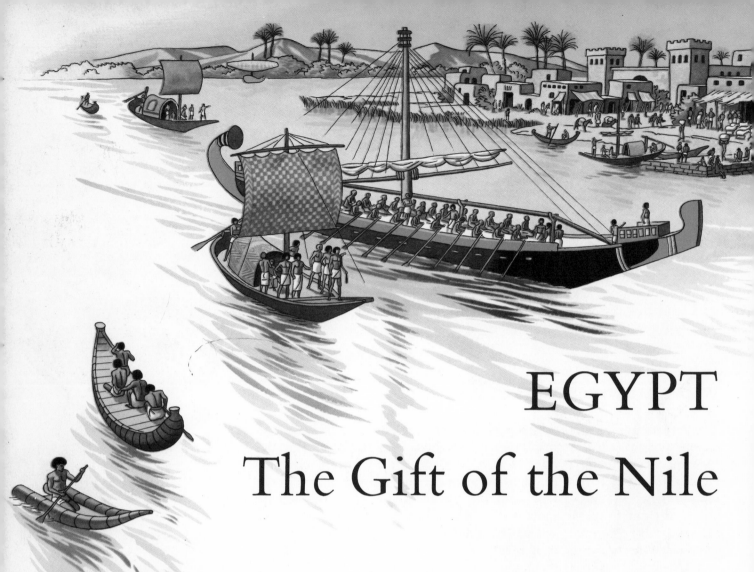

EGYPT
The Gift of the Nile

A typical port city on Egypt's highway, the Nile. In the river traffic are a one-man canoe, reed skiffs, cargo boats, pleasure boats with deck cabins, and a many-oared warship.

God sneezed, and the world was born. Then a goddess wept in heaven, and her tears splashed down to the earth in a stream. And that, said the ancient Egyptians, was how the Nile began.

The Nile is the longest river in the world. It rises in the highlands on the equator and flows north to the Mediterranean Sea. From prehistoric times, the Nile acted like a giant gardener. It brought down rich dirt and spread it over the barren sands. The dirt rose thirty feet high—the Nile had created a land where plants could grow and men live. That's why Egypt has been called "the gift of the Nile."

The Nile Valley is about twelve miles wide except at the Delta, where the river fans out. Deserts on both sides rise into limestone and sandstone mountains. The climate is one long summer. The landscape is flat and unchanging. Today's Egypt spreads east and west, but 99 per cent of her people live on less than 4 per cent of her land—on the snakelike stretch of land that was ancient Egypt.

The never-changing quality of Egypt has made it the most conservative country in the world. What is time in Egypt? The age during which the ancient Egyptians built their pyramids lasted longer than the whole history of America from the time Columbus landed until today. Life is so unchanging that today's peasants celebrate a holiday in mid-June called the Night of the Drop. It's the night the first tear dropped from heaven to form the Nile.

34

Egyptians lived to the rhythm of the Nile. In spring and early summer the river fell to its lowest level. The blistering sun shot the temperature up to 110 degrees in the shade. If a man touched a rock, it branded his skin like a red-hot iron. Hot winds blew fine desert sand over everything. Trees and shrubs dropped, the earth was parched and cracked, and the wells ran dry.

Then, as if by magic, the Nile waters began to rise. Farmers watched anxiously as the water changed from green to blood-red. The blood of their god Osiris was said to be flowing through the Nile.

The Egyptians had another explanation. The sun-god Re decided to slay mankind because it had sinned against him. He ordered the goddess of violence to destroy everyone. The goddess slaughtered mankind until she waded in a river of blood. But Re had a change of heart and pitied the Egyptians. He had 7000 jars of beer brewed, dyed the beer red, and poured it over the field where the goddess was next expected. When she arrived in the dazzling morning sunlight, she looked down at the flood of what she took to be blood. She bent down and drank the liquid. It tasted so good that she drank more. She began to feel happy. Gradually she grew so drunk that she could barely stagger back to the home of the gods. She had forgotten her deadly mission.

Man was spared destruction by the Nile's blood-red flood. No, it wasn't blood in the Nile, or beer. It was rich red clay from the African highlands, bringing life. No wonder the faces of the farmers broke out in a broad grin at floodtime! "Every mouth laughs," said an old hymn, "till every tooth shows."

By September 15 the flood rose to its peak; the farmlands were under water. It was New Year's Day, a day for celebrating and giving gifts. The Egyptians even threw presents of flowers, cakes, and beer into the Nile. Why not? Hadn't the Nile given them gifts with the generosity of a god?

When the waters receded, lumps of black mud crackled in the hot sun as if alive. Flowers burst into bloom. Fish teemed in the river, and ducks and geese returned to the marshes. Dry wells had filled again. To an Egyptian, there was nothing like good Nile water. When he was away from home, he sent for a skin of Nile water to bring back the sweet taste of his land.

After the flood, barefoot farmers, ankle-deep in mud, hoed the soil and sowed their seed. Other farmers guided a plow pulled by yoked cows or bulls. Sometimes slaves, yoked like animals, pulled the plow. After the furrows were seeded, some farmers didn't have to hoe the soil. They left that job to sheep. The farmer tempted the bellwether of the flock—the leader of the sheep—with some tasty forage. He thus led the flock across his fields, their hoofs trampling the seed into the soil.

The long- and short-horned cattle of the farms of the ancient Egyptians were stabled in open-air mangers, fed on hay, and milked by a farm girl. The milk-maid often sat directly underneath the cow, balancing her pottery milk pail on her knee. Farmers had to pay a tax on each head of cattle. At tax time, the rich estate owner sat on a reviewing stand while his cowhands drove the herd past him. His scribes, sitting cross-legged at his feet, wrote down the numbers and breeds of cattle. The overseer of the cattle held a baton or short stick, which was his badge of office. Occasionally he used it to slap an animal on the rump to move it forward. All foremen and overseers in Egypt carried batons. From this custom people later mistakenly thought that all Egyptian officials held whips with which to beat man and beast.

At harvest time, the reaper used a wooden sickle with a saw-edged flint blade to cut the grain. He loaded the grain in baskets and slung them over a donkey's back. If he worked on a big estate, he led the donkey to the granary. The grain bins had doors that slid up in grooves to let out the stored grain, but the granary had no roof. Storage bins in Egypt today are often roofless, since rain falls only in the Delta.

The ancient Greeks used to believe that Egyptian soil was so rich that all a farmer had to do was scatter his seed and wait for the harvest. The farmer's life was not so easy. His land was owned by the state, a temple, or a nobleman, and he worked as a serf, paying a portion to the owner and taxes to the government. If his land was on one of the canals fanning from the river, he had to dig out the rocks and stumps clogging them when the water level was low. When the flood rose too high, his house, his cows, and his whole family might be swept away. To irrigate his crops, he poured water by the bucketful all day long from his shaduf, or water-lifting bucket. His modern descendant uses the same device.

FERTILE WATER

If the Nile didn't rise one single year, Egypt would starve to death. This is as true today as it was in ancient times. But the Nile never fails. Sometimes, however, it doesn't rise high enough to reach all the fields. Ancient man solved this problem by building canals. When villagers banded together to build and regulate a canal, they took the first step toward civilization and government.

Egypt became a group of states divided into two kingdoms, northern and southern. Southern or Upper Egypt (so called because it was on the upper

Egyptian roundup. In this model from a tomb a cattle rancher is seated in a pavilion with his scribes while his cattle hands drive the herd past him.

reaches of the Nile) began at the first cataract of the Nile at Aswan and ended where the Delta began. Northern or Lower Egypt consisted of the Delta. The king of Upper Egypt conquered the northern kingdom about 2900 B.C. and made Egypt one country. Egyptian kings thereafter called themselves "King of Upper and Lower Egypt" and "wearer of the double crown." The southern crown was a tall white hat, while the northern was red. The crowns were combined into a double crown.

This first king is said to have built the first dam on the Nile. Every king after him made the Nile his chief concern. Today, in Egypt, the Aswan dam is the government's biggest project.

All along the Nile, in ancient times, were devices for measuring the river's rise. The wall of a city dock or a temple beside the river was marked with a graduated scale. As the river rose, officials at the docks and temples recorded the water level on these Nilometers and sent the information to the king. The readings of past years had been written down, and with this information the king predicted how high the river would rise. A low rise meant, in our terms, a depression, whereas a high rise promised prosperity. The king then based the country's taxes on his prediction. Many a king was accused of falsifying the figures to stuff his pockets.

The king of Egypt lived in a mud-brick palace plastered with clay. Brightly striped wooden pillars shaped like bundles of papyrus or lotus buds held up the roof. A double gate led into the palace grounds, a symbol of the double kingdom. Before the palace, flags fluttered on tall wooden flagpoles. The flags bore a picture of a falcon or some other animal, the symbol of the state from which the royal family came.

Smaller palaces, belonging to the nobles, surrounded the king's. Here the government officials lived. Every morning, the king held a conference with his prime minister, the vizier. The vizier was practically a one-man "cabinet." He was chief justice, secretary of the interior (in charge of canals, mines, and forests), secretary of the church (in charge of the state religion), and secretary of war. Those who came to him for justice called him "father of the orphan

Sun worship. A pharaoh, his queen, and his children hold up lotus blossoms, symbols promising that the sun will rise again. The queen also holds up a sistrum (see facing page).

and husband of the widow." He kept forty papyrus rolls of laws before him when he acted as judge, but his decision was sometimes based on the size of the bribe offered.

All government decrees were issued from the king's palace, called *pr-'o*, "Great House." When the President of the United States makes a statement, we often read or hear: "The White House today declared..." Now, the Egyptian king's orders were stated similarly: "The Great House today declared..." The king came to be referred to as pharaoh, from the Egyptian word for Great House—especially in the days when the kings ruled an empire, from the sixteenth to the twelfth century B.C.

Of all the pharaohs of Egypt, the most peculiar was Hatshepsut. The pharaoh was believed to be a god, the son of the sun-god. But Hatshepsut was a woman. She wore men's clothes and tied a false beard—the sign of high office—over her chin on state occasions. She even had her artists carve her picture on a temple wall as a newborn baby boy.

BEAUTY AND THE BATH

Egyptian customs fascinated the other ancient peoples as they do us. The ancient Greeks joked about them. Why, they said, Egyptians shaved their eyebrows and went into mourning for a dead cat! A Greek would have skinned it. Egyptians worshiped eels. Greeks would have eaten them. The whole Egyptian world was topsy-turvy! Didn't Egyptians knead dough with their feet and mud with their hands?

They did. But the Egyptians were among the cleanest people in the ancient world. Rich and poor washed morning and evening and before meals. The rich used fingerbowls at the end of dinner and dried their hands on linen napkins. They had bathrooms in their houses. In the days of their empire, they even had toilets that could be flushed.

To take a bath, an Egyptian sat on a stool in a room with a stone floor and limestone walls. A servant poured water over him, and he washed with soda. After the bath, he rubbed oil on his body to keep his skin from drying. Then he perfumed himself. Egyptians called perfume "fragrance of the gods." Our perfume advertisements use the same words today.

Men shaved their beards with a bronze razor. Women used it to shave body hair. They also plucked their brows with tweezers. Priests shaved their heads as a purification rite, just as monks do in our day. But Egyptians loved a fine head of black hair. And they worried as much as we do when their hair turned gray or fell out. Doctors had all kinds of prescriptions for restoring the natural color. Oil mixed with the blood of a black ox or the fat of a black snake worked wonders. But if it didn't, the gray-haired Egyptian could always dye his hair. Henna was a favorite hair dye—as it is today. It was extracted by grinding the leaves of a bush known as Egyptian henna or privet. Baldheaded men tried as many sure "cures" then as they do today. The Egyptian doctor recommended a pomade made of six fats: lion, hippopotamus, cat, crocodile, snake, and ibex fat. Rubbed on the bald head, it guaranteed a new crop of hair.

Men and women wore their hair straight and curled, long and short, and plaited. At first, the nobles at court and the pharaoh wore wigs on ceremonial occasions. These hot and heavy things were worn over the hair. Such is

Sistrum, a musical instrument used in religious services. When the player shakes it, the bars with metal rings jingle.

A wooden pillow. Headrests like this are still used in Polynesia, South America, and Africa because a wooden pillow is cooler than a feather one.

Kohl pot, used in eye make-up.

Polished bronze mirror with carved handle.

fashion that soon anyone who could afford one had a wig. The wigmaker turned out short wigs with overlapping rows of little curls and long wigs sometimes ending in pigtails. The pharaoh wore a false beard for certain rites. He fitted this over his chin by tying two straps attached to it behind the ears or under the wig. Pharaohs' statues often wore such false beards. The Great Sphinx originally had a stone beard, but it has almost completely worn off.

Men and women first used eye make-up because it had magic powers. A painter going blind wrote a desperate note to his son: "Bring me some honey for my eyes and some fat . . . and real eyepaint as soon as possible . . . I want to have my eyes, and they're missing." Eyepaint, he believed, would restore his failing sight.

The earliest pharaoh we have record of is Narmer, who may have been the king who united the two kingdoms. He left us a slate palette on which he ground the green malachite he painted around his eyes. We may be tempted to smile at this magic eye shadow. But malachite is actually a germ killer, and Africans still use it to keep away flies and gnats.

The brown-skinned Egyptian woman had many beauty aids. She used a kohl pot with a long brush to make up her eyes and paint her brows. Holding a rouge pot and mirror in her left hand, she brushed red ocher on her cheeks and lips. She had bottles of oils for her hair, pots of creams for her face and body, and vials of perfumes. She combed her hair with wooden, bone, and ivory combs and held up her hairdo with hairpins. She kept a supply of henna on hand to tint not only her hair and fingernails, but the palms of her hands and the soles of her feet as well. She brushed the flies away with feather fans set in wooden or ivory handles. She kept a pillbox with little pills that she swallowed to sweeten her breath.

FROM LOINCLOTH TO SKIRT

When the north wind blew, the nights were cool, and Egyptians slept under a blanket. The days were hot, and to keep the sun off their heads they wore linen hats and headdresses. But they wore brief clothing. From farmer to

40

pharaoh, all Egyptians originally wore a kind of loincloth, a short skirt around the hips that knotted in front. They added tunics and capes not because they were cold, and certainly not because of modesty, but because more elaborate clothing became the fashion. Eventually the loincloth turned into a ruffled or pleated skirt. Women wore a slim slip that fitted tightly from breast to ankle—in today's dressmaking terms, we would call it a sheath. But no woman, ancient or modern, could work in a sheath. When she worked over her millstone or danced for her lord, she wore a loincloth like a man's.

In the ancient world, Egyptian linen was unmatched anywhere. Flax, from which linen is made, has about double the strength of cotton. Linen doesn't soil easily, and it keeps the wearer cool. Egyptians could turn out linen cloth as smooth and gossamerlike as today's silk. In the period of the empire, Egyptians wore linen underskirts with linen robes on top so fine that you could see through them.

When an Egyptian didn't go barefoot, he wore sandals. These, made of reed or leather, had the curled-up toe that makes us think of characters in the *Arabian Nights*.

Both men and women wore jewelry—gold bracelets, necklaces, and anklets; rings of turquoise and lapis lazuli; pins in the shape of bees and beetles. These jewels lent the wearer not only beauty, but magic protection. They were amulets or charms, with power to keep away evil spirits, disease, and death. They didn't keep away thieves, for Egyptians had their jewel robberies, too. Men and women also wore elaborately embroidered or jeweled necklets, and men often carried walking sticks with carved heads. Today's canes and umbrella handles descend from these. The Egyptian cane, however, was a badge of office or showed a man's place in the social scale.

BEER, BREAD, AND ROAST GOOSE

Someone once said that a history of ancient food would turn out to be a history of beer. The two staples of Egyptian diet were bread and beer, both

A stone amulet, called a scarab, carved in the shape of a beetle.

An Egyptian lady kneels on a reed mat while her servants bathe, oil, and perfume her.

made from grain. A good daily ration for a laborer consisted of three loaves of bread, two jugs of beer, and a bunch of onions. Even a schoolboy drank two jars of beer a day.

Fish ran in such abundance that they almost leaped out of the Nile. Egyptians ate fish raw, roasted, boiled, sun-dried, and pickled. But their favorite dish was plump goose roasted on a spit over a charcoal fire. They drank milk and ate beef, but considered the pig unclean and didn't eat its flesh. A farmer wouldn't even think of having his daughter marry a swineherd.

Vegetables like onions, garlic, and beans, and fruits like dates, figs, olives and grapes, grew abundantly. When the figs ripened on the tree, Egyptians sometimes sent pet monkeys scampering up it to pluck the fruit and throw it down. The Egyptian cook fried with olive oil and sweetened his puddings with honey.

To make flour, a farm girl tied a cloth over her head to keep meal dust out of her hair. Then she kneeled behind a large red millstone and rubbed the grain with a smaller stone. The flour ran down the sloping millstone into a trough. "Crush well!" the bakery foreman shouted. "I'm crushing with all my might," she answered. (Their words were carved on a tomb wall.)

Bread was made from wheat and barley flour. Shepherds and poor farmers kneaded the flour into dough in earthen bowls, baked flat round breads over hot reed fires or ashes, and picked the loaves out of the fire with little sticks for forks. Indoors, bread was kneaded in baskets, then shaped like fancy pastries and baked on the hearth or on a clay stove. The stove was cone-shaped, wider at the bottom than at the top, where it was open. Dung or straw was burned inside, and bakers stuck their loaf-shaped dough on the sloping sides. In the Great House, where hundreds or thousands of loaves had to be baked daily, men kneaded the huge amounts of dough with their feet. Here the bread was baked inside open ovens. Next to the bakery stood the brewery, where beer was brewed from barley bread, as it still is in modern Egypt.

FISHERMEN, FOWLERS, AND MARSHMEN

Many Egyptians worked, ate, and slept outdoors—especially the fishermen, the bird catchers, and the herdsmen. The fishermen scooped up their catch in nets that looked like butterfly nets. From their boats they lowered large draw nets with corks to float the upper edge and weights to sink the lower edge. Then they drew the ropes of the net together, to trap hundreds of fish at a time. They strung the fish through the gills and carried their catch to the fish peddlers. The bird catchers spread nets like the fishermen's over nesting places in the marshes, trapping wild game, ducks, and geese. They also baited bird traps in the marshes and lay in wait for a nibble.

Before floodtime, when the pastures in the south were almost gone, the large herds of cattle were sent north to the marshy Delta area, where grass still grew. The Delta marshmen who herded these cattle were a rough lot. They didn't shave cleanly, sometimes grew beards, and dressed in reed instead of linen skirts. The rest of the people made fun of them, but admired their skill with cattle and the expert way they plaited reed mats. Like our cowboys, these herdsmen had to keep track of their herds. They roped them, tied their legs together, and branded them on the back with a hot iron. They moved with the herds, setting up reed huts whenever they settled down.

Wooden statuette of a servant placed in tomb. She carries a basket of food on her head and holds a duck with which to feed her master after death.

The enclosed garden of a country estate. The girls in front of the pool are playing a game similar to checkers.

HOME LIFE

Farmers built their earliest houses of reeds and mud. Later they built square houses of sun-baked mud-brick. In fact, our word "adobe" for the Indian brick house comes from the ancient Egyptian word for "sun-baked mud-brick." Egyptians who lived at the Delta plastered the brick with black mud; those in the south, with yellow desert clay.

Craftsmen in town—carpenters, jewelers, sandalmakers—lived in one-story mud-brick houses with two or three rooms. The houses were crowded close to each other in double rows, leaving a narrow alley between for a street. This blocked off the sun and kept the rooms cool.

People paid taxes with the grain they grew, the fish they caught, or the things they made. They bought the same way, bartering in open-air markets. The fish peddler's catch hung on a string. The jeweler displayed his beads so they would sparkle in the sun. In the market a farmer exchanged a sack of grain for several pairs of sandals, or a woman bargained for a string of beads, offering ostrich feathers in return.

Beyond the market or bazaar, in a separate part of town, rose the high walls that screened the houses of the rich. These houses, with mud-brick walls, wooden pillars, and palm-trunk rafters, were usually built around a courtyard. The windows were high, the doors small, to keep out sun and let in air. Mats that could be rolled up like shades covered the windows. There

Wall painting of a party, from a tomb at Thebes. As one girl plays her double pipes, others clap hands to keep time for the dancers. The cones of perfumed oil on their heads will melt over their wigs and clothes.

were rugs on the floor and bright carpets on the walls. Pillars were built in the shape of trees, with the column painted reddish brown and the leafy top, or capital, bright green. Like the sky, the ceiling was blue. Including workrooms and servants' quarters, these houses sometimes had as many as seventy rooms.

The farmer or the craftsman slept on a floor mat or on a clay bunk. In the marshy region of the Delta, men used the nets they fished with by day as a kind of insect netting. They spread the nets over the ground, then crawled underneath to go to sleep. The rich man in his house slept on a wood-frame bed made of interlaced cords, with folded sheets for a mattress and with a wooden headrest. Under his bed was a chamberpot.

To light their houses and temples, Egyptians used saucers and lamps of salt soaked with castor oil, with a floating wick. A lump of tallow stuck on a stick made a large torch. These torches could be carried at night and stuck in the ground outside the house or temple or in tubs of earth indoors.

To tell time at night, the Egyptian looked at his water clock, which resembled a flowerpot with a hole near the bottom. The inside had lines that marked off the twelve hours of night. It was filled with water, and as the water trickled out, the level lowered and the hours could be told. To tell time by day, he had a shadow clock, or sun dial.

The wealthy Egyptian loved to give a good "beer house," as he called a dinner party. In early times, men squatted at mealtime on rugs and cushions.

Servants placed a small stand before every two persons and served the food in bowls and the beer in jugs. In later times, there were tables and chairs—even chairs that could be folded up and put away in the chests and baskets that served as cupboards. A good host decorated everything with flowers—the table, the beer jugs, and the guests. Servants placed cones of perfumed ointment on the heads of the guests. These looked like large ice-cream cones and, like them, melted. They dripped over wigs and clothes, staining everything yellow, but they added a delightful scent to the air.

Musicians played during the meal. An Egyptian orchestra during the period of the empire might consist of a twenty-stringed harp as tall as a man, a lyre, a lute, and a double pipe that, if it had a reed in the mouthpiece, would have sounded like a clarinet. Many were all-girl orchestras.

The guests were served many courses and several beers and wines. The party was considered a great success if most of the guests ended up drunk and sick.

DUCK AND HIPPO HUNTING

After the hurly-burly of court functions and routine, the rich Egyptian retreated to the quiet of his country house. He sat under a covered patio to enjoy his arbor and vines, the poppies and daisies in his garden, the lilies and lotuses in his pool. Here in the country he kept pet greyhounds, cats, monkeys, and ichneumons—mongooses which were especially popular because they were supposed to eat up crocodile eggs.

With his pack of giant greyhounds, he hunted gazelles in the desert. Sometimes he took his wife and child and family cat on a duck hunt. He paddled his reed skiff silently into the marshes at the Nile's banks where game birds nested. Like our duck hunters, he often used decoys. His were live herons, which he held by the neck in one hand. In his other hand he held a bent wooden throwing stick, a kind of boomerang. When he was close to the ducks, he stood up, startled them, and, while his wife held onto his leg so that he wouldn't fall overboard, threw his stick at the flying birds. Like our

Hippopotamus hunt. The hunters harpooned the hippo and hauled him in by the ropes attached to the harpoons.

hunting dog, the cat leaped out of the boat, landed on the marsh bank, retrieved the hit bird, and leaped back onto the skiff with her prize.

A hippopotamus is said to have carried the first pharaoh out of history. Probably, he had gone on a hippopotamus hunt. Egyptians harpooned hippos as nineteenth-century whalers harpooned whales. Standing on a skiff, the hunter poled into the marshes where the hippos fed, watered, and lazed. Sizing up his prey, he hurled a harpoon into the hippo, letting out his line.

Bellowing with pain, the hippo, like the harpooned whale, quickly submerged, dragging the boat with him. The hunter played out his line skillfully. The hippo, weighing about four tons, could pull the boat under and feed the hunter to the ever-waiting crocodiles. The hunter's attendants used to stand by with pieces of pig meat to decoy the crocodiles.

If the hunter had made a lucky strike, the hippo grew weak and had to come up for air. The hunter speared him again and again with a short lance, then threw a rope over the hippo's head, and dragged him to shore.

The pharaohs were Egypt's greatest hunters. One pharaoh, after a report of a huge herd of wild cattle loose in the Delta, sailed all night down the Nile to the spot. He hopped into his chariot and in one day brought down fifty-six cattle with his arrows. Another pharaoh, Thutmose III, was the Davy Crockett of his day. It was said that he could shoot an arrow clear through a copper target. He killed seven lions in one moment, carried off a herd of wild cattle within an hour, and finished off 120 elephants while returning from a battle. Or so he wrote on a temple wall.

Riding piggyback, girls play a game of ball.

MARRIAGE AND CHILDREN

Years of play ended early for Egyptian boys and girls. Girls married when they reached twelve or thirteen, boys at fifteen or sixteen. Pharaohs married even younger. The father arranged the marriages of his children. Parents didn't like to see their sons and daughters leaving home and usually married them to neighbors or even cousins. Since property and titles were inherited from women, brother often married his "sister." "Sister" could mean almost any female relative, usually a cousin. However, the pharaoh had to marry his sister to become king. In the city of Arsinoë when Rome ruled Egypt, two thirds of the inhabitants were "brothers" married to "sisters."

Families were large, especially those of rich men, for they married as many wives as they could keep. A poor man had only one wife—all he could afford. A wise old Egyptian advised husbands to give their wives plenty of food and good clothes and to persuade them rather than beat them.

The pharaoh's harem, where his wives lived, was called the House of the Isolated. Once a princess entered, she never went out again into the world. Ramses II fathered 170 children. Though Egyptians loved large families, many of their children died young. An Egyptian's life expectancy was, perhaps, twenty-five years. Still, some Egyptians managed to live to a ripe old age. Pepi II became pharaoh at the age of six and reigned till his death at the age of one hundred—the longest reign in history.

An Egyptian mother nursed her child for three years, as Egyptian peasant women still do today. She watched over her child carefully, to keep evil spirits away. To protect a sleeping child at night, she might tie a magic packet around his neck. This contained clover, onions, fish roe, fish jawbone, and the backbone of a perch.

During their first four years, boys and girls ran around without clothes. They played games with each other and with toys like a crocodile that moved its jaws, a jumping jack, dolls with movable arms, and a figure on a stick that crushed grain when a string was pulled.

Children were given names like Little, Riches, and Strong. Pharaohs used

names like Amenhotep, which means "God Is Satisfied." Actually, our own names are not so different. Take Paul and Elizabeth. What is Paul but the Latin word for Little? And Little was a good Egyptian name. Elizabeth is Hebrew for "God Has Sworn," and that's not too far from Amenhotep.

CARPENTERS AND BARBERS

When a boy turned five, he put away his toys and went to work or to school. In modern Egypt, when a man goes into a different line of business from his father's, he may still be known by his father's trade. His neighbors may call him the Shoemaker even though he's a government clerk. In ancient Egypt, a boy almost invariably followed in his father's footsteps. Families had seven or eight generations of painters—or even barbers. A father could, however, apprentice his boy to a different trade, paying the craftsman for teaching the lad. The father also had to pay for the days his son played hookey.

The boy could become a carpenter. Egyptian carpenters invented plywood, gluing together six different layers of woods. They used wooden pegs for nails and planed the wood surface with an adze—a blade tied with leather thongs to a wooden handle. Today, Egyptian carpenters still use an adze rather than a plane.

Glassmakers heated powdered quartz with natron (sodium carbonate) and cast vases and statuettes in molds, or dipped sand cores in the molten glass mixture. They wound thin glass threads around copper wire, slipped out the wire, and had a glass bead for a necklace. Glass wasn't blown until Roman times.

Leatherworkers made sandals, chair seats, and leather tires for chariot wheels. Blacksmiths cast copper tools. First they put copper ore into a crucible with a stoppered hole in the side. Then they blew through long tubes to fan the fire under the crucible. The stopper was removed, and the molten metal poured into a mold.

The barber carried a block of wood for his customer to sit on or to stand on himself. Under his belt was his razor. He roamed through the village or city streets and shaved customers where he found them.

Even in ancient Egypt, however, fathers had ambitions for their sons. A man named Khety was such a father. He had entered his son Pepi in school, but the boy was reluctant to go. On the boat trip to school, Khety tried to convince him that learning to write and becoming a scribe was the best trade a boy could choose.

"I've seen the metalworker working at the mouth of his furnace," said Khety. "His fingers were as tough and wrinkled as crocodile skin, and he stank worse than fish roe." The carpenter, he went on, worked as hard with his adze as a farmer with his hoe. The jewelrymaker ended up at night with a back as stiff as the gems he cut. The barber buzzed like a bee through the streets,

Wrestling match. An adaptation from a tomb mural showing the many holds in wrestling.

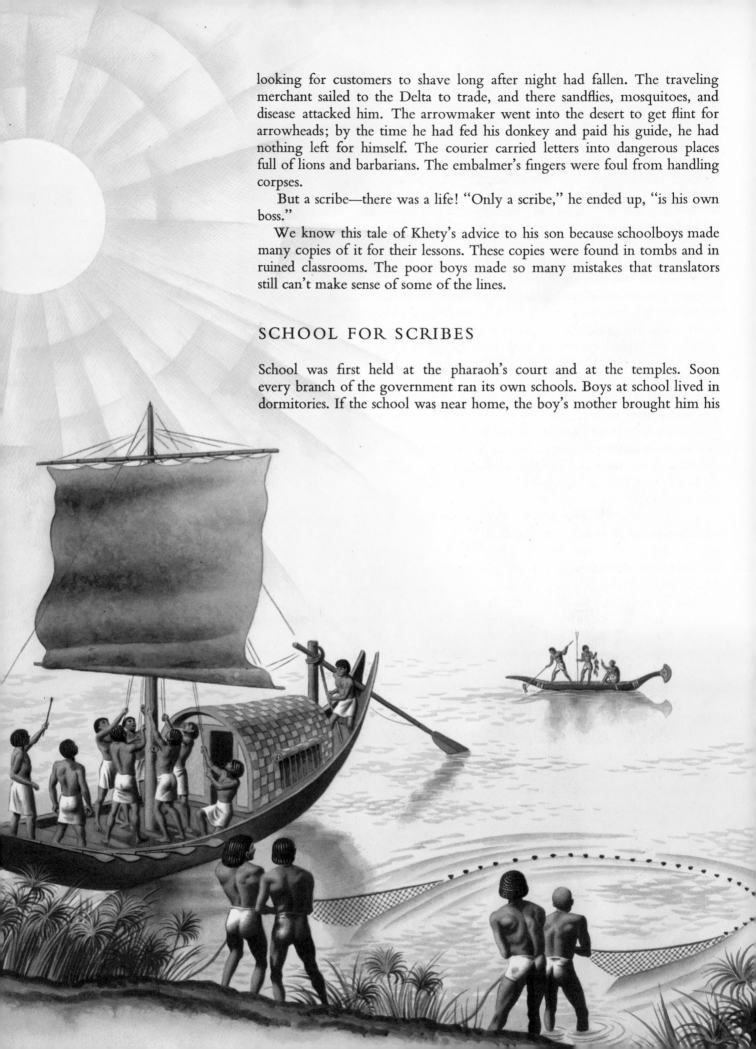

looking for customers to shave long after night had fallen. The traveling merchant sailed to the Delta to trade, and there sandflies, mosquitoes, and disease attacked him. The arrowmaker went into the desert to get flint for arrowheads; by the time he had fed his donkey and paid his guide, he had nothing left for himself. The courier carried letters into dangerous places full of lions and barbarians. The embalmer's fingers were foul from handling corpses.

But a scribe—there was a life! "Only a scribe," he ended up, "is his own boss."

We know this tale of Khety's advice to his son because schoolboys made many copies of it for their lessons. These copies were found in tombs and in ruined classrooms. The poor boys made so many mistakes that translators still can't make sense of some of the lines.

SCHOOL FOR SCRIBES

School was first held at the pharaoh's court and at the temples. Soon every branch of the government ran its own schools. Boys at school lived in dormitories. If the school was near home, the boy's mother brought him his food. Otherwise, he had to live on the three loaves of bread and two jugs of beer a day the school provided.

The teacher woke up the boys early in the morning. They grabbed their clothes and dashed for class. Latecomers were paddled. The youngest boys learned to draw the letters, while the older ones copied lines from a poem or a religious book. When they were good at copying, they were given a book of "instructions." These were proverbs and rules of conduct written by wise men. This way, the teacher taught a boy how to write well and, at the same time, how to behave. Boys kept notebooks, in which they wrote their lessons. The teacher looked them over and made corrections in the margin.

The Egyptians had a proverb: "The ears of the young are placed on the back—a boy hears when he's whipped." To them, a schoolboy was a wild animal that had to be tamed. The teacher was the animal trainer. Boys didn't mind the whipping too much. A former student wrote to his old teacher: "You beat my back, but your instructions went in my ear." If a boy was unruly or lazy, he might even be tied up and put into a school jail. No wonder that when noontime was announced, and lessons were over, boys rushed out with whoops of joy! Khety had warned Pepi not to mix with the rowdies after school let out.

By the time he was twelve, the student acted as a junior scribe after school hours. He filled the back of his notebook with drafts of business letters he had to write and bills he had to add up. Like all schoolboys, he drew pictures of animals on the back of his notebooks to amuse himself. His notebook wasn't like ours, however. It was a roll of papyrus.

HOW TO MAKE PAPYRUS PAPER

Papyrus reeds grew as high as fifteen feet in the Nile marshes. Naked workers pulled up the reeds, tied them into bundles, and shipped them to market.

Fishing and fowling on the Nile. From left to right: Hoisting sail for a day's boating; casting a large net for fish; spear-fishing from a skiff; using a live bird as a decoy, a throwing stick for a weapon, and a "bird cat" for retrieving; fishermen hauling in a seine or net.

Papyrus had many uses. The roots were used as firewood. The pith was cooked or eaten raw. The head of the plant made wreaths for statues of the gods. The stem was made into paper, boats, ropes, mats, sails, and sandals. The "ark of bulrushes" in which the baby Moses floated down the Nile was a chest made of papyrus.

To make papyrus paper, the stalk was sliced into long strips. The paper-maker laid these strips side by side on a table. Then he laid another layer of strips in the opposite direction on top. He poured Nile water over the sheet, hammered it flat with a wooden mallet, and set it in the sun to dry. If there were rough spots, he smoothed them out with a shell or a piece of ivory. To make a roll or a "book," he pasted several sheets together. His book looked somewhat like our school diploma.

Papyrus rolls ran from 6 to 17 inches wide—from the width of a book to that of a sheet of wallpaper. They could be made into any length. The longest we know of is 135 feet long and 8 inches wide. The rolls were tied with a piece of papyrus string. If the roll was a contract or a letter, the writer sealed the string with a bit of clay, then pressed his ring or scarab into the clay.

Egyptians wrote not only on papyrus, but also on parchment, leather, stone, clay, ivory, linen, wood, and metal. They carved ten-inch brushes or pens out of reeds and wrote with ink. In fact, they invented ordinary ink—a mixture of lampblack and vegetable gum in water. By using colored pigments, they made inks of all colors. But these inks weren't liquid. They were dry cakes like the watercolor paints in our paintboxes. Scribes held a palette in one hand and a pen in the other. Shaped like our old-fashioned pencil boxes, these palettes had a panel through which the scribes could stick several pens, and hollows on top for the cakes of ink.

An important scribe might have a palette made of ivory or alabaster, but a schoolboy had a plain wooden one with two hollows, one for black ink and the other for red. Squatting on the floor of his classroom, with a spare pen behind his ear, he dipped his pen into a small pot of water, rubbed it on the cake of black ink, and wrote his lessons. If he wanted to make an initial letter or write a title, he dipped his spare pen into the red ink. Papyrus paper wasn't cheap. He often used the same roll several times, washing off the earlier writing.

THE PICTURE WRITING CALLED HIEROGLYPHICS

When the ancient Greeks went to Egypt, they saw a strange kind of picture writing carved on the temples, tombs, and coffins. They called it "sacred carving," or hieroglyphic. We still use the term. Hieroglyphics on temples had, of course, been carved with a chisel. When scribes used pen and ink to write on papyrus, it took them too long to draw pictures of birds, animals, plants, and men. They simplified the pictures into a kind of handwriting. This script was later condensed into a sort of shorthand, called hieratic writing, that was used for everyday writing.

The Greeks had given Egyptian picture writing an apt name. The Egyptians themselves called it the "sacred writing." In Mesopotamia, writing developed because of temple business and the need to record amounts of grain and cattle paid in. In Egypt, writing developed for sacred or magic reasons. To an Egyptian, merely speaking a name was an act of magic. If you spoke a

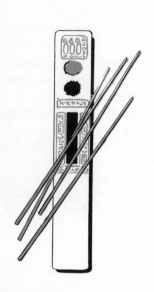

A scribe or professional public "secretary." Shown with him are his rolls of papyrus, a case for his "books," and a palette with two inkwells. He has a spare pen behind his ear.

god's name, you could even bring him under your power. If you drew a bull, which was a form of the god Ptah, you summoned up his spirit. Ptah then gave you his protection. Now, the pharaoh was also a god. His name had great power, too. But how could you write a man's name?

The priests discovered the answer in Narmer's time. There is a fish in the Nile called the *nar*. Now, if an Egyptian drew a picture of this fish, all he meant was the fish itself. If he drew a chisel, he was drawing that and nothing more. But in Egyptian "chisel" was pronounced *mer*, and the fish *nar*. By the gods, that was the answer! Use the *sounds* of the words, not the meaning.

On the same palette on which Narmer ground his eyepaint, an artist had carved the earliest kinds of hieroglyphics. By combining the fish, *nar*, with a chisel, *mer*, he had written the name of the pharaoh, Narmer.

1, 11	a reed leaf
2, 13	mouth
3	hare
4, 5, 19	surface of water
6, 16	basket with handle
7, 23	owl

From right to left this reads: "If you should be a well-favored man, and you beget a son by god's grace...." This is a kind of shorthand script based on the picture writing, or hieroglyphics, at the right.

THE PYRAMID—STAIRWAY TO HEAVEN

"The king is not dead—he is alive!" Such were the magic hieroglyphics written on the tomb walls in the pyramids. They were part of a magic spell that would guarantee a dead pharaoh a future life.

The Egyptian built his house of mud brick and wood because it didn't have to outlast his own lifetime. But if he could afford it, he built his tomb of stone because it had to last to eternity.

At first only the pharaoh could become immortal. A god, he walked up to heaven to join his father, the sun. This cost him and his people a pyramid. The rich made the heavenly flight by building a tomb. The common people could not afford to build pyramids and tombs for themselves, and were unworthy of going to the sun. They walked instead to the underworld, to the land of the god Osiris, where they could rest in the cool shade of trees. In time, the Egyptian afterworld became a mixture of the underworld of the poor and the heaven of the pharaoh and the rich.

Pharaohs erected their pyramids on the west bank of the Nile, for the sun sank there. To an Egyptian, "to go west" meant to die. We use the same expression today. The Egyptians called the east "God's land," because the sun rose there. To them the sun was the god Re traveling through the sky. Egyptians always traveled by boat. What was more natural than that Re traveled by boat? By day his ship sailed across the sky to the west. At night it passed through the underworld, emerging at the east at dawn.

The Egyptians had another explanation for sunset and sunrise. The greenish scarab or dung beetle is common in Egypt. It lays its eggs in a ball of dung, pushes the ball backward with its hind legs till the ball grows almost two inches big. Finally, it drops the ball into a hole in the sand. Here the larvae feed on the ball, then hatch. The Egyptians didn't know that the beetle had laid eggs. They thought that the young beetles were self-hatched. They therefore

8	bolt of a door
9, 18	seated man
10, 27	stroke
12	hill
14, 25	sealed roll of papyrus
15	eye
17	pintail duck
20	folded cloth
21	sickle
22	Egyptian vulture
24	tree + branch
26	emblem: cloth wound around pole

53

saw the sun as a huge ball that a giant, invisible beetle pushed across the sky, dumping it into a hole in the desert. It, too, would hatch the next morning.

Scarabs or images of this beetle were carved of basalt, jasper, and precious stones. They magically guaranteed that a man, like the sun and the ball of the beetle, would be reborn after he was laid beneath the desert sand. Scarabs on a chain were placed around the corpse's neck, worn by the living as pins and rings, and used as seals to sign papers.

The sun in the sky and the sun on the earth, or the pharaoh, were both buried in the western desert. Early Egyptians had been wrapped in animal skins and buried in pits with whatever food, drink, and tools they thought they might need in the other world. Later, the body was wrapped in linen and the pit became a room with corridor belowground. On top, a brick rectangle with sloping sides and flat roof had been erected. Partly covered by drifting sand, this tomb looks like a stone bench. In later times, the Arabs called it a *mastaba*, their word for "bench."

Pharaohs grew richer and more powerful. Now they wanted to take as many things from their daily life into the other world as they could. They had larger rooms built below and heavier brick structures erected on top. Then Imhotep, the pharaoh Zoser's architect, built a stone mastaba. Not satisfied, he placed five successive shells of solid stone over it. The mastaba towered 204 feet into the air. Imhotep had invented the pyramid.

Today, this pyramid, called the Step Pyramid because it has six tiers, stands alone in the desert. Originally, a wall a mile long enclosed the pyramid, its temple, a false tomb, and statues. Below the Step Pyramid was no brick-lined room, but a room of solid pink granite brought from Aswan. A hole had been bored into the roof slab. The king's sarcophagus—a stone outer coffin containing the inner wooden coffins—was lowered into his room through the hole. A granite plug then sealed it.

THE GREAT PYRAMID AND THE SPHINX

The Step Pyramid was one of about eighty pyramids that still stand on the west bank of the Nile. The ancient Greeks called the Great Pyramid of Giza, with its companion pyramids, the first of the Seven Wonders of the World.

The architects of the pharaoh Khufu chose a rocky site for his tomb. In fact, they left a platform of rock to form the core of the pyramid. Through this core, they dug shafts and excavated rooms and corridors. On top, they

Shaduf, a seesaw device for lifting water. It is still used on the Nile.

piled 2,300,000 blocks of limestone. Each block averages 2½ tons, and some weigh as much as fifteen tons. When complete, the Great Pyramid covered thirteen acres—almost ten times as much ground as the Capital covers in Washington. If sawed into cubes measuring a foot on every side, the stones of the Great Pyramid, placed end to end, would encircle two thirds of the earth around the equator. When Napoleon was in Egypt, he calculated that the stones in the three pyramids at Giza could be used to build a wall ten feet high and one foot wide around France.

Through the ages, the Great Pyramid has been stripped of its outer casing of white limestone and its capstone, which may have been gilded. Now 451 feet high, it had originally been 481 feet high, or the size of a modern forty-story building. Inside the pyramid, Khufu's body once lay in a granite sarcophagus in a room with a ceiling made of nine granite slabs weighing 400 tons.

The middle pyramid of the Giza group was built by a pharaoh whose face is known throughout the world. For the Great Sphinx, which lies south of the pyramids, is a portrait of the pharaoh Khafre. The stonemasons who built the Great Pyramid tossed the waste limestone and granite over the cliffs to north and south and left a knoll of rock near by. Khafre had the rock carved into a sphinx, with pieces of stone added where needed—to make the paws, for instance. Since the sphinx—half man, half lion—also represented the sun-god, he had his sculptors model the face after his own.

The sphinx is the dreaded guardian of the dead. A lion—even a stone one—could pounce on anyone trying to rob the pyramids and temples. So the pharaoh believed. And the Great Sphinx is no ordinary lion. About 240 feet long and 66 feet high, it stretches out paws 50 feet long.

Down the ages, men speculated about the lost art that enabled the Egyptians to build their pyramids. What secret engineering methods had they possessed? The answer is: manpower. One hundred thousand men spent twenty years building Khufu's Great Pyramid. It took ten years to build the temple causeway. About 4000 of the men—masons, stonecutters, sculptors, laborers—lived with their families in barracks all year long. The rest of the workers were peasants.

PYRAMID WORK GANGS

The peasant worked from sunrise to sunset. Schoolboys learning to write used to copy an essay that told of his hard life. "The worm has taken half the wheat, the hippopotamus the rest. The fields are full of mice, and the locusts have descended. The cattle devour, and the sparrows steal. Poor miserable farmer! What was left on the threshing floor, thieves made away with." Then the tax collector, with armed guards, arrived for his share of the harvest. If none was left, the farmer was beaten, tied up, and thrown into the canal.

Plowing and seeding. The sower scattered his seed, the plow turned over the mud, and the sheep trampled in the seed.

During the three months of the Nile flood, the peasant couldn't work his farm because the fields were under water. Then the pharaoh's men came to his hut and took him away to build roads, temples, or pyramids. The peasant was put into a gang that lived and worked together. A foreman over each gang kept records of how much stone was hauled, how much time it took, how much food was distributed, and which men were absent from work and why.

The pyramid gangs were not an unhappy lot, and sang as they worked. They were building for the greater glory of their king—and they could go home after three months. It wasn't till a thousand years later, when Egyptians brought hordes of slaves into Egypt as war prisoners, that public-work gangs led a miserable life. The Hebrew slaves of the Bible never labored on the pyramids, but they may have built cities, tombs, and monuments for the pharaohs of the empire.

The pyramid gangs were paid in bread, beer, oils, clothing, and firewood. Sometimes a stingy pharaoh who gave 600 sacks of grain a day to one temple couldn't spare a few sacks to feed his tomb builders. Sometimes the men starved, or went on strike, refusing to work till they were fed.

The limestone for the pyramids was quarried locally and from Tura, on the east bank of the Nile. For granite, the men sailed 500 miles up the Nile

Harvesting flax, as shown on tomb walls. Top: Removing heads from stalks. Right: Cutting grain with a sickle. Farther right: Bundling flax. Below: Man and woman pulling up stalks.

to Aswan. To quarry limestone, they used copper chisels and saws and split the rocks with wooden wedges. To quarry granite, which is harder, they probably rubbed an abrasive powder like quartz sand with a stone to make slots in the granite six inches deep at six-inch intervals. With a mallet, they hammered wooden wedges into these slots, then poured water over the wedges. The wedges swelled, causing the granite to split.

Once the block was cut, a gang pushed and levered it onto a wooden sled, then lashed it with ropes. As the foreman gave the order and clapped his hands, the gang pulled the sled with ropes. To reduce friction so the sled wouldn't burn, one of the men poured water over the ground in front of it. Sometimes, if the blocks were especially heavy, wooden rollers were placed under the sled. Barges filled with sand were waiting on the swollen river. A mud embankment led into the barges. The gang hauled the giant rocks up the embankment and into the barges.

In floodtime the river came within yards of where the pyramid was being built. The blocks were unloaded and hauled by a gang to the building site. A gang of eight men could haul ten 2½-ton blocks in the three months

they worked, so the men must have moved 115,000 blocks a year for the Great Pyramid.

Our construction workers sometimes chalk their names on steel girders. The pyramid work gangs sometimes wrote their names in red ocher on the limestone blocks—"Boat Gang," "Vigorous Gang," "North Gang." A block in the Great Pyramid has "Craftsman Gang" written on it.

The pulley was not invented till Roman times. The pyramid builders used ropes, wooden levers, and muscle power to move the giant stones. Masons first smoothed the bottom of the blocks, leaving sides and top rough. Then a work gang pulled each block up an inclined mud-and-brick supply ramp. Slippery wet mortar was plastered over the blocks already in place. The new blocks were then levered and slid into place. The last stones set in were the slanted casing stones of white limestone. Masons then smoothed the tops of the blocks in position, so the next row could be placed on top. So expert were the stonecutters that the face of the casing stones varied only 1/100 of an inch from a straight line.

In life, the pharaoh had been surrounded by men and women of the court. So he was in death. The courtiers built their tombs near the pyramids. Out of an estimated population of five million during the pyramid age, about 700 persons built tombs—about 700 persons could afford heaven.

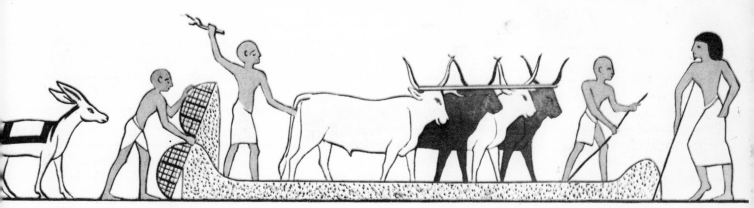

THE TOMB ROBBERS

Pouring out grain for threshing by cattle.

The pyramid was supposed to protect the pharaoh's body from Nile floods, wild animals, and robbers. The Egyptians believed that they were born with a double, another self, called the *ka*. When the body died, a soul flew out, sent a life spark through the *ka*, and then traveled to the other world. Now the *ka* could go in and out of the tomb and dine on the food and drink left at the temple near the tomb. But it had to return to the body.

If the body was destroyed, the Egyptians feared that their *ka* would be destroyed, too. So they invented embalming, to preserve the dead body in unguents and linen bandages. But they knew that accidents happened and the best mummies disintegrated. The pharaoh therefore had a model body—a stone statue of himself—placed in his tomb.

At first, the pharaoh made a contract with a temple to supply him with food and drink for centuries to come. One pharaoh gave twelve towns to a temple to guarantee a steady supply. But priests were human, and within a hundred years the contract was forgotten. To guard against this, the pharaoh

All-girl orchestra, from a tomb painting. The girls play a harp, a lute, double pipes, and a lyre. The little girl in the middle is dancing.

also provided himself with model food—details of his food and drink were inscribed on tombstones.

The pharaoh never had to work in heaven, but his courtiers were afraid that they might have to plow, spin, and cook in the hereafter. To protect themselves, they had artists fashion model servants and tools, which were placed in their tombs. These figures were called "answerers." When a courtier in the hereafter needed something, he called on one of these model servants to do the work. The model was supposed to spring to life and say, "Here I am!"

Pharaohs and courtiers wrote dire threats on their tomb walls. They built passages leading to dead ends. Tons of stone sealed the burial chamber. The entrance to the pyramid, high up the wall face, was so carefully blocked in that it couldn't be detected. Yet every protective device proved in vain. The Great Sphinx must have fallen asleep. Robbers managed to steal the treasures, even the gold- and jewel-laden bodies, out of all the pyramids and most of the tombs. Not in modern times, but in ancient times. Often, the masons who had built the tombs later robbed them. While building a new tomb, they also tunneled into an old one next door.

Thieves defeated the pharaohs in their plans to live forever. But the pyramids themselves have been standing for almost 5000 years. Geologists say that when the last man has disappeared from our planet, the pyramids will still be standing.

THE VALLEY OF THE GREAT TOMBS

The pyramids had been built near Memphis (near modern Cairo). In the days of the empire, the pharaohs built their tombs in a valley behind a wall of cliffs west of Thebes, in Upper Egypt, near the capital. They had their tombs hewn out of solid rock in this desolate valley. Robbers had to scale cliffs and drop down into the valley or enter by one road leading in. The entrance was heavily guarded, and police patrolled the road. The tomb doors were made small,

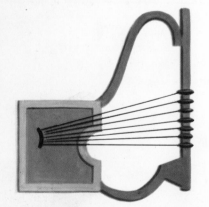

Lute from above scene. Its seven strings are plucked with a metal, ivory, or wooden plectrum.

then covered with natural boulders. The rock that had been excavated was carefully removed and scattered. Builders and priests were sworn to fearful oaths of secrecy. On the distant plain, the pharaohs set up the temples where their food and drink were placed. Poor pharaoh's *ka* or double had to walk over a mile for refreshment.

More than sixty pharaohs honeycombed the cliffs with these secret tombs. Yet the only one not robbed in ancient times was the tomb of a nineteen-year-old pharaoh who did nothing more memorable than die. Tutankhamun had been buried in one of the smallest tombs in the Valley of the Kings' Tombs. But it lay undisturbed for about 3270 years. A later pharaoh had cut his tomb immediately above Tutankhamun's, and tons of stone rubble had buried it. When the tomb was discovered and opened in 1922, there were signs that it had been broken into. But the robbers had been caught in the act and the tomb resealed.

What riches lay in the tomb! The storerooms were piled up with gold-plated statuettes, wooden chests inlaid with ivory, carved and gilded shrines, the royal couch framed by carved animals, the throne with a jeweled and gilded back picturing the king and his young queen, alabaster lamps and vases, ebony stools inlaid with ivory, and gilded chariots.

Two life-size statuettes, decorated in beaten gold, guarded the entrance to the burial room. Four golden shrines with folding doors enclosed a yellow quartzite sarcophagus. Inside rested Tutankhamun's mummy, encased in a nest of three golden coffins. The innermost one, six feet long and a quarter inch thick, was made of solid gold. The metal in it alone was said to be worth $250,000. As a work of antique art, it was priceless. The pharaoh's head was covered by a portrait mask of beaten gold, and his feet were shod with golden sandals. Beneath the linen wrappings the body wore golden jewels.

Since the discovery of this tomb, people have used the words "as rich as

Harp (from all-girl orchestra). The sounding board is covered with a leopard skin.

A tomb painting of porters from a royal household bringing offerings on behalf of the dead.

59

Canopic jar for internal organs of mummy.

King Tut" to mean unbelievable wealth. Yet Tutankhamun was an unimportant pharaoh who died young. What wealth must have been in those tombs—fifty times the size of Tutankhamun's—which the great pharaohs had hewn in the Valley of the Kings' Tombs!

HOW TO MAKE A MUMMY

Few men and women could afford to protect their bodies—and therefore their spirits—under tons of granite the way the pharaohs and rich nobles could. But all could afford one form of protection—embalming.

The word "mummy" is not Egyptian. It comes from the Arabic word for bitumen or pitch. The mummies the Arabs first discovered were poorly made mummies, heavily coated and filled with pitch. When handled, they cracked like a piece of stale peanut brittle. The Arabs thought that these mummies had magic powers, and sold mummy pieces as a drug. They were supposed to be especially good for healing wounds.

The ancient Egyptians also thought that mummies had magic powers. For them, the mummy meant a body in which a man could live after death. But how could they preserve the body? They found the answer in the fish market. Here fish were salted and dried in the sun. Fresh fish rotted in a few days, but salted fish kept for months. As the fish dealer salted his fishes to preserve them, so the embalmers salted the human body.

When mummies were first discovered in modern times, the world believed that the Egyptians had possessed a secret formula for preserving the body. But mummies were later found buried deep in the sand, where they had lain for over three thousand years. They were perfect mummies—yet nothing had been done to preserve their bodies! Scientists discovered the ancient "secret formula." It was nothing else than the intense dry heat of the sun and the porous, sterile sand.

Coffinmakers putting the finishing touches to a mummy case.

A poor man was mummified by the cheapest process. His body was salted with natron (sodium carbonate) or steeped in pitch. A few magic charms were placed on top, then the body was wrapped in linen. His family buried him in a cave or in the sand. With him went his sandals and a staff, to support his body on the difficult trip to the underworld. Cats, dogs, bulls, and crocodiles sometimes were given better treatment. Even kittens were carefully salted, bandaged, and placed in cat-shaped bronze or wooden cases.

If a man couldn't afford to build a tomb, he could rent space in a public tomb built and run by priests. Here his mummy would be piled on top of others like boxes in a warehouse. But a man of importance wanted his own tomb and to be made into a first-class mummy. Let us follow such a man—the scribe Ani, who lived in the days of the empire—from death to the tomb.

When Ani died, he was taken to the embalming house. Here the chief embalmer, who was a priest, and his assistants chanted magic formulas as they turned Ani into a mummy. First, the body's inner organs were removed, washed in spiced palm wine, smeared with resins, and bandaged in linen. Except for the heart, they went into four alabaster jars, each one protected by a god. The god would see that each organ performed its functions later on. The brain was extracted through the nostrils, dried, and later buried with the body. The body was placed in a wooden box and covered with natron. Our bodies are seventy-five per cent water. The natron dried up the water.

After seventy days, the shrunken body was taken out of the box. The skull was filled with natron and plaster, and obsidian eyes were set into the sockets. The heart was put back, and the chest and stomach were packed with resin-soaked rags. A golden disk with a magic eye engraved on it was placed on the chest, and Ani's scarab ring was slipped over his finger. A scarab on a chain went round the neck. The body was now smeared with unguents and resins.

Ani's mummy was bandaged from head to foot in linen, the arms close to the side and the hands resting on the stomach. Magic formulas were written on the bandages to protect Ani from demons, and a stone scarab was placed over his heart. Linen pads were put under the feet, for the mummy had to stand upright. The mummy was bandaged again and tied with strips of linen.

The coffinmakers had made a wooden replica of Ani's mummy. An artist painted his portrait on top while Ani was in the box of natron. Two other coffins were made, painted inside and out with figures of the gods and with Ani's name. The mummy was placed inside, and the coffins were taken to Ani's house for the funeral procession to the tomb.

At the tomb entrance, Ani's coffin was set upright. The mourners bade him good-by, then the coffin was lowered by rope into the burial room. Priests and close relatives now walked down the steps to the burial room. The jars containing his organs were set at the four corners of the coffin stand.

The priests performed a ceremony called "opening the mouth." Ani's mouth had been bandaged up. The priest's wand and words magically opened it again so he could eat, drink, and talk.

In a niche in the wall his friends placed a book that he had copied and his artist friends had illustrated. This book contained religious verses.

In the pyramids, magic spells and formulas had been carved on the walls of the inner corridors and rooms. Later, they were written on the inside and

A partly unwrapped mummy, said to be that of the pharaoh Seti I, who ruled almost 3300 years ago.

outside of the coffin, where they would be handier for the mummy. In Ani's day, the spells and formulas had increased so in number and length that they had to be written on papyrus rolls. These have been called the Book of the Dead. Favorite verses were copied and placed in the tomb, in the coffin, or between the mummy's bandaged legs. Priests sold rolls of these verses guaranteeing the buyer entry into paradise. Blank spaces were left next to the magic formulas. All the buyer had to do was sign his name in the right places.

When the mourners and priests had left Ani's tomb, masons set up a stone slab at the entrance and sealed it. Inside the tomb, Ani's soul brought the mummy to life, then flew out of the tomb as a human-headed hawk. It began the journey to the west.

A SOUL JOURNEYS TO THE WEST

The west, as we know, was the land of the dead in Egypt. Jackals lived in the western desert, and the jackal was called the dog of the dead. Perhaps that's why so many peoples believe in the superstition that a dog howling in the night means that someone will die.

Ani's soul had to climb dangerous peaks, ford streams, and avoid apes that fished with nets for souls. Finally, it reached the judgment hall of Osiris, god

Gold mask, inlaid with lapis and other stones, that covered the mummy of Tutankhamun (about 1361– 1352 B.C.).

of the dead. Here, before a jury of forty-two gods, the soul confessed that Ani had not committed forty-two sins: "I have not committed evil against men, I have not mistreated cattle . . . I have not made anyone sick, I have not made anyone weep, I have not killed." Then the soul recited a verse from the Book of the Dead, swearing that Ani had given bread to the hungry, water to the thirsty, clothing to the naked, and a lift to the man who was marooned.

On a balance, the jackal-headed god Anubis now weighed Ani's heart against the feather of truth. The god of the scribes, ibis-headed Thoth, waited for the report, his palette in one hand and his pen in the other. If the balance hung uneven, a beast with the head of a crocodile, the forequarters of a lion, and the hindquarters of a hippo would eat the soul, destroying Ani forever. But Ani had no cause to worry. Hadn't the embalmer placed a magic scarab over his heart? This prevented his heart from crying out the truth if he had committed any wrongs.

Truth did not outweigh the heart. The balance hung even. Anubis reported the good news to Thoth, who wrote it down. Then Ani's soul was led to the great god Osiris. Now it became a spirit-body and went to paradise.

There in the land of the Heavenly Nile Ani found his wife Tutu, who had died before him and whose mummy lay in the same tomb. As they had lived on earth, so they lived here. Ani and Tutu had loved a quiet game of checkers at home. Now they played contentedly in paradise.

Funeral procession. Bulls draw a sledge holding a funeral barge with a coffin. Many of those following the procession are hired mourners.

Statue of Akhnaton, a name meaning "splendor of the sun," a pharaoh who made the worship of the sun's energy the national religion.

A stone carver putting the finishing touches on a statuette.

SAILING ON THE NILE

When the sun sank in the west, Egyptians believed that the sun boat had to be towed through the underworld, for there was no breeze. Their ideas were based on observations of their life on the river. The Nile was in their blood and on their lips. An Egyptian didn't say he was going north or south. He went "downstream" or "upstream." He peppered his speech with nautical expressions. A man who spoke too much was "a hurricane of words." A talkative woman, the Egyptian said, should tie her tongue to a mooring place.

What the car is to us the boat was to the Egyptian. A poor man had a boat made of reeds. A rich man had several wooden boats that he called for whenever he had to travel, like a man in our day calling for his car. A kitchen boat followed behind. Here on deck women ground flour and bakers made bread, joints of meat hung on ropes, and stews simmered over stoves burning charcoal. At mealtime, the kitchen boat pulled up alongside the main boat and was moored to it.

We have a car radio. The rich Egyptian brought his musicians aboard and listened to the harp and singing as he sailed. There were traffic jams on the Nile, ships crashed into each other, shell horns honked incessantly, and it was difficult to find a parking place to moor a boat along the busy city docks.

Early Egyptian boats were bundles of papyrus reeds bound together. Hunters poled these skiffs through the shallow marsh waters. But the Nile is deep, and paddles were invented. The hunter used to throw a reed mat on the bottom of his boat to keep out dampness. The day he held it up against his pole and caught a breeze, the sailboat was born.

64

The first sailboats carried a square or oblong sail on a mast shaped like the letter A. The mast could be unhitched and laid on deck. Since the wind blows mainly from the north, all an Egyptian sailor had to do to go south or upstream was to raise his mast and sail. He had two paddles lashed to the stern to steer with. If the boat carried a passenger, he sat amidships in his own elegant chair, while his pet monkey clambered up the mast. Going downstream, the boat was carried by the current. The sailor furled the sail, unhitched the mast, and laid it on deck.

The earliest wooden boats were copies of the spoon-shaped reed skiffs. Passengers, crew, and cargo, all rode on deck. Facing the stern, sailors sat on little stools and rowed with long oars. Egyptian shipbuilders could put together a masted ship 100 feet long by 50 feet in the beam in only seventeen days. The back of the boat was always raised like the skiff. If the boat hit a sandbank, the men could pole it off.

Egyptians named their ships just as we do. *The Glory of Memphis* sounds like a Mississippi river boat, but it was a bright-blue Egyptian passenger ship. These ships now had cabins on deck, to protect passengers from the hot sun. The cabins were fitted with linen or mat shades that could be rolled up or down at the sides. They could be pushed from one end of the deck to the other. Eventually the cabins became small houses on deck—gaily painted and furnished.

THE ANCIENT SUEZ CANAL AND A VOYAGE TO PUNT

In their inscriptions, pharaohs had written of ships and sea captains dispatched to the Sinai copper mines. The Nile was not naturally connected to the Red

The magnificent temple at Deir el-Bahri. It was built into the limestone cliffs west of Thebes during the reign of Queen Hatshepsut.

A wooden model of a funeral boat found in a tomb dating from about 2000 B.C. By the magic of this model, an Egyptian believed his body would sail to the heavenly Nile of paradise.

Sea. How could a ship sail over the desert? The answer was found in modern times, when engineers began to dig the Suez Canal. A dry channel ran through the Bitter Lakes in the Isthmus of Suez. It must have been the bed of an old canal. The modern Suez engineers dug their canal alongside the ancient one.

This old Suez canal connected the Red Sea with the Mediterranean via the Nile. A ship sailed from the Red Sea, through the Bitter Lakes, westward on the canal to the Nile, then north to the Mediterranean. It took 25,000 peasants five years to build the sweet-water branch of today's Suez Canal, which parallels the ancient one. We can't even guess how much time and how many men were spent on the ancient one.

To sail on the Mediterranean and the Red Sea, the Egyptians built ships 180 feet long by 60 feet in the beam. Columbus' flagship the *Santa Maria* and his favorite *Niña* could have fitted on the deck, with a little room left over. Crews of over a hundred men sailed the ships. The ancient Suez canal must have been enormous to accommodate such large ships.

The seagoing ships sailed to Crete, the coast of Asia Minor, and the fabulous land of Punt. In the oldest "fish story" ever recorded, an Egyptian told of sailing to Punt in a huge ship manned by 150 sailors with "hearts as strong as a lion's." Gale winds blew up, giant waves swamped the ship, and it foundered. Only the hero was saved, washed up on the shore of a desert isle. A giant blue-and-gold snake over fifty feet long, wearing a long beard, picked him up in his mouth and carried him to his palace. Here the snake entertained him until another ship came along to rescue him. The snake gave him gifts of myrrh, ivory, and monkeys, then said good-by. As soon as the sailor left the

66

isle, the snake told him, it would magically turn into water and never be seen again. An ancient Sindbad the Sailor had made his first voyage.

A famous real voyage to Punt took place when Hatshepsut was pharaoh. A fleet of five ships lay moored to trees in a Red Sea harbor. The 65-foot ships, with thirty sailors at the oars of each, had sailed from the capital city of Thebes down the Nile to the Suez canal and into the Red Sea. The bow of the ships was shaped like a gondola, and the stern curled up into a lotus flower. The sails stood out wider than the ships.

Sailors in rowboats brought jars of provisions aboard. The commander of the expedition, his soldiers, and royal dancers to entertain the troops came aboard. On shore an animal sacrifice was offered for the gods to send a fair wind. The captain, standing with the lookout in a sort of openwork fo'c'sle, shouted his orders. The sails were hoisted, the ropes made fast, and 150 oars dipped into the sea. Like giant wooden birds with a vast wingspread, the ships began the magical voyage to Punt.

A month at sea, and the lookout sighted no desert isle with a talking snake. But soon the coast of Somaliland came into view. For this was Punt. Giant trees and tropical plants lined the shore. Beyond were villages of huts raised on pilings. The native chief and his fat wife came down to welcome the ships. The Egyptian commander disembarked with his soldiers and set up a table with Egyptian articles on it—necklets, daggers, and axes. In return, the Somali natives piled up incense, brought out potted myrrh trees, and led forward monkeys and two live panthers on leashes. Bearers went up and down the gangways, loading the ships with the incense trees and bags of incense, sandalwood, green gold, panther skins, ebony, ivory tusks, eye cosmetics, baboons, monkeys, giant greyhounds, and slaves.

The ships then made the homeward voyage. When the commander and

The judgment of the dead, a scene from a papyrus found in the tomb of the scribe Ani. Above, the great gods act as jury. Below, Anubis, the jackal-headed god of the dead, weighs Ani's heart against the feather of truth. To the left, Ani and his wife await the verdict. To the right, ibis-headed Thoth, god of scribes, stands with Amenit, the soul-eating monster.

Aerial view of Giza, showing the pyramids, built more than 4500 years ago, of pharaohs Khufu (also known as Cheops), Khafre, and Menkaure.

his men moored at Thebes, the whole city turned out to welcome them. Thirty-one growing incense trees and two live panthers—no one had seen the like "since the world began," they said. "Nothing like this had even been brought to any other king."

The "king"—the woman pharaoh Hatshepsut—had built a magnificent temple-tomb against the western cliffs of Thebes. Three colonnaded terraces led from the plain to the distant cliffs. She had planted a granite garden. Then she wanted to beautify it with trees—incense trees that would send a heavenly fragrance up to the gods. That was why she had sent a fleet to Punt.

SETTING UP AN OBELISK

Egyptian kings celebrated anniversaries of their reigns—jubilees—by setting up obelisks. In memory of her father, Hatshepsut set up two granite obelisks at the temple of Karnak. One still stands in the temple ruins. Ninety-seven and a half feet high, it weighs 700,000 pounds. The top was once covered with glittering electrum, a gold and silver alloy, which made it seem to pierce heaven. Hatshepsut said that she measured out twelve bushels of electrum like sacks of grain to decorate these obelisks.

The obelisks were carved and set up by skillful yet simple means. An unfinished obelisk lies today in the Aswan quarries. It is 137 feet long and would have weighed 1170 tons if it had been finished. But after it had been

68

smoothed and partly detached from the surrounding rock, engineers found a flaw in the granite and stopped work. This half-born obelisk tells us how the Egyptians carved such monuments.

First, masons built a fire on top of the rock, then poured water on the heated surface. The rock split in several places, and the top layers could be chipped away. Masons then pounded the surface with balls of a hard greenish stone called dolerite. These balls weighed between nine and fourteen pounds, and a mason had to hold the ball in both hands. After the top of the rock was flattened, the architect drew the outline of the obelisk on it. Now, the masons didn't cut out the obelisk. They didn't have tools strong enough. They bashed it out with the dolerite balls. Perhaps for this phase of the work the balls were attached to wooden hammers.

The obelisk was shipped on a barge to Thebes, where masons smoothed the surface, sculptors carved the hieroglyphics, and metalworkers fitted on the shiny metal cap.

Hatshepsut wanted her obelisks set up practically in front of a colonnaded hall of the Karnak temple. According to her, she had to take the roof off the hall to get the obelisks in. But that still doesn't explain how such a heavy, tall monument could be set up in the middle of buildings, without machinery.

The most probable answer is that a mud-and-brick ramp was built over the

Cross section of the Great Pyramid. The entrance (right) leads to an unfinished room below the rock core on which the pyramid is built. Another corridor rises (left) to a room (in the center) originally intended for the burial chamber. The grand gallery above leads to the king's chamber, where his sarcophagus lay.

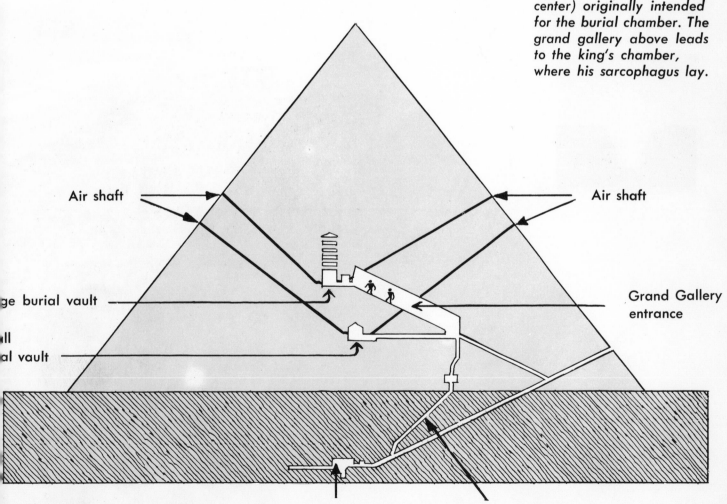

Air shaft

Air shaft

ge burial vault

Grand Gallery entrance

ll
al vault

Underground chamber

Connecting shaft

spot the obelisk was to stand on. Perhaps it went through the hall of the temple, making it necessary to remove the roof. Near the top of the ramp a rectangular pit was dug out to the pedestal. The sides of the pit tapered to the size of the pedestal, which was already in place at the bottom. The pit was filled with sand.

Men pulled the obelisk on a sled up the ramp and more than halfway across the filled-in pit. Outside the ramp a tunnel led to the bottom of the pit, where workmen slowly removed the sand. As the sand lowered, the base of the obelisk sank slowly into the pit. When all the sand was gone, the obelisk rested on the notch in the pedestal. Men with ropes then pulled the obelisk upright into position. The ramp was removed, and the obelisk stood free.

THE PHARAOHS GO TO WAR

The obelisks now in Istanbul, Rome, London, and New York had originally been set up in Egypt by Thutmose III. This warrior-pharaoh has been called the Napoleon of Egypt, for his skill in battle.

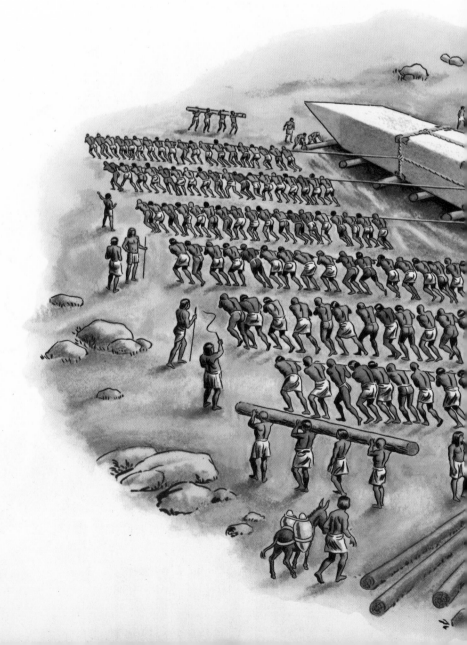

Thutmose's army of about 20,000 men was made up of archers, spearmen, and charioteers. Before the days of the empire, archers had carried their arrows loose in their hand. They copied the quiver from their Asiatic enemies. Asiatic invaders of Egypt had brought in the horse and chariot, and the Egyptians modified the chariot and made it a swifter vehicle of attack. To fight a battle, the pharaoh and his generals took most of the first day to draw up a battle line facing the enemy. Although the pharaoh claimed he led his troops into every charge, it is unlikely that he did. If anything happened to him, the god and leader, it would have been the end of the Egyptian army. The men would have fled in panic.

The archers usually went first into battle. They swarmed out, fired volleys of arrows, then drew back again. Now the charioteers charged and tried to break enemy ranks. The foot soldiers closed in. Clad in leather or metal coat-of-mail, they fought with spears and battle-axes, protecting themselves with shields. At the first sign of trouble, the enemy usually turned and fled. Once, when the Egyptian army attacked the enemy in front of a city's walls, the inhabitants stood on top of the walls and pulled the soldiers up by their clothing.

Raising an obelisk. After it was quarried, the shaft was hauled by rope to a barge on the Nile. Then it was inscribed and pulled up a ramp and set up. The the diagrams at left show one way it may have been raised: first, the base was tipped into a sand pit covering the pedestal; then, as the sand was emptied out of the bottom of the pit, the obelisk sank slowly into position; afterward, the ramp was removed.

When an Egyptian soldier killed an enemy, he cut off the dead man's hand and brought it to his commander. Just as we give soldiers medals for bravery, the pharaoh awarded the Gold of Valor to soldiers who "carried away hands." The soldiers piled up the hands in mounds, and after battle the scribes counted them.

An Egyptian general once captured the city of Joppa, in Palestine, by a trick. While the pharaoh and the prince of Joppa were holding a parley before battle, the general hid 200 Egyptian soldiers in 200 huge baskets. He had 500 more of his men carry them. Then he sent word to the prince of Joppa's charioteer that the Egyptians had surrendered. The baskets, he said, were full of tribute for the prince's wife. The charioteers rode ahead of the men to bring the good news. "We have captured the pharaoh!" he shouted, and the city gates flew open for him and the men carrying baskets of "tribute." As soon as the men were within the gates, they put down their baskets, let out their companions, and captured the city. It was the same trick the thieves were to use in *Ali Baba and the Forty Thieves*.

FOREIGNERS, ANIMALS, AND GODS

The pharaohs' victories brought hordes of Asiatic slaves to Egypt. They were marched in with their hands in wooden handcuffs or their arms crossed over

Great temple of Ramses II at Abu Simbel. It is carved out of solid rock and the four colossal seated statues on its face are of the pharaoh himself. Since Egypt's new Aswan Dam will completely flood it, engineers hope to slice off the whole tomb in a solid block and shift it to higher ground.

Columns from the Great Hall of the temple at Karnak. The greatest colonnaded hall ever built, it has 134 columns in 16 rows.

their heads and bound together. They were sent to work in the harem and on temple estates and to build the great monuments. The pharaoh Ramses II used this slave-labor force to turn Egypt into a granite memorial to himself. In one city he erected no fewer than fourteen obelisks, and a colossal statue of himself over ninety feet high. He planted in the Ramesseum, the temple to serve his tomb, another colossus of himself weighing over 1000 tons. Four more, each hewn out of solid rock, flank the entrance to a gigantic temple carved out of solid rock to a depth of 185 feet. More than sixty-five feet high, these portrait statues sit at Abu Simbel. When he finished adding to the temple of Amon at Karnak, it was the largest building in the ancient world. Its hall of 134 columns could hold the Cathedral of Notre Dame of Paris. The main columns are so huge that it would take six men with outstretched arms to encircle one of them.

Ramses didn't care where he got his stone, using his ancestors' monuments as a rock quarry. Modesty never troubled him. He signed his name on his own momuments and on many built by other pharaohs. He had their names routed out and his chiseled in.

Foreign slaves lived and died building these monuments. To the Egyptians, foreigners weren't real human beings. A man once complained to the pharaoh about the terrible times they were living in. Why, he said, a woman who used to be satisfied with looking at herself in the water now owned a mirror! Laundrymen were growing so independent that they wouldn't carry their bundles any more. But worse, he said, foreigners were becoming "people" everywhere. In other words, Libyans and Nubians were adopting Egyptian customs, and Egyptians were accepting them socially. This Egyptian was outraged—weren't Nubians said to have buttocks instead of hearts?

73

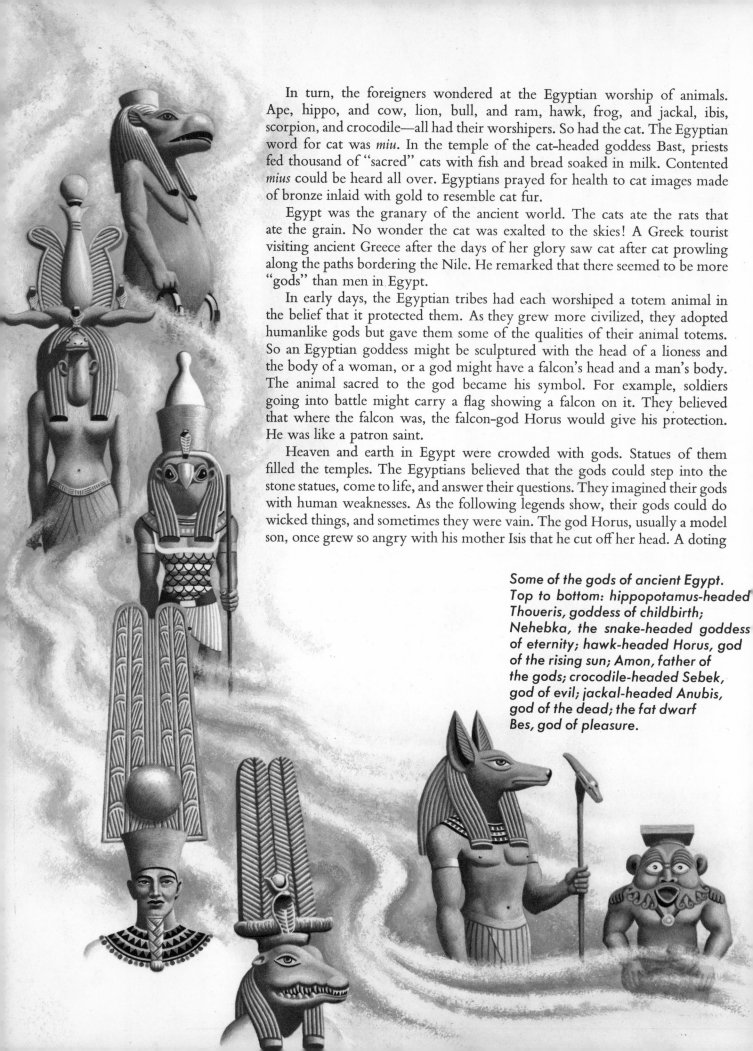

In turn, the foreigners wondered at the Egyptian worship of animals. Ape, hippo, and cow, lion, bull, and ram, hawk, frog, and jackal, ibis, scorpion, and crocodile—all had their worshipers. So had the cat. The Egyptian word for cat was *miu*. In the temple of the cat-headed goddess Bast, priests fed thousand of "sacred" cats with fish and bread soaked in milk. Contented *mius* could be heard all over. Egyptians prayed for health to cat images made of bronze inlaid with gold to resemble cat fur.

Egypt was the granary of the ancient world. The cats ate the rats that ate the grain. No wonder the cat was exalted to the skies! A Greek tourist visiting ancient Greece after the days of her glory saw cat after cat prowling along the paths bordering the Nile. He remarked that there seemed to be more "gods" than men in Egypt.

In early days, the Egyptian tribes had each worshiped a totem animal in the belief that it protected them. As they grew more civilized, they adopted humanlike gods but gave them some of the qualities of their animal totems. So an Egyptian goddess might be sculptured with the head of a lioness and the body of a woman, or a god might have a falcon's head and a man's body. The animal sacred to the god became his symbol. For example, soldiers going into battle might carry a flag showing a falcon on it. They believed that where the falcon was, the falcon-god Horus would give his protection. He was like a patron saint.

Heaven and earth in Egypt were crowded with gods. Statues of them filled the temples. The Egyptians believed that the gods could step into the stone statues, come to life, and answer their questions. They imagined their gods with human weaknesses. As the following legends show, their gods could do wicked things, and sometimes they were vain. The god Horus, usually a model son, once grew so angry with his mother Isis that he cut off her head. A doting

Some of the gods of ancient Egypt. Top to bottom: hippopotamus-headed Thoueris, goddess of childbirth; Nehebka, the snake-headed goddess of eternity; hawk-headed Horus, god of the rising sun; Amon, father of the gods; crocodile-headed Sebek, god of evil; jackal-headed Anubis, god of the dead; the fat dwarf Bes, god of pleasure.

mother, she soon forgave him. Being a goddess, she could function with or without her head. Another god in a moment of anger insulted the god Re by saying, "Your temple is empty!" Re was so hurt by this cutting remark that he lay down on his back for a whole day, feeling perfectly miserable.

Since the gods were so human, men sometimes treated them with less than respect. It was not unusual for an Egyptian to rebuke a god. "What's the matter with thee, Amon!" scolded a pharaoh after he had lost a battle. The pharaoh had a fierce prayer to use as a last resort if the gods thwarted his plans. He threatened to eat them in paradise. Later, the common people adopted this prayer as their own. In it, they threatened to eat the biggest gods for breakfast, the middle-sized ones for dinner, and the little ones for supper, if the gods didn't answer their prayers.

Each part of his body, an Egyptian believed, was protected by one of thirty-six gods. When he had a nose cold, for example, he appealed to the god in charge of his nose, bringing gifts to the god's temple. If the cold persisted, he could pay a priest to recite a magic spell to drive it out: "Depart, cold, son of a cold! Go out on the floor—stink! stink! stink!"

To an Egyptian, disease and bad luck were caused by evil spirits or by offending the gods. He called on a specialist in heavenly matters—the priest— to set things right. The priesthood grew until it specialized in many fields. Mortuary priests knew how to embalm the body. From their embalming

Top to bottom: Nut, goddess of the sky; Osiris, god who judged the dead; Isis, goddess of motherhood; hawk-headed Re, the sun-god from whom all pharaohs claimed descent; Neith, goddess of Lower Egypt, called mother of the gods; lion-headed Sekhet, goddess of violence.

practices, priests learned to be doctors. Doctors used magic spells as well as medicine as part of their cures. A woman breaking out in boils might call on a temple priest and have him write a letter of complaint to a god. She then prayed to the god, left a live duck or a jar of beer at his temple, and went home hoping to wake up next day cured. If the boils didn't disappear, she called in a doctor-priest. He might prescribe pills made of ground malachite (a copper ore) and bread dough, to be gulped down with sweet beer.

Egyptian doctors became famous in the ancient world. They were the world's first medical specialists. There were Egyptian dentists, oculists, veterinarians, and surgeons. Egyptian surgeons were highly skilled in sewing up cuts and in setting and splinting fractured bones. They were the first doctors to us splints, bandages, and compresses.

In the pyramid age, priests were government officials, not professionals. But through the centuries they grew into a powerful class from the gifts pharaohs and common people alike made to the temples. One pharaoh gave 169 towns, 100,000 slaves, and a million head of cattle to the temples of the city god of Thebes, Amon.

As the Egyptian king became an emperor, so Amon became the emperor of the gods. One pharaoh declared a holy war on Amon and his priests. Amenhotep IV forbade the worship of Amon and for the thousand gods of Egypt substituted one—Aton, the sun disk. He and his followers prayed to a golden disk from which radiated rays of light. The rays ended in hands, for the sun gave life to everything with a generous hand.

The pharaoh changed his name to Akhnaton, "He Who Serves Aton." With his beautiful wife Nefertiti and his daughters, he sailed from Thebes down the Nile to a place where, he said, he could "live in truth." Here his architects, engineers, and artists built a city said to be like a glimpse of heaven.

But Egypt wasn't ready for monotheism, the worship of one god. That would be given to the world by a subject nation of the Egyptian empire, Palestine. The Hebrews had learned many proverbs from their Egyptian masters. Later they would incorporate this wisdom into the Bible. The Egyptians in times of trouble believed that a savior would appear in Egypt to rescue the people from oppression and bring justice to earth. The Hebrews inherited this tradition.

THE LAST OF THE PHARAOHS

After Akhnaton's death, the old gods returned more powerful than ever. Eventually they sat on the throne as pharaohs. Egypt became a spoil for

The Great Sphinx at Giza. This sphinx, guardian of the dead, has the body of a lion and the head of the pharaoh Khafre, near whose pyramid it crouches. It is about 240 feet long and 66 feet high.

foreign nations. Conquerors, like rats, nibbled away at the wheat from the great barn that was Egypt. Peasants used pharaohs' stone inscriptions as millstones to grind their grain and pulled down blocks from the pyramids to bridge the canals. Sand and mystery settled over the monuments. Colossal statues were said to move their lips and sigh when the sun came up.

For a thousand years the sacred writing couldn't be read. Then a soldier of Napoleon's army found a black stone at Rosetta, in the delta of the Nile. It was covered with inscriptions in Greek, hieroglyphics, and the simplified form called demotic. With the help of the Rosetta stone, hieroglyphics were deciphered. The pharaohs at last had their wishes fulfilled. They lived again.

Modern and ancient Egypt meet. Shepherds tend their flocks in the shadows of the pyramids.

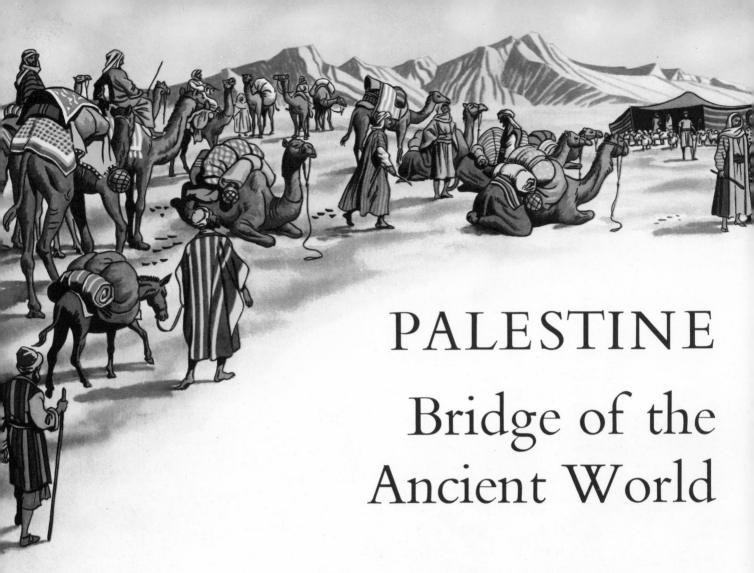

PALESTINE
Bridge of the Ancient World

A caravan halts at a "movable city"—a tent city of nomads. A crossroad of the ancient world, Palestine was the home of many peoples—Canaanites, Amorites, Edomites, Israelites, Philistines and Phoenicians.

In the Bible, Father Abraham led his family westward from Ur, in Mesopotamia. Hundreds of years later, Moses led his people out of bondage eastward from Egypt. The Bible reflects the two great forces that brought civilization into Palestine.

For the tiny, fertile land of Palestine lay between the world's two oldest civilizations. Egypt and Mesopotamia fought their battles in Palestine. In peacetime, merchants used the land as a bridge from one empire to the other. They sold their wares and their way of life to the inhabitants. For Abraham the Mesopotamian and for Moses the Egyptian, Palestine was the Promised Land. Here, perhaps, men might live in peace, enjoying the fruits of both civilizations.

Ancient Palestine was about the size of the state of Vermont. Yet it helped give the world one of its greatest inventions, the alphabet. And from it came the world's greatest book, the Bible.

THE PURPLE LAND—CANAAN

Palestine is the modern name for the old land of Canaan. Curiously, the name comes from the Philistines. The ancient Philistines were one of the Sea Peoples from the Aegean isles and Asia Minor who roamed the shores of the Mediterranean looking for a place to live. The Philistines settled on the southern

78

coast of Canaan in the twelfth century B.C. The Biblical giant Goliath and Samson's betrayer, Delilah, were both Philistines.

Palestine's older name, Canaan, means "land of purple." For that part of Canaan between the cities of Tyre and Haifa was the ancient center of the purple-dye industry. The ancient Greeks called northern Canaan Phoenicia, which also means "land of purple."

The Canaanites or Phoenicians—we might call them the Purple People—had a secret process for making purple dye. A mollusk or shellfish called the murex is washed up in great numbers along the Mediterranean coast. A sea snail living in a shell, the murex has a gland that secretes a purplish substance. The dyemakers cut out this tissue, ground it, then boiled it in a weak salt solution for three days. The result was a reddish-purple dye envied and sought by the rest of the ancient world. The dye was expensive, and only kings and rich men could afford to buy it. To wear purple came to mean being a person of rank or wealth.

The streets of Tyre were said to have had a horrible stench. No wonder, for the dyemakers used only a tiny part of the sea snail and threw the rest into the street, to rot in the sun.

Certain towns in Palestine specialized in dyeing. The dyer wore gloves to protect his hands. He mixed his dye in a stone or pottery vat, dipped in a piece of cloth to test the strength of the dye, then soaked the wool. Wool was dyed before it was woven. After soaking, the wool was removed from the dye vat, the excess water squeezed out, and the wool laid on a bench to dry. The dyed wool was then stored in leather bags or wrapped in animal hides so that sun and rain wouldn't fade or run the color.

THE WALLS OF JERICHO COME TUMBLING DOWN

The Hebrews that Moses led out of Egypt knew little about Canaan. It wasn't the "purple land" to them, but the Promised Land, the land flowing with milk and honey. Moses never entered Canaan. Joshua, who followed him as chief of the tribes, was to lead the chosen people into Canaan. First, he decided to spy out the land.

The cities of Canaan were then little independent kingdoms. The fields surrounding the cities were sown with crops or had flocks grazing on them. In summer, the people lived mainly outdoors. But in winter, when it rained, they moved into their houses inside the city. The cities were small hilltop fortresses, with tiny one-room houses crowded together behind high walls.

Joshua's spies went to Jericho, one of Canaan's main cities. Today, Jericho is a mound of ruins beside the Jordan River. But excavations of the ruins have shown that Jericho may be one of the oldest inhabited cities in the world.

According to the Bible, Joshua's spies stayed in the house of a woman who lived on the walls of Jericho. When the king's men came looking for the spies, she hid them on the roof of her house, covering them with flax drying in the sun. Later, she lowered them down by rope over the city wall.

A house on a wall—it was just a story, people said. Today we know better. The ancient city of Jericho has been dug out of its ruins. Two walls about twenty feet high and from twelve to fifteen feet apart encircled the city. The outer wall was six feet thick, the inner wall twelve. Jericho was only six acres in size. It was so overcrowded that people built their little houses in the space between the two walls, on top of the walls, and on timbers laid across the two walls. To defenders of the city, these houses would become a serious obstacle.

Joshua's soldiers surrounded Jericho. No one could enter or leave the city's gates. It was a war of nerves, for news of the approaching nomadic warriors had frightened the Canaanites. Joshua instructed his soldiers to walk around the city but to make no noise. For six days the only sound the walled-in Canaanites

A winged ivory cherub from the "house of ivory" that King Ahab of Israel (c. 874–853 B.C.) built at Samaria.

Fattened geese, an ancient delicacy, being brought to court, possibly as a tax payment. This ivory from the fortress-city of Megiddo is more than 3000 years old.

heard from the outside was the nerve-shattering blasts of the priests' trumpets. On the seventh day, the trumpets blew, the Hebrews shouted, and the walls of Jericho came tumbling down. So said the Bible. Modern excavators discovered that about 1400-1385 B.C. the outer wall of Jericho slid down the hill, while the inner one cracked and crumbled. Houses showed signs of life—dinner ready—till the moment they caught on fire. What had happened?

Jericho is in a volcanic zone. In 1927 an earthquake shook the area and sent cliffs crashing into the Jordan River, damming it up. Arabs walked across the dry river bed just as the Bible has Joshua's soldiers do. The walls of Jericho showed every sign of having been destroyed by earthquake. Then Joshua's men could have poured into the terrified city and burned it down.

Joshua laid a curse against anyone rebuilding the city. Archeologists have found that for five hundred years after the walls came tumbling down Jericho remained uninhabited. Other archeologists believe that the Hebrews entered Canaan in the mid-thirteenth century B.C.—after the walls of Jericho fell. Still others place the entry of the Hebrews between 1400 and 1250 B.C.

OUR ALPHABET IS INVENTED

When Joshua and his army were conquering Canaan, writing was a state monopoly in Mesopotamia and Egypt. Only a chosen few, the scribes, ever learned to write. They had to be trained for years by the priesthood or government officials, for cuneiform writing and hieroglyphics were difficult to master. Kings as well as merchants hired scribes to write for them. When a king could write, he proudly boasted of the fact on stone columns or clay tablets.

Canaan or Palestine had no state government and no organized priesthood. The city officials and the merchants hired scribes to write letters and documents in cuneiform. Most likely, these scribes were trained in foreign schools.

The language of Palestine was Semitic, with different dialects spoken wherever different tribes lived. The term "Semitic" is modern, invented to indicate the races that Noah's eldest son, Shem, fathered. Canaanite, Hebrew, and Phoenician were all dialects of the same Semitic language.

Between the years 1800 and 1600 B.C. Canaanites working in the Sinai turquoise mines borrowed Egyptian hieroglyphics, simplified the signs, and wrote their language in it. It was an early attempt at an alphabet. Between the years 1400 and 1200 B.C. other Semites living on the north Syrian coast opposite the isle of Cyprus, in the city of Ugarit, developed a cuneiform alphabet. But our alphabet was really invented in one of the cities of Canaan between the years 1400 and 1000 B.C. and perfected by the Canaanites or Phoenicians in the north.

These two lines show the development of the letters A and B. According to one theory, the letters of the alphabet began as pictures called hieroglyphs (left). They then developed into a script, called hieratic (middle), and, after that, into letters such as those in the Semitic alphabet (right).

The invention of the alphabet was a democratic revolution. For now anyone could learn to write. Writing wasn't clumsy and difficult, but easy. With the alphabet, hundreds of signs didn't have to be memorized. Why, it was as simple as ABC. No one ever said as simple as cuneiform or hieroglyphics.

We should say "as simple as ABG," for A, B, and G were the first three letters of the new alphabet. It had twenty-two letters, all consonants. The letters were based on the sound of consonants and named after familiar objects. For example, the Hebrew or Phoenician letter A is *aleph*, which means "ox." And the letter A looked roughly like an oxhead. (A in Semitic languages is a consonant, not a vowel.) The alphabet inventor chose *aleph* for A because it was easy to remem-

Dyeing purple cloth. The most prized dye of the ancient world was made from the gland of a sea snail called murex (see inset) found in huge numbers on the Palestinian coast between Tyre and Haifa. The dye was so expensive that only kings and nobles could afford it, and it became known as "royal purple." Actually it was not purple but various shades, including black-purple and red-violet.

ber. Only the initial sound mattered, not the word. The letter B was *beth*, which means "house." The letter B originally was shaped like a house.

A Canaanite reciting the alphabet would say *aleph*, *beth*, *gimel*, and so on, or *ox*, *house*, *camel*. When we learn our alphabet we do something similar. To remember the alphabet, we're taught to connect the letters with objects we know. "A as in apple, B as in boat, C as in cat, D as in door." When we see BAD, we don't read "boat, apple, door"—but the word "bad." The Canaanites and Phoenicians used their alphabet the same way.

There was only one basic alphabet—the original Semitic one. All other alphabets, including our own, are only variations of this. The Phoenicians were the traders of the ancient world. In their ships, they carried a cargo more precious than dyes and oils. They carried the alphabet. The Greeks adopted it and renamed the letters *alpha*, *beta*, *gamma*, and so on. The names of these letters mean nothing in Greek. They are merely Greek versions of the Semitic *aleph*, *beth*, *gimel*. The Greeks added vowels, then passed the alphabet on to the Romans. The Romans changed the shapes of the letters somewhat and spread the alphabet throughout Europe. And that's how we got our alphabet. The word *alphabet* itself comes from the first two letters of the Greek alphabet—*alpha*, *beta*.

FARMERS AND SHEPHERDS

One of the earliest inscriptions in the new alphabet—about 925 B.C.—is a limestone tablet written in the Hebrew of the Old Testament. A boy in ancient Gezer wrote it as a school composition. This tablet, called the Gezer Calendar, lists the seasons for planting and harvesting.

Palestine has always been primarily an agricultural country. Where there were soil and water, crops were planted. Where there were only grass and rocks, shepherds tended flocks of goats and fat-tailed sheep. According to the Gezer Calendar, the olive harvest lasted two months, grain planting two months, late planting two months, and flax hoeing, the barley harvest, the wheat harvest, and the gathering of summer fruits one month each.

The Hebrews didn't plant the olive groves in Palestine. This "king of trees," as the Bible calls it, had long been grown by the Canaanites. Nomads wander and can't tend olive trees; settled people are needed for this. In fact, the olive tree is a symbol of the peaceful, settled way of life. Even today, when we talk about a peace offer, we speak of holding out an olive branch.

The olive tree is grown from a slip. When it is three years old, it is grafted so that it will bear fruit. To harvest the olives, the trees were shaken or beaten with long poles and the olives caught in baskets.

Grapes were also grown in Palestine from the most ancient times. In the Bible, Noah is said to have planted the vine after he came out of the ark. Oddly enough, the vine is now believed to have been grown originally in eastern Anatolia. It was there, on Mount Ararat, that Noah's ark supposedly landed.

To make a vineyard, the Canaanites and the Hebrews removed the stones from a field and built a wall with them. Then they planted vines, trained them to grow up trees or sticks, dug the soil around the plants, and pruned the vines till they bore grapes. Near by, where there was rocky ground, they made a winepress. Two hollows were cut in the rock, one lower than the other. After the harvest, the grapes were put into the upper hollow. Barefoot men and women stamped on the grapes, singing and shouting. The grape juice then flowed into the lower hollow. Pots were dipped into the juice, and the liquid was stored in pottery or wooden vats until it fermented and turned to wine.

Men who owned large vineyards built watchtowers at the edge of their vineyards. During the grape season, the whole family lived in the watchtower. Here they could look out for jackals and wild pigs that trampled down the vines and thieves who stole the grapes. According to Hebrew law and probably Canaanite custom, some of the grapes were left on the vines. Passing strangers and the poor were allowed to eat these grapes, though they couldn't carry any away with them. This same custom applied to the olive trees and to the fields of wheat and barley. A neighbor or a stranger could come into the grove or field, pluck off olives or ears of ripe grain, and eat as much as he wanted.

Where barley and the vine wouldn't grow, sheep and goats could graze. The shepherd led the animals to their pasturelands in the hills. Near a cave or where he pitched his tent, he built a rock wall to enclose his flock at night. This is called a sheepfold. At night he slept in the cave or his tent, his slingshot close at hand.

A Phoenician shipyard. The Phoenicians were the great seafarers of the ancient world and even manned King Solomon's navy.

Flocks weren't kept in cities; the cities were scarcely large enough for the inhabitants. A city family might, however, keep a sheep or a goat for milk. The large flocks were enclosed in sheepfolds outside the city. Some of these folds had high stone walls with watchtowers where armed men guarded the flock. Not only wild animals tried to make off with the sheep, but desert raiders —ancient rustlers—swooped down on horseback to steal the sheep.

Cattle also grazed in Palestine, but usually in the agricultural districts. For cattle need better pastures than sheep and goats. Besides, they pulled the plows at planting time and treaded out the grain after the harvest. The Canaanites used to yoke a bull and an ass together as a plowing team. Hebrew law forbade this, but the custom has continued down to the present. Palestinian cattle are not the large animals we know, but short-horned beasts about the size of asses.

LAND OF MILK AND HONEY

When Moses led the Hebrews through the wilderness of Sinai, they were starving until manna fell from heaven. Manna isn't a myth. A sweetish, fruit-tasting juice oozes from the thin branches of the tamarisk tree in June and July, just as maple sirup flows from maple trees when they're tapped. A tiny scale insect taps the tamarisk. It punctures the bark, and the juice drips from the branches. In the cold of early morning, these drops become solid and fall to the ground like little gum-drop candies. This may have been the manna that Moses found on the ground to feed his people. Of course, when the sun grows hot, the drops melt and mix with the dirt. Men and animals still eat manna from the tamarisk tree.

In Canaan, men didn't live off manna from heaven. People plucked the fresh ears of barley or wheat, rubbed the husk off by hand or in a mortar, and ate the raw grain. They also "parched" the grain. A bundle of ears of ripe grain were held over a blazing fire or roasted on a metal plate or a hot stone.

Barley or wheat was ground into flour in a mortar or between millstones. The flour was then mixed with honey and oil to make a kind of porridge. Honey was usually made from dates or by boiling grape juice, but honey from wild bees may have been used. Bread was, of course, the staff of life. Flat circular cakes of bread were baked on hot stones, on pottery griddles, and in dung fires. The griddles had perforations on one side that helped conduct the heat through the dough. Bread was also baked in a pottery oven shaped like a beehive. A fire was lit inside; then, when the oven was hot enough, the fire was raked out, the dough put in, and the bread baked. Country people all over the world still bake bread this way, using a brick oven.

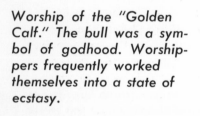

Worship of the "Golden Calf." The bull was a symbol of godhood. Worshippers frequently worked themselves into a state of ecstasy.

Only the rich could afford to eat meat throughout the year. The poor ate meat at religious festivals, when animals were sacrificed to the Baals or nature gods of the Canaanites or the God of the Hebrews. In a hot climate like that of Palestine, the animal was slaughtered, dressed, and cooked right away, before the meat spoiled.

Both meat and bread were flavored with salt. The inhabitants of Palestine, like the Mesopotamians, believed that salt had magic powers. And, indeed, it has. It preserves food. Salted fish last for months, whereas fresh fish rot in a day or two. The waters of the Dead Sea were scooped up in clay pans and set in the hot sun. The water evaporated, leaving salt in the bottom of the pan. Rock salt near the Dead Sea, where Sodom may have been, juts out like cliffs. Winds fashion these cliffs into shapes that sometimes resemble human figures. Perhaps the story of Lot's wife turning to a pillar of salt had its origin in one of these changing cliffs of crystallized rock salt.

Salt was sold in lumps or cakes. To use it, the housewife crushed it in a mortar. Salt was added to oil lamps and to poor fuel like camel dung to make the fire burn brighter.

Oil pressed from olives was used for lamps, cooking, medicines, and cosmetics. Ointment makers steeped flowers, roots, and herbs in hot oil to make perfumes and fragrant unguents for the hair and body. When flies fell into the ointment pots, their dead bodies caused the ointments to stink instead of to smell sweet. For this reason, we still use the expression "a fly in the ointment" when we mean that something has gone wrong.

In a land flowing with milk and honey, milk was an important drink. Our milk comes from milch cows, but in Palestine milk usually came from sheep and goats, asses and camels. Often, the milk was allowed to sour or ferment before being drunk. It tasted more refreshing to these people.

CITIES THAT MOVED AND CITIES BEHIND WALLS

Down to the present day, Palestine has had not only stationary but movable cities—cities of tents. Nomads, then as now, traveled in tribes or families, along with their sheep, goats, and other animals. When they reached a stream or a spring, they pitched their tents and stayed until the weather changed or their herds had eaten the available fodder. Sometimes they planted small crops and remained till they reaped the harvest.

In a view based on the Bible, Israelites are shown carrying the Ark of the Covenant, the most sacred of Israelite ritual objects. Under the two carved cherubim on the lid, the Ark held the stone tablets of the Ten Commandments.

The women usually wove strips of goat's-hair cloth. These they sewed together to make the tent covering. Poles six or seven feet high held up the tents, with cords tied to tent pegs driven into the ground to strengthen the structure. Curtains were hung from the tent poles to make sections or rooms. Small tents had only two sections, one for men and the other for women. Larger tents had another section for entertaining guests. Rich nomads traveled with tents having as many as seven sections.

The whole family lived in the tent. When the family grew too large for it, the eldest son set up housekeeping for himself and his family in a separate tent. The Hebrew nomads who entered Canaan carried a special tent with them that served as a sanctuary or temple where they worshiped their God.

Since they were always on the move, nomads didn't have much furniture. They sat and slept on mats or rugs. The women had a loom to weave cloth and a mortar and pestle or two millstones to grind grain. Clay pots and bowls for drawing water and for cooking made up the rest of the kitchen equipment. For cooking, the men set up primitive stone hearths or burned desert brush or animal dung in the open air.

Among the nomads, the tribal elders decided when to take down the poles, fold the tents, and move on. They judged their fellows according to their tribal laws, dealing out a primitive kind of justice. King Saul of the Hebrews held his court sitting under the shade of a tamarisk tree.

Tent cities were a cluster of big and small tents in barren land or desert sand. The permanent walled cities of ancient Palestine covered no more than from six to fifteen acres. Before Joshua and his army entered the land, city walls had been high and thick. After the Hebrew conquest, city walls dwindled to half the

A vineyard with a watch-tower where a man could guard against thieves, jackals and boars.

size they had been. The former nomads wouldn't submit to the discipline needed to build and repair giant walls.

To enter a city, you climbed a pathway up the hill leading to the town gate. The gateway didn't lead directly into the city, but turned at an angle. This way, if enemy troops attacked the city, broke through the gate, and opened arrow fire, they wouldn't hit the defending soldiers or the townspeople. The arrows would glance off the gate walls.

Some cities had towers on several parts of the wall, so that lookouts could guard every direction of enemy attack. But every city had a tower at the gate. Stone benches lined the tower walls. Here the local judges sat to hear lawsuits. There were no lawyers. The two quarreling parties brought their witnesses and told their stories to the judges. If a merchant was accused of giving short weight, he had to open his pouch of weights, set up his balance, and prove that he hadn't cheated on the measure. Of course, this was difficult, for every merchant had his own weights, and they varied from merchant to merchant. Justice didn't always triumph. The Bible speaks of judges who took bribes before making decisions.

In Hebrew times, if a man was accused and convicted of a crime punished by death, he was led outside the city walls. The witnesses placed their hands on his head as a kind of oath and then picked up a stone and hit him with it. After the witnesses had "cast the first stone," people from the town who had followed the "court" outside the city then picked up rocks and stoned him to death.

From the gate a cobblestone road led to the "palace," if the city was important and had a king living in it. Until the time of King David (about 1012–972 B.C.) and perhaps even then, these palaces were merely houses larger than the others.

An olive press. Olives were placed in a basket on a platform and pressed out with a beam used as a lever. The oil ran down through a hole in the platform and was stored in jars. Similar presses were used in making wine from grapes.

Nothing in Palestine approached the magnificence of Egyptian and Mesopotamian palaces. The city streets stank from garbage and poor drainage and were narrow, dark, and dirty. Children didn't play in the streets, which we would call alleyways. They played in the bazaar or market place, the only open part of the city. Here merchants and craftsmen set up their booths for business.

PHILISTINE HOMES AND IVORY HOUSES

Canaanite houses, which the Hebrews copied, were built on a plan still seen in the Near East today. A small court opened into a one-room house. Often, the room was divided into two sections, one slightly higher than the other. During the day, the cooking and other household chores were performed on the lower level. At night, the family brought in their ass or goat and tethered it in the lower section. They used the upper level for their own sleeping quarters. It was easy to enlarge this house, which was done when a son married and raised a family. Another room was simply built on to the court.

The house walls were made of mud brick or stone and plastered over with mud. The outside walls were often whitewashed, and the inside walls were sometimes painted. But paints were expensive. The floors were made of beaten clay. The roof was flat, supported by wooden beams laid from wall to wall. The rooms were tiny, and ordinary timbers spanned the distance easily. The roof was thatched—the timbers covered with straw, leaves, dead branches—then covered with a coat of clay or lime. It was never completely rainproof and needed constant repair. As in Mesopotamia, the family climbed an outside stairway to the roof during the summer to sleep in the cool night air. Hebrew law required homeowners to build a balustrade around the roof to protect persons in the streets and those on the roof.

A house at Gezer dating to the days when the Philistines controlled the city has been excavated in modern times. Since the room was too wide to be spanned by a single roof beam, two lengths of wood had been used. Wooden columns supported these double roof beams, each column resting on a stone slab. Perhaps it was just such a building that Samson pulled down on the heads of the Philistines. It wouldn't have been difficult for a strong man to slip the pillars off their stone bases.

The houses of the rich had stone foundations, which kept them dry when the rains poured down. The sun-dried brick walls were plastered outside and paneled inside with wood, sometimes with cedar imported from the north. The windows were closed in with latticework to screen out the sun's rays. In crowded cities like Jerusalem and Samaria, the lower walls were very thick, for they supported an upper story built of brick or wood. The kitchen, the storerooms, and the servants' quarters were located on the lower story, and the family lived on the second floor.

In early days in Palestine—and always in the case of the poor—people slept

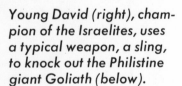

Young David (right), champion of the Israelites, uses a typical weapon, a sling, to knock out the Philistine giant Goliath (below).

on mats or rugs. These were rolled up by day and spread out at night along a wall. In summer, the sleeper carried his rug to the roof and rolled it out there. At dinnertime, cushions or rugs were laid on the floor, and the family squatted cross-legged on them. Sometimes a row of cushions was set along a wall to make a divan. Low, movable tables like trays were placed in front of the diners, or boards were laid over wooden props. The house boasted a wooden stand to hold the lamp. This could be moved wherever needed. The lamp, which burned oil and salt, was a piece of pottery shaped like a saucer. One end was pinched in to hold a wick made of flax threads. Though the king's palace might have a fountain in the courtyard, the average family washed out of a pottery basin.

Nothing remains of the cedar palaces Phoenician architects and workers built for King David and King Solomon. And the "ivory house" of King Ahab (about 874–853 B.C.) in Samaria, mentioned in the Bible, was long thought an exaggeration. However, archeologists have since dug into the ruins of Samaria and discovered many pieces of carved ivory. Some are decorated with gold leaf; others have insets of colored glass and semiprecious stones like lapis. The ivory may have come from Africa by way of Egypt. It may also have come from the upper Euphrates or northern Syria, for herds of elephants still roamed these districts in the ninth century B.C. Rich merchants of Tyre had so much ivory that they even used it to inlay the decks of their ships.

Ahab's "ivory house" wasn't made of pure ivory—any more than the "glass rooms" of a museum are made of glass. The ivory house was so called because there were ivories in it, just as there are glass exhibits in a museum's glass rooms. The Samarian ivories are in the shape of plaques or panels. Most likely, Ahab's house had cedar-paneled walls with the plaques inlaid in the wood paneling. Ahab's wife, Jezebel, was a Phoenician princess, and the ivories had probably been carved by Phoenician artists.

SPRINGS, CISTERNS, WELLS, WATER BOTTLES

Palestine has two seasons, dry and rainy. The rainy season lasts almost two months. Irrigation farming, as in Egypt and Mesopotamia, was not widely practiced in Palestine. Palestine didn't have the rivers for it. The Jordan is no Nile or Euphrates, and its bed is too low to irrigate any land but the Jordan Valley. The farmers of Palestine practiced "dry farming"—farming to conserve the moisture of the soil without using irrigation.

Much of Palestine is rocky. The rain falls on soft limestone rock and trickles through to the hard rock underneath. Where the layer of hard rock juts out of the earth, water spouts out as though from an underground river. This is called a spring. Palestinian cities were usually built near a spring. Naturally, the spring was located outside the city walls. For the spring gushed from the base of the hill, whereas the city was built on the top of the hill.

In early Canaanite days, the city dwellers dug a shaft through their hill, then cut a passage through the rock leading to the spring. The spring water then flowed to the bottom of the shaft. Whenever the city was besieged, the inhabitants were guaranteed their water supply. The townswomen stood on a platform over the shaft and lowered their jars into the pool of water below.

In 701 B.C., the Assyrians invaded Palestine and besieged Jerusalem. The Bible states that King Hezekiah built a tunnel to lead water into the city and at

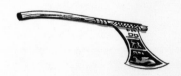

89

the same time keep the water out of the Assyrians' hands. Hezekiah's tunnel has been excavated in modern times. The tunnel carried water from the spring of Gihon outside the city walls to the pool of Siloam within the city. About 1760 feet long, the tunnel was bored through solid rock by miners using wedges, hammers, and picks. Miners began the tunnel at both ends, to meet in the middle. It is a miracle that they met, for the tunnel twists and winds so much.

An inscription inside the tunnel recorded the story of how the tunnel had been bored. The miners were guided by the sound of their picks. When both teams were within a few feet of each other, they could hear each other's voices. Then a pick broke through, the miners could see each other, and soon the water flowed from the spring to the city pool. In some places the tunnel is as tall as a man. In others, it is wide enough for two men to pass each other. It has been estimated that the tunnel took from six to nine months to build. Once again, today, it brings water to the inhabitants of one of Jerusalem's hills.

Rainwater is precious and must be saved and stored in Palestine. The cistern was one of Palestine's earliest water-storage devices. How it was developed is easy to imagine. Natural rock caves dot the country. When the rain fell, some of these caves filled up with rainwater, where it lasted long after the rain had stopped. The next step was to carve an imitation cave. A circular shaft was cut through the rock, below which a square or circular room was hollowed out. The walls were plastered so that the water wouldn't seep away. Roughly, the cistern was a large rock bottle with a narrow mouth and a wide base. Cisterns uncovered in Gezer had a shaft three by five feet leading to a storage room twenty feet deep and from thirteen to twenty-five feet in diameter.

Sometimes cisterns were used for more sinister purposes than storing rainwater. Empty cisterns were turned into jails. The top of a cistern could be covered and the room below used as a secret storage place. Sometimes fugitives used an empty cistern as a hideout from the police.

Smaller cisterns were hewn from blocks of stone and placed in the courtyard or under the corner of the roof. The rain poured off the roof into a clay gutter and splashed into the cistern below. This kind of cistern is just like our country rain barrel placed beneath the eaves of barns and houses.

In the desert areas or barren places, men searched for green oases or any growing vegetation. Oases meant underground water. Here they sank wells. The word "Beer" that precedes the names of many Palestine desert towns, as in Beersheba, means "well." The well was the gossip center of Palestine's villages. Here the women, carrying clay water pots on head or shoulder, met

An Egyptian fresco showing two Canaanite tribute-bearers wearing magnificent clothing.

and exchanged the latest news. Often, the mouth of the well was covered with a stone so that sand wouldn't blow into it and muddy it or animals fall in and poison the water.

"The pot that goes too often to the well breaks," says an old proverb. Merchants, soldiers, shepherds, and nomads, who traveled distances, carried unbreakable water bottles. These were made of goatskin or sheepskin. The whole skin of the animal was sewn together to make it watertight, except for the end of one leg. This was tied with cord. When a man wanted a drink, he untied the cord and used the leg as a spout. When the water bottle was empty, he filled it through this same leg. Water bottles were practical on journeys, for when empty they could be folded up.

TAKING THE CLOTHES OFF A MAN'S BACK

Like its neighbors, Palestine had slaves from early times. War captives were usually made slaves. Kings, army officers, and rich merchants and farmers naturally owned the most slaves. The slaves worked in the fields, on public works like walls and roads, and took care of household chores. When slaves served their masters, they always appeared with head covered and feet bare. Bare feet and covered head were the mark of respect of a person in the presence of his betters. The master, in the presence of his master, his God, also covered his head and removed his sandals.

The custom still holds true for orthodox Jews. And today, outside mosques, turbaned Moslems remove their shoes at the door before they enter to pray. A stranger can always tell how full the mosque is by counting the pairs of shoes or sandals outside the mosque entrance.

Another clothing custom—though this has nothing to do with slavery—still persists in the Near East. When an Arab has to move with speed, he lifts up the bottom of his robe and tucks it under the cloth belt wound around his waist, freeing his legs. In the Bible, this is called "girding up the loins." Men girded

Solomon's Temple. According to the Bible, it was built with beams of cedar and was overlaid with gold. Although only about 90 feet long and 45 feet high, it was celebrated for its sumptuous adornment. In the Temple courtyard stood the "brazen sea," a gigantic bronze bowl holding water for ritual purification. After standing three and a half centuries, the Temple was destroyed by the soldiers of Nebuchadrezzar in 587–586 B.C.

Copper mine. Between the Dead Sea and the Gulf of Aqaba was a chain of copper mines that were worked as early as the Bronze Age (about 2500 B.C.). These mines supplied Solomon with copper to mold such objects as the "brazen sea."

Smelting copper. Using a bellows, a smith forces air into the furnace to increase the heat.

up their loins usually before battle, so they could move about with greater ease.

Slavery in Palestine didn't necessarily mean oppression. Slaves were often treated as part of the family, sometimes were adopted and made heirs, and often were freed by their masters. Under the Hebrews, a master who injured a slave had to set him free. If a man died owing a debt, the creditor could seize his children and work them as slaves until the debt was paid off.

The life of a slave was sometimes better than that of a poor man. A poor man owing money could have his clothes taken off his back by the man to whom he owed the money. His clothes were held till he made good his debt. But at night, his clothes had to be returned to him. That was Hebrew law. For rich and poor slept in their clothes on cool nights.

SOLOMON IN ALL HIS GLORY

Of all the kings who ruled little and big states in Palestine, Solomon was the richest and mightiest. He had hundreds of wives in his harem, many of them princesses from foreign kingdoms. Throughout his realm, he owned thousands of slaves. His merchant fleets sailed to faraway Africa and India, bringing to Palestine "gold, and silver, ivory, apes, and peacocks." He built the great Temple of the Hebrews on a hill of Jerusalem, which became the symbol of the religion of Judaism.

Yet, outside of the Bible, no mention of Solomon's name has thus far been found. Part of the reason may be that both Assyria and Egypt recorded only their victories, not their defeats. Besides, both were weak powers when Solomon ruled Palestine (about 971–931 B.C.). Another reason, perhaps more telling, may be that many of the sites where Solomon built have since become Moslem shrines. They cannot be excavated. Still, inscriptions of his reign may one day turn up. After all, the only mention of the Hittites was in the Bible, until nineteenth-century archeologists began to turn up Hittite records.

In the Bible, Solomon was said to have kept "chariot cities" at Megiddo, Hazor, and Gezer and to have supplied his allies with horses and chariots. Archeologists have dug up ancient Megiddo. In a level dating back to Solomon's reign, they found a huge stable—a kind of giant horse-and-chariot garage. Stone pillars held up the stable roof and also served to separate the mangers or stalls. Each pillar had a hole bored through it at a level where halters could be tied through the hole. Between each pillar was a stone manger with cobble-stoned flooring to prevent the horses from slipping in their stalls. Broad, paved streets led into the stables. Solomon's stables at Megiddo could house 150 chariots and 450 horses.

In front of the Temple Solomon built in Jerusalem stood two bronze pillars about forty feet high. In the Temple court stood the "brazen sea." This was a huge bronze bowl resting on twelve bronze oxen arranged in groups of three. It could hold an estimated 16,000 gallons of water. From a hole in the side, water poured down in a stream. Here the Temple priests washed their hands and feet before holy services. The bowl alone has been estimated to have weighed 200 tons.

Bronze is an alloy of copper and tin. To use bronze so lavishly Palestine needed a good supply of copper. But Palestine was not noted for mineral resources. And then, not too many years ago, an archeologist exploring the region south of the Dead Sea found King Solomon's mines. Copper mines had been worked all along the Wadi el-Arabah, a depression that runs from the Dead Sea to the Gulf of Aqabah on the Red Sea. Solomon was said to have built a great seaport called Ezion-geber on the Red Sea. But where had it been located?

Ezion-geber was unearthed from a mound on the gulf, bringing to light the largest and most elaborate refineries yet discovered in the ancient world.

The raw copper ore was dug in open mines along the wadi and given a first roasting on the spot. Some of the stone furnaces are still in place. The metal was then sent to Ezion-geber for smelting, refining, and casting. Piles of waste slag mark the ancient copper route to the Red Sea.

The winds at Ezion-geber blow steadily and gustily from the north. The furnace rooms were set at an angle to catch the winds. Walls were pierced with flues and built with air channels. Instead of hand bellows to fan the flames, nature herself did the job. The heat of the furnace fires must have been intense. They were truly blast furnaces.

Clay molds to cast the bronze have also been excavated at Ezion-geber. To mold the "brazen sea," a pit would be dug in front of the furnaces, with ropes running down into it. Workmen covered the ropes and the bottom and sides of the pit with clay and broken bits of pots. When the pit was shaped like a smooth bowl, a core was suspended in it so that the bowl would be hollow. Then the molten metal was poured. After the metal had cooled and hardened, the core was removed, and men pulled the ends of the ropes to lift up the bowl.

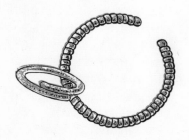

Bronze objects. Left to right: bracelet, necklace and dish. Top to bottom: ladle, hairpin, and a primitive ax.

BY THE RIVERS OF BABYLON

Nearly four hundred years after the bronze "sea" was cast for Solomon, Nebuchadrezzar and his Babylonian warriors conquered Jerusalem. They broke up the bronze pillars and the bronze "sea," and every other bronze object in the Temple, and carried the pieces to Babylon. More importantly, they carried away the best part of the population into captivity.

"By the rivers of Babylon," sang the Psalmist of the Bible, "there we sat down, yea, we wept when we remembered Zion." Zion was the hill where the Temple had stood. The Babylonian captivity ended when Babylon fell to Cyrus of Persia in 539 B.C. Thousands of the Israelites girded up their loins and trekked back to Palestine. The exiles found a ruined, poverty-stricken land. It took centuries before Palestine grew prosperous again. But Palestine became more than a country and Zion more than a hill. They became an idea that swept over Western civilization like a whirlwind. The message of Zion was simple. Earth was to become one city where all mankind lived under God.

93

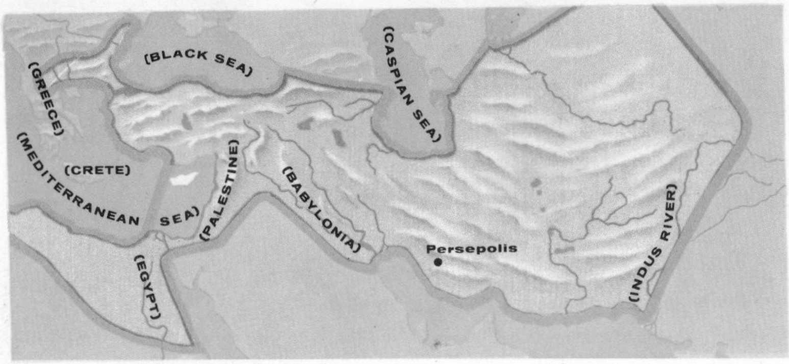
(BLACK SEA)
(CASPIAN SEA)
(GREECE)
(MEDITERRANEAN SEA)
(CRETE)
(PALESTINE)
(BABYLONIA)
Persepolis
(EGYPT)
(INDUS RIVER)

Extent of the Iranian empire about 500 B.C.

The army of the empire marched to battle hundreds of thousands strong. When the trumpets blared for attack, a sea of soldiers swept over the battlefield—horsemen and footmen, camel corps and elephant corps.

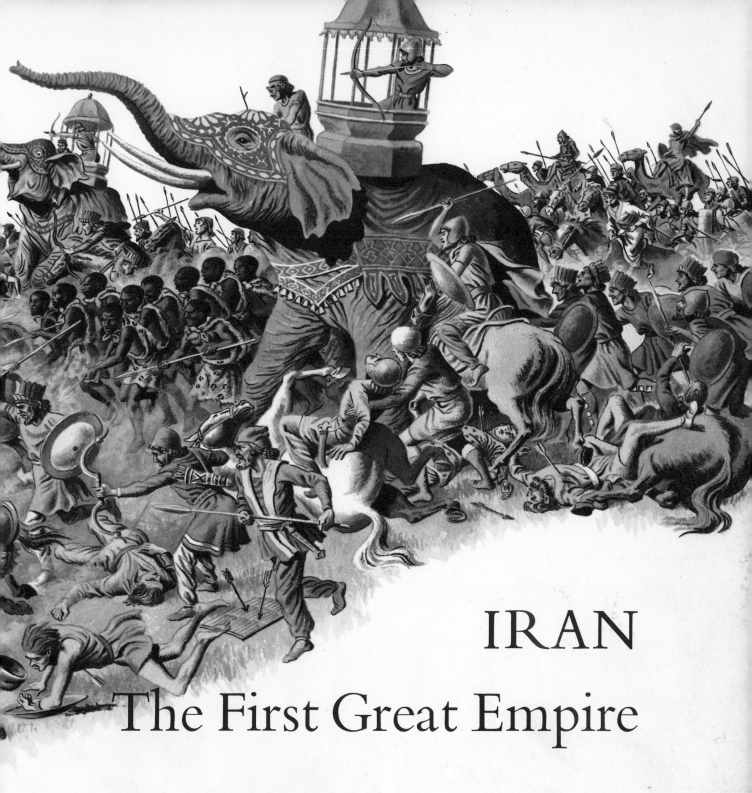

IRAN
The First Great Empire

The Israelites who trekked home to Palestine after the fall of Babylon called Cyrus the Great the Lord's "anointed." For the Persian liberator not only let them go home, but also let them worship their God once more.

With Cyrus a new spirit swept over the Near East. Persian horsemen, shouting and singing, still charged into battle with rival armies. But the conquered people were no longer butchered or carried into exile. The camel corps waddled back home laden with riches—but these were "gifts" or taxes from the conquered people to their new ruler. The defeated cities were not burned to the ground. The inhabitants kept their gods, local government, homes, and businesses. How else could they pay taxes to their new king? For now the defeated nations became provinces of a new empire.

A later king boasted that the Persian empire stretched so far south that men couldn't live there because of the heat and so far north that they couldn't live there because of the cold. Actually, it extended 3000 miles from east to west and from 500 to 1500 miles from north to south.

The Persians who ruled the ancient world for two hundred years were an Iranian tribe. For Persia was only a part of ancient Iran. The word "Iran" means "Land of the Aryans." Much has been written about the ancient Aryans, but we really know little about them except the language they spoke.

Since history began, there have been many languages. One family of languages, called Semitic-Hamitic, was spoken in Assyria and Babylonia. Modern Hebrew and Arabic belong to the same family. Another language family—the main one in the world today—is called Indo-European, from the tribes which had once lived in the northern grasslands stretching from the Danube River to central Asia. Originally, they had spoken a similar language. But in 2000 B.C. they began to move west, south, and east—toward Europe and India. As they drifted apart, their dialects became different languages. Today, we can still trace words they had all spoken. Take our English word "father." We can go from Ireland to India with it. In Old Irish, it was *athir*. In Dutch, it is *vader*; in German, *vater*. In the Latin of Rome it is *pater*. In ancient Greek it is *pater*; in Old Persian, *pitar*; and in Sanskrit of old India, *pitr*.

From such words, scholars have tried to reconstruct the life of the original "Aryan" tribes. The "Aryans" had similar words for bear and pine tree, but none for crocodile and palm tree. So, they argue, the original tribesmen fought the bear, cut down pine trees, and lived where it snowed. There is no common word for sea, and so they must have lived inland. These deductions are interest-

A seal showing a lion hunt.

ing, but not proof. As one scholar pointed out, there is no common word for milk. Did "Aryan" babies, then, drink something else?

The Aryans of Iran—we call them Iranians—reached the plateau about 900 B.C. The Iranian plateau extends from the Caspian Sea in the west to the Hindu Kush, a mountain range, in the east. From north to south it runs from the steppes of Turkistan to the Persian Gulf. The temperature varies from freezing cold and snow in the mountains to stifling heat (130°) on the plains and in the gulf. In the center of Iran lies a great salt desert that was a giant lake in prehistoric times. Eight hundred miles long and from 100 to 200 miles wide, this desert is almost as large as California. By comparison, a traveler once said, it makes the Gobi—the desert in Mongolia—seem almost an oasis.

The Iranian tribes, like our Western homesteaders, were looking for a land of opportunity. They drove their herds of cattle and flocks of sheep with them. Horses pulled wagons and carts loaded with household goods and women and children. When they settled down, they planted crops, bred horses, and built wooden houses. Villages turned into walled towns topped with towers. Warriors on horseback fought for their chiefs and created kingdoms—the Medes in the north and the Persians in the south. Medes and Persians were both Iranians. By the sixth century B.C., they were united under the kingship of a Persian family, the Achaemenids.

The Iranians of course didn't find a deserted land. Native tribes of darker skin color had lived on the plateau since civilization began. In the southwest, where the Persians settled, there had been an ancient kingdom called Elam. Its history dated back almost to the time of the Sumerians. Though Mesopotamia had ruled it for centuries, Elam grew powerful enough in the twelfth century B.C. to raid its neighbor and carry off a famous black stone as a war trophy. This was the law code of Hammurabi, which archeologists dug up, in 1901, in the ruins of Susa, the capital of Elam.

Detail from an Iranian seal: a Greek soldier with characteristic plumed helmet and round shield.

HOW CUNEIFORM WAS DECIPHERED

We owe our knowledge of the ancient kingdoms of Mesopotamia—Sumer, Babylonia, and Assyria—to the ancient Persians. Some time near the birth of Christ, the last men who could read and write in cuneiform died. Cuneiform was forgotten, not to be read again until our nineteenth century.

Two days' trip by caravan from the Iranian city of Ecbatana (modern Hamadan), a mountain peak rises along the main road. Today it is called the Rock of Behistun or Bisutun, from the village near by. The rock can be seen miles before it is reached. A spring gushes out into a pool at the rock, and here for centuries caravans stopped and watered their animals. High up on the face of the mountain, from 300 to 500 feet above the road, you can see many columns of carved writing and a relief—a picture carved in stone—showing a king and some men. Legends had grown up about the rock. It was carved, some said, by a queen of Babylon. Others claimed that it pictured the twelve Apostles. It even became a sacred Moslem shrine.

In the middle of the nineteenth century, Henry Rawlinson, an English soldier-scholar, killed the legends. Swinging on a rope lowered from the top of the cliff, he copied some of the inscriptions. It was no easy job. The relief is about twenty feet long and ten feet wide, but the columns of writing stretch sixty feet across. Below the relief, some of the columns of writing are six feet

Iranian boys were trained to ride a horse, shoot an arrow, and speak the truth. Above: Mounting at full gallop. Below: Shooting from horseback.

wide. To the left, a chasm cuts into the rock, behind which are other inscriptions. Above these, a boulder sticks out with more inscriptions. Rawlinson figured out part of the inscription, and this led to the solution of all them.

The Rock of Behistun turned out to be carved in three languages—Old Persian, Elamitic, and Akkadian. Persian cuneiform gave the key to all the other systems of cuneiform writing. The clay tablets from Mesopotamia became, once again after centuries, living documents.

Darius the Great, the third Persian king, knew that tablets and papyrus could be destroyed and palace walls leveled to the ground. So he engraved the tale of his reign on the side of this mountain. The paths leading up the rock face were chopped away. No one could climb up and remove his words and deeds. The paint or gold leaf that once overlaid the cuneiform characters has worn off. But Darius' story can still be seen from the road below.

Today, cars and trucks drive past Darius' rock, for the old caravan road has become the main highway from Hamadan to Baghdad. The most famous Iranian road of ancient times has, however, disappeared. This was the Royal Road. It ran from Susa in the southwest, through Mesopotamia and Asia Minor, to Sardis, in Lydia. It passed through gorges in the mountains, ran up steep hills, and sometimes ended at a fording place in the river, then continued on the other bank. Forts manned by the king's soldiers guarded the gorges and fording places, for here bandits could waylay caravans. The Royal Road was over 1600 miles long.

A Persian king had his soldiers test how far a horse could gallop in one day. Then he built a chain of post stations along the Royal Road, each one a day's ride apart. Fresh horses were stabled at the stations, and food and lodging could be had. With an empire to rule, the Persian kings sent a steady stream of messengers from the court at Susa to cities in the west. They had the fastest messenger service in the world. In fact, its speed wasn't bettered until after Napoleon's day.

If the king wanted to send an edict to his governor in Lydia, the scribe handed the document to a courier. The courier leaped on his horse and galloped to the first post station. Here a second courier waited with a fresh horse. He in turn galloped to the next station, handing over the king's edict to a third courier. And so the document went, from courier to courier, until Lydia was reached. These couriers rode through rain and snow, through scorching heat and bitter cold, night and day. It was the Pony Express of the Persian empire.

The stages on the Royal Road were about nineteen miles apart. (Our Western Pony Express stations were ten miles apart.) Relay messengers could travel from Susa to Babylon in a day and a half. They could cover the whole length of the road in a week to nine days. This was ten times faster than caravans or soldiers could travel along the road.

The roads of Iran spread Eastern ideas and products to the West and Western products to the East. Iranian merchants brought the chicken to Europe. Originally a wild bird from India, it was domesticated in India and Iran and sold by Iranians to the Greek cities of Asia Minor. From here the bird reached Europe. The ancient Greeks called the rooster the Persian bird.

Persian words for things strange to the West took root in the Greek language. In turn, ancient Greek passed along the Persian words to English. The rose is said to have originated in Persia, and the rose gardens of Shiraz are still famous. The word "julep" in mint julep comes from the Persian for "rose water." Roses went westward along with other flowers like jasmine, lilac, and narcissus. All these flower names come from Persian. Peaches and oranges, asparagus and spinach—these too traveled the roads of Iran to the West, and ended up as our European plants and English words.

Ancient Persians and Medes wore a felt cap with earflaps, whereas the king wore a stiff fluted hat with a golden headband around it. Our word "tiara" comes from this cap and royal hat, though our tiaras are jeweled crowns that ladies wear to fancy-dress balls. The peacock with his jeweled tail traveled westward. Our word "peacock" comes from ancient Iran. In the old language of Iran, the word for arrow was *tighri*, which meant "swift." Like an arrow, the tiger speeds through the jungle. Our word "tiger"—the beast as fast as an arrow—comes from Iran. Rice, pistachio, and tapestry did not originate in Iran, but Iranians first sent these products to Europe—and the words to us.

When you sit next time on a veranda, think of ancient Iran with its caravan inns along the roads. For "veranda" comes from the Persian word that meant the covered porch in front of a caravan inn. Here the camel drivers unloaded their goods.

THE KING'S EYES AND EARS

Safe roads meant prosperity to merchants. The roads of Iran were protected by soldiers because trade roads also meant possible trouble roads. Invaders could also march in through them. In an empire that stretched from Egypt to Mt. Caucasus and from the Danube River to the Indus in India, the king had to know where trouble was brewing. He set up what was probably the world's earliest secret-service system.

Every province of the Persian empire was ruled by a satrap appointed by the king. "Satrap" means merely "governor of a province." Under Cyrus, each province gave the king a yearly gift. When Darius became king, he fixed yearly taxes for each province. For this he was called "the huckster." Media, for example, paid 450 talents of silver and 100,000 sheep and 50,000 horses. (A talent was an ancient weight in which gold and silver were weighed.) Babylonia and Assyria paid 1000 talents and 500 boy eunuchs to serve at the

A game of bat-ball, an early form of polo. It was played on foot as well as on horseback.

king's palaces. India paid the highest taxes—360 talents of gold dust. Every year, gold and silver that would amount to about $20,000,000 in our money flowed into the royal treasury. When in 331 B.C. Alexander the Great captured the city of Susa, he needed 10,000 mule carts and 5000 camels to ship the gold out of the treasury.

The king set the taxes, then sent his secret-service men into the various provinces. Through these men, the king was said to have a thousand ears and eyes. The King's Ears or Eyes, as they were called, traveled to the provinces to see if the people could afford to pay the taxes he had set. Sometimes a satrap doubled the royal tax, keeping half for himself and sending the other half to the king's treasury. If the King's Ears reported such a situation, the king might cut his tax in half, to spare the people of the province.

The King's Ears also made yearly trips to see how a satrap was running his province. Often, they paid surprise visits, for a satrap could fool the king's agents on an official visit. The King's Ears also kept watch against rebellion. They reported any sign of disobedience or trouble directly to the king.

COINS AND "ARCHERS"

The King's Ears listened to discontented voices within the empire—and outside, too. They kept in touch with prominent citizens of states outside the empire. Persian gold flowed in two directions—into the king's treasury and into the hands of men we would call fifth-columnists.

When the gold and silver bars from the provinces of the empire reached the treasury, they were melted, then poured into clay pots. After the metal cooled, the pot was shattered, leaving lumps of gold and silver called bullion. When the king needed money for his secret agents, he ordered goldsmiths to chop off pieces of bullion and mint coins.

Coins were not invented in Iran. In fact, coins were not invented, but, like Topsy, just sort of "growed." As we have seen in Egypt and Mesopotamia, barter was the earliest kind of "money." Boys barter, for example, when one says to another, "I'll trade you my baseball glove for your goldfish and a top." Barter will work for small numbers of persons, but when an estate owner has to pay his farm hands for their work, he needs a medium of exchange. Food was the first medium of exchange. "Money" was figured out in bushels of barley. As business grew complicated and merchants traded from country to country, bushels of barley took up too much space. They were bulky to transport. Merchants and kings substituted bars of gold and silver for the barley. They stamped these bars according to weight, guaranteeing the purity of the metal. There were no standard weights. The metal "ingots" varied from merchant to merchant, city to city, country to country. A strong ruler sometimes standardized the weights for his country.

The metal ingots grew smaller until finally they turned into coins. Ingots had to be weighed on scales. Coins contained so many grains of gold or silver, as the coiner guaranteed. Our coins are minted by the government. Ancient coins, however, were probably first minted by bankers for their own convenience. No one knows who issued the first coins. Some time between the eighth and seventh centuries B.C., bankers and merchants in the Greek cities on the coast of Asia Minor first used coins. Tradition indicates that the neighboring kingdom of Lydia may have minted the earliest coins. The first

Two sides of a silver coin. Above: The king adores a star or sun set between the horns of a crescent.

Lydian coins were made of electrum or "white gold," a natural alloy of gold and silver. They didn't look like modern coins, but were shaped like beans. On the face of the coin, the engraver pictured a snarling lion.

When we want to say how rich a man is, we sometimes say, "He's as rich as Croesus." For Croesus, the last king of Lydia, issued the first gold and silver coins. The capital city of Lydia was incredibly rich in gold. After shearing their sheep, Lydian shepherds dipped the fleece into the river flowing through the city, to wash it. When they pulled it out, it glittered with grains of gold. For the river cascaded down a mountain rich in gold, cutting the gold ore like a liquid pickax. The shepherds "panned" the gold with fleece.

In 546 B.C. Cyrus the Great defeated Croesus and added Lydia to his empire. His satraps continued coining staters, as Croesus' gold coins were called. Coinage had spread throughout Asia Minor. Now it spread east through the Persian empire. Darius the Great adopted the new money system, coining the purest gold coins known in the ancient world. They contained 97 per cent gold, with 3 per cent of an alloy to harden them. These gold coins, called "darics" after the king, showed a bearded, crowned king with a spear in one hand, a quiver over the shoulder, and a bow in the other hand. They were popularly called "archers" not only because of the design, but because they did as deadly work as the king's bowmen. The king sent thousands of "archers" into the temples, treasuries, and private pockets of the citizens of the Greek city-states, buying their allegiance.

The coinmaker engraved a small metal die, then secured it in an anvil. He cut a slug of gold, put it over the die, and held it in place with a metal bar. With a sledgehammer he struck the other end of the bar, driving the gold slug into the die. The result was that all early coins showed a design on the face and a square imprint of the bar on the reverse.

Like the Greeks, the Persians also struck silver coins. Only the king could issue gold coins, but the satraps of the provinces could mint silver coins. Once, an Egyptian satrap decided to imitate his king and mint silver coins as pure as the king's gold ones. He did it out of a sense of loyalty. His coins compared so favorably with the king's that the king rewarded him by executing him.

Coins were minted in great numbers throughout the Persian and Greek world. A wealthy Lydian merchant handed over four million gold darics to the Persian king Xerxes—about $22,000,000 in our money.

FAT-TAILED SHEEP AND UNDERGROUND CANALS

The Persian nobles hated business because they believed that the market place bred lies and deceit. Their wealth was in their land rather than in hoards of gold coins. Farming and shepherding were considered honorable occupations for Iranians. Most of Iran was divided into huge estates owned by the nobles and worked by laborers who kept a share of the crops. Iran was thus mainly an agricultural country.

Herds of cattle and flocks of sheep and goats grazed on the plateau. The sheep were the fat-tailed variety, with tails weighing as much as nineteen pounds in late spring. The tails shrank in winter as the animals' food supply dwindled. Iranian housewives used the tail fat for cooking oil.

In the summer, the herds and flocks were pastured on the near-by mountains. In autumn, shepherds and cattle drovers led their beasts back to the valleys.

Head and tail of a gold coin. Above: A bearded god with long wavy hair. Below: Victory driving a four-horse chariot.

Cylindrical clay seals were used in Persia as elsewhere in the ancient world to make a mark showing ownership and as good-luck amulets. Of King Darius' cylinder seals, this is the most famous. The winged figure at the top represents Ahura Mazda, which stands for light and goodness.

Here they were sheltered in stables and folds for the winter. Like the farms, the herds were also owned by of the wealthy nobles.

On the plains, however, there were a few independent small farmers and shepherds. The poor farmer made his own plow. He cut down a tree where three branches formed a crotch. He or a blacksmith shod the tip of the thickest branch with iron, and this became the plowshare.

Near the Caspian Sea, heavy rain falls. On the plains there is little water, and a farmer has to depend on mountain streams or springs. The Iranians dug underground canals from a near-by mountain spring to the plain. These canals sometimes covered twenty-five miles. To dispose of tunneled-out rock and soil, shafts were dug at intervals to the surface of the ground. The workmen piled up the debris around the openings. These shafts also allowed workmen to go down into the canal and clear out any part of the tunnel that had collapsed or caved in. The tunnels were dug underground to keep the water from evaporating in the hot sun. From a distance, the path of the canal could be detected by the piles of debris at the tunnel openings. A row of giant ant hills seemed to stretch from the mountain to the fields.

Usually, the canal came out of the ground at the end as a spring. Otherwise it ended in a well. When the king built the canal, the farmers using the water paid a fixed amount to the royal treasury for each measure of water they drew. Today, landowners in Iran still build these underground canals. They charge the farmer so much money per gallon of water.

STRANGE CUSTOMS

It was no dishonor to be poor in Iran, but the Iranians considered a man in debt to be dishonorable. For, they said, a man who owes money tells lies.

102

The sport of kings: the lion hunt. Iranian kings also hunted in a park or "paradise."

Iranian society was sharply divided into classes—the king, the nobles, the soldiers, the artisans and poor farmers, and the priests. Men "pulled rank," as we would say, when dealing with each other. A poor man coming before a noble to ask a favor had to fall down full length on the ground before him. In turn, the noble had to prostrate himself the same way before the king until ordered to rise. Men of the same rank greeted each other with a kiss on the lips. If a man felt that his visitor held lower rank, he offered his cheek instead. If the visitor was even lower down on the social scale, he merely bowed.

Men of rank traveled about on horseback or were carried in a litter. They didn't like to be seen walking—only the lower classes traveled on foot. They wore their hair and beards long and curled, used face make-up, colored their eyelids, and perfumed themselves. The Persians wore a fluted tiara, a flowing robe, and soft leather shoes with three straps. The Medes wore a domed hat, long trousers and a tunic, a topcoat over the shoulder, and laced-up shoes. Like all Orientals, they wore earrings and bracelets.

As the king ruled his empire, so the father ruled his family. His word was law, and he believed in strict discipline. Families were large, and the king sent yearly gifts to the father in Iran with the most children. Boys and girls in poor families had to help with their parents' work. Children of the nobles were cared for by their mother until the age of five, then by slaves. They lived in the harem or women's quarters and often never saw their fathers until they had grown up.

Women of the upper classes lived sheltered lives, watched over constantly by slaves and eunuchs. If they were allowed to leave the harem for a visit, they stepped into a curtained litter carried by servants and traveled unseen. Women of the poorer classes had more freedom. They lived in a one-room house, not a harem. Poor families worked, ate, and slept together.

Rich or poor, king or peasant, each celebrated one day as lavishly as he

103

could—his birthday. If a family could afford it, a whole ox, horse, or camel was roasted for the guests invited to the birthday party. The guest of honor was always seated on the right of the host. The right hand was considered the honorable one. Men concluded deals and agreements by clasping the right hand. In battle, a messenger arriving on the field raised his right hand to show that he came on a peaceful mission. The right hand was, of course, the hand that could wield a dagger.

When the king won a victory in battle, the Persians strewed the streets with boughs of myrtle, burned incense, and made merry outdoors. At any other time, it was considered unbecoming to eat or drink in the street. When a general was killed on the battlefield, his soldiers shaved their heads in mourning and even cut off the manes of their horses and mules.

TO RIDE AND TO DRAW A BOW

Persian "Pony Express." The king's messengers could gallop over the 1600-mile-long Royal Road from Susa, in Iran, to Sardis, in Lydia, in about a week.

According to the Greeks, the Persians taught their sons three things: to ride a horse, to shoot with bow and arrow, and to tell the truth. In the royal cities, boys met for school in the square next to the king's palace or in a building next to the law court. In country towns, the boys met at the gates of the town governor's palace. Teachers never held classes near the market place, for here their students might hear lying, swearing, and cheating.

With musicians playing, or accompanying himself on a lute, the teacher told his students tales of the great Aryan heroes. Not many boys, even at school, learned how to read. Persians usually imported their scribes from Meso-potamia or Palestine. The teacher knew the Aryan laws by heart and had his students memorize them. A boy studying to be a priest usually learned the sacred writings by memory, too.

Iran was a land mainly of military schools. Trumpets blaring at dawn woke the boys. They dashed to the place of assembly and were divided into companies of fifty, led by a prince or the son of a satrap. The boys had to learn difficult feats of horsemanship. They had to mount and alight from a horse galloping at breakneck speed. They practiced long-distance racing. They threw the javelin on foot and on horseback.

Iranians were the most famous archers of the ancient world. On the ground and on horseback, the boys learned to shoot still and moving targets. They swam the rivers, hunted game in the forests, and performed farm chores. They were even called out by the local police to join in chasing robbers. To help their breath control, they held yelling contests. Weighted down with their equipment, they went on long marches in the hot sun or up the mountains where cold winds blew and frost and snow bit their skin. They forded swift rivers and stayed up on all-night watches in rough weather. When they finished cadet training, they were toughened soldiers.

Iranians were great sportsmen. They raced on foot and on horseback, wrestled, threw the javelin, and played dice. Even women threw the javelin, practiced archery, and tossed dice. But the sport of king and courtiers was the chase. They hunted stags, antelopes, wild asses and boars, bears, and leopards. On the royal hunt, the king and his courtiers rode in chariots driven by charioteers. They held their bows in readiness for sight of the game, but no one dared let go his arrow until the king had had the first shot. Giant dogs, imported from India, dashed through the thickets, flushing out the game.

Sometimes the king didn't feel up to hunting in the forest. Then he went to a special game preserve. This was a park with thickets of trees, running brooks, and wild animals roaming about. It was completely fenced in. When the king grew tired or wanted to eat, he was driven to a pavilion built in the park. This hunting park was called *pairidaeza*. Our ancestors visualized Adam and Eve in a place as beautiful as a Persian hunting park—a paradise. And so our word "paradise" comes from the old Persian word for "park" or "enclosure."

Ball-bat, an early form of polo, was played by young and old, by rich and poor. Children played it on foot; men played it on horseback. As many as fifty players on horseback lined up to form a team. Two teams faced each other, holding reins in one hand and a wooden bat in the other. Spectators lined the playing field, and a band of musicians signaled the start of the game by playing their fifes, drums, and trumpets. The referee threw the ball high into the air between the two teams. The player who caught the ball with his bat hit it with all his might to send it high over the heads of his opponents.

The game was like a fast and furious game of tennis on horseback, with a hundred "tennis" players and no net. Unlike polo, in bat-ball the players tried not to let the ball hit the ground. They kept the ball in the air, and scored whenever the opposing team couldn't return it.

TO SPEAK THE TRUTH

To ride a horse and to hit a bull's-eye were important lessons for a boy. But the most important lesson of all was to speak the truth. It was the first law of his religion. The Aryans or Iranians who settled on the plateau worshiped nature. The sun and the moon, fire, water, and wind—all were holy. And Iranians sacrificed horses and oxen to these mighty powers. According to the Greeks, the Persians thought it foolish to picture God as a man. They set up no statues of the gods, built no temples in the Greek or Mesopotamian sense of a temple, and erected no altars for their sacrifices. On their altars and in their small, square temples, the priests tended the sacred fire.

The Iranians were not fire worshipers. Fire symbolized the power of their god, Ahura Mazda, whose name means "Lord Wisdom." Iran, we know today, is rich in oil deposits. Possibly the Aryans entering the plateau saw lightning strike an oil bed or a natural-gas spring and burn without letup night and day. Their first sacred-fire altars may have been built over these sites.

The Iranian priests who kept the sacred fire burning eternally and sprinkled incense on it came from a special tribe, called the Magi. The Magi interpreted the king's dreams, read omens from strange happenings, and performed feats of magic with spells and incantations. Our word "magic" came to us from these Iranian priests. The Magi were skilled astrologers, and so in the Bible the wise men from the East who followed the star to Bethlehem to find the Christ child were Magi.

In the Aryan religion, any man could perform his own sacrifice to the elements. He prayed for all Iranians. Then the Magi recited holy prayers over the slain beast. The Magi also prepared a sacred drink called *haoma*, which was offered to the elements and then to the worshipers. It made them drunk.

The Magi were also the physicians of Iran. There were three kinds of

doctors—those who healed with holiness or prayer; those who healed with herbs; and those who healed with the knife, or surgeons. Doctors on horseback traveled from town to town. With a whip they beat out disease demons and with a rod or knife they killed snakes and insects. When attending a patient, the doctor wore a cloth over his head to keep his breath from contaminating anything. It covered the face from the bridge of the nose to below the chin, and was tied behind the head with strings. It was like a modern surgeon's mask.

A man from northern Iran, one of the great religious reformers of the world, began to teach against sacrificing, against worshiping many gods, and against drinking *haoma*. His name was Zoroaster, and he probably lived in the days of Darius the Great's father, about 570 B.C. Zoroaster taught that you could love God only by loving mankind. He didn't believe in religious fasting. The world, he said, lived by eating. He preached that two powers, good and evil, fought each other in the universe. In the end, good would win.

After Zoroaster's death, old Aryan and Magian practices were grafted onto his religion. The Persians used to bury their dead after coating the body with wax. The Magi exposed the dead bodies on mountains or specially built towers. On these towers of silence, as they were called, the body was weighted with stones so that an animal couldn't drag it off and defile the purity of water and

Iranian engineers spanned the Hellespont, the strait between Asia Minor and Greece, with a temporary bridge supported on hundreds of ships—a boat bridge.

vegetation. Birds of prey picked the corpses bare, then the clean bones were put into an urn and into a tomb.

In Zoroastrianism, the sun was considered the great cleansing power. Modern medicine also knows the sterilizing power of the sun. Bodies were carried to the towers of silence during the day, never at night. Clothes soiled by blood or other matter had to be exposed to the sun for long periods of time.

Zoroastrianism is still a living religion. When the Moslems conquered Persia and persecuted those who wouldn't become Moslems, a band of Iranians

107

Stairway leading to a palace of Persepolis, the royal city built on a terrace. The graceful columns once held up the roof of the king's audience hall or throne room.

fled to India. Here they continued to practice the teachings of Zoroaster. They are called Parsis. The word Parsi means "Persian."

PERSIAN DOGS

We know nothing about ancient Persian cats, but we do know something of Persian dogs. In the Zoroastrian religion, the dog was a sacred animal. When a man died, a dog was brought into his house to gaze at his body. The dog was supposed to chase away the demon of defilement. Puppies had to be looked after for six months. When a dog became sick, the veterinarian had to be called. In cold weather, the dog had to have bedding and a warm fire. A mad dog was to be cared for as if he were an insane man. If medicine couldn't cure him, he was muzzled and tied to a post.

Every household in ancient Iran had a dog. The shepherd's dog held first place in the Iranian's heart, for the dog guarded the flocks of sheep and herds of cattle. At night, he couldn't sleep because he had to go the rounds of the flock or fold three times before daybreak. Second in popularity was the watchdog, which guarded fields and groves, houses and children. Watchdogs were

108

taken along on caravans to protect the merchants' goods against bandits. Iranian dogs were huge—about the size of our mastiffs. Third in favor was the hunting dog. No dog was allowed to be beaten severely. A man who treated a dog cruelly was punished by law. Iranians thought it just as sinful to offer rotten food to a dog as to a man or a woman. How badly, in comparison, is the dog treated today in Iran! The dog is an impure animal to the Moslems, and he has to lead the life of a scavenger.

GABLED HOUSES AND GLITTERING PALACES

The houses the dogs guarded had a different look from those in other parts of the Near East. Most Mesopotamian houses had flat roofs. The Iranians brought the gabled roof with them from their northern homeland. The gabled roof covered the main and only room of the average man's house. A porch led into this room. It had a flat roof held up by wooden columns that rested on stone bases. The porch faced the sun, for the Iranians feared cold, not heat. The same sort of house is still built in modern Iran.

Like other cities in ancient civilizations, the old Iranian cities have disappeared. Still, ruins of slender sixty-five-foot columns and crenelated stairways bring to life some of the glories of the empire. The palaces of the kings were built on heights, with the workers' houses huddled below on the plain. Like the temples and ziggurats of Babylon, the palaces stood on huge terraces. They glittered in the hot sun like the king himself in all his jeweled splendor.

Darius the Great built a huge winter palace at Susa, which was his capital city. All the peoples of the empire shared in making it a work of art. Babylonians molded sun-dried bricks. Assyrians brought cedars from Lebanon to Babylon, and Carians and Ionians delivered the wood to Susa. The king sent to Gandara and Carmania for teakwood. Gold came from Sardis and Bactria, lapis lazuli and carnelian from Sogdiana, turquoise from Chorasmia, and silver and ebony from Egypt. Wall ornaments came from Ionia, ivory from Ethiopia and Sind. Ionians and Sardians cut the stone blocks. Medes and Egyptians fashioned the gold decorations. Sardians and Egyptians carved the wood. Babylonians baked the bright enameled tiles that lined the palace walls.

In a great hall, called the apadana, the king received ambassadors from all over the world. The roof was held up by thirty-six stone columns. Here the king sat in half light, for royalty was too splendid to be seen in full light except on special occasions.

Darius also began building Persepolis, which his son Xerxes and later kings added to. A giant terrace with its back to the mountain, it was partly quarried out of rock and partly built of large stone blocks joined by iron clamps. No cement was used. An elaborate staircase led up to the terrace. Troops of horsemen ten abreast rode up and down it with ease. The stairway led to the gate of Xerxes, which was really a gatehouse, guarded by huge stone winged bulls. The apadana or audience hall took thirty years to build. Thick sun-dried brick walls enclosed the hall, and seventy-two fluted columns held up the cedar roof. At the four corners of the building, stairways led to roof towers.

Up the double stairway of the apadana came delegations from the countries ruled by the Persian king, bringing their tribute and taxes. Xerxes was not satisfied with his father's apadana and built an even more imposing one—a hall of a hundred columns.

Close-up of a figure from the great staircase at Persepolis.

109

About ten miles from Persepolis, Darius and his successors carved their tombs in the face of a rock cliff. Shaped like a Greek cross seventy feet high by sixty feet wide, the tombs begin about thirty feet above the ground. There isn't a stairway or path leading up. The Magian priests hoisted up the king's sarcophagus by rope, placed it in the tomb, then lowered themselves and cut the ropes. Still, robbers managed to climb the crevices in the rock wall and remove the contents of the tombs. Today they are empty. But Darius' inscription can still be read: "I am Darius the Great King, King of Kings."

KING OF KINGS

The law of the Medes and Persians, says the Bible, did not change. For the law was the king's word, and it couldn't be changed or undone. The king was Chief Justice, though he appointed seven judges for life. These men, who had to be Persians, judged civil cases, interpreted civil laws, and advised the king. The last job sometimes placed their lives in danger. The king often asked if there was a law that allowed him to do something he wanted to do. If there was no such law and the judges told him so, he might have them killed because he *was* the law. If a law seemed to permit the action he wanted to take, and they advised him that he was legally right, he might have them killed because he felt they were misinterpreting and therefore breaking the law.

The king dealt harshly with judges who took bribes. King Cambyses discovered that one of his judges had taken a bribe and given an unjust verdict. He had the judge put to death, then flayed. The judge's skin was tanned like leather and used to cover his old seat in court. Cambyses then appointed the judge's son to serve in his father's place. "Remember," Cambyses warned, "what you sit on."

The king never put his foot on earth outside his palace. An attendant always placed a golden footstool for him to step on when entering his chariot or litter. In the chariot, he sat on another gilded stool. An attendant held a tent-shaped parasol to keep the sun off his head. When he appeared in public on great state occasions or on his birthday, he wore his richest jewels, a gold spiked crown, and the costliest robe in the ancient world.

During a royal procession, guards lined the way four deep, and horsemen, foot soldiers, and charioteers went before and after the king. If he left his

Persepolis burning. Alexander the Great set fire to the city, destroying, among other treasures, 21 sacred books of the Zoroastrians written in gold on 12,000 oxhides.

palace to perform a sacrifice, the bulls or horses to be killed came out of the royal gates first. They wore golden crowns on their heads. The sacred fire, carried by the priests, followed, then the king in royal purple. Javelin bearers rode behind the king, then a thousand horsemen, with chariots four abreast.

When the king held an audience, his subject prostrated himself. When told to rise, he placed his hands in the sleeves of his robe. Now he could not reach the dagger at his side. If a visitor entered the apadana and dared sit on the king's throne, the guards seized him and he was quickly put to death. Men holding an audience with the king couldn't make demands as human beings. They couldn't even appeal to the king in the name of law. They could only beg a favor.

The king rarely had any privacy. Guards, attendants, and eunuchs surrounded him. Court astrologers stood near him to interpret his dreams and foretell the future. Scribes wrote the letters and edicts he dictated. They then read back his words to him and affixed the royal seal to the documents. The king was above even that little task. From all parts of his empire came messages from satraps and generals. These the scribe read aloud to the king. Only when the King's Ears arrived were the words spoken in secrecy.

In his private apartments, the king dined with the queen mother if she was still alive or with his favorite wife. He sometimes played dice with his wives, relatives, and courtiers. The stakes were high—eunuchs, slaves, and gold.

Like all Iranians, the king gave a great birthday party, inviting as many as 15,000 guests. The king dined on an elevated platform, for everyone had to be seated lower than he was. A thin curtain separated him from his guests. Though he could see them through the curtain, they couldn't see him. Musicians played throughout the feast, and harem girls sang and danced. As a token of royal

Right: bronze bit from Luristan made by an elite clan of nomadic warrior horsemen. Below: Bronze vessel handle in the shape of a winged ibex.

favor, the king sent food from his table to an honored guest. A thousand animals and large numbers of game and poultry were served at such a feast. What the guests couldn't eat, they took home with them.

The king drank water only from the river that flowed outside of Susa. When he went to war or traveled, the water was boiled, poured into large silver flagons, and carted off on mule-drawn wagons.

THE ARMY AND THE IMMORTALS

Persians were intensely loyal to their king. When Xerxes was sailing back from a campaign, the ship was in danger of sinking at sea because it was overloaded. Persians jumped overboard to their death to lighten the cargo and save the king. The king didn't demand such loyalty; he expected it. When he issued the call to arms in wartime, every able-bodied man had to serve. Once, a Persian nobleman with four sons in the army begged a favor of his friend the king. An old man, he asked if his fifth son might stay home. The king graciously consented. The father found his son's body cut in half and placed on both sides of the road over which the army was marching off to war.

When war was declared, the king sent messengers to the satraps with lists of the troops, horses, ships, and supplies each had to contribute. Counting the troops that poured into the capital was done in this way: the first ten thousand men were herded tightly together; a circle was drawn round them on the ground, the men were disbanded, and a circular fence was set up on the marking. As new troops arrived, they were herded into the enclosure. The king could now tell if his troop orders had been filled. When the empire marched to war, the army numbered in the hundreds of thousands.

112

Soldiers wore their native costumes, used their native weapons, and spoke their own language. When Xerxes marched to conquer Europe, sixty different nations were represented in his army. The Assyrians wore twisted bronze helmets and carried wooden clubs studded with iron. Indians in cotton loincloths were armed with reed bows and iron-tipped arrows. Ethiopians, clad in leopard skins, carried bows, spears, and clubs. Before they went into battle, the Ethiopians put on warpaint, painting their bodies half white and half red. Other nations could be identified by their leather coats, by foxskin hats, and by helmets made of skinned horses' foreheads with the ears and mane left on the pelt.

Six Persian commanders directed the movements of this vast army. Their task was as difficult as it would be to take all the inhabitants of a city the size of Toledo, Ohio, and march them over the Rockies to California. The commanders appointed captains over units of ten thousand. These captains then appointed captains in charge of thousands and hundreds. All commanders and captains were either Persians or Medes, but the army was organized according to nations, not according to infantry, cavalry, and charioteers.

On the march to the battle front, the king sent heralds ahead to prepare the towns on his route to feast him and his army. An Iranian army could pick a town clean of its food supply. When provisions ran out, captains gave orders to slaughter some of the horses, mules, and camels to feed the troops.

The king rode in the royal chariot, surrounded by crack Persian troops and followed by 10,000 Immortals on foot carrying lances topped with golden pomegranates. They were called Immortals because their number never fell below 10,000. When an Immortal grew sick, was wounded, or died, another soldier took his place. In peacetime, the Immortals were the regular army.

The camel corps usually came last because the camels made the horses bolt. Cyrus the Great, however, defeated Croesus of Lydia by sending the camel corps first and causing Croesus' cavalry to disperse when the horses bolted.

Battles took place by day, often by arrangement. Enemies lined up like players on opposing teams. Trumpets blared, drums beat, and the two enemy lines began to move toward each other. The Persian troops burst into war songs. The charioteers whipped their horses and drove at top speed through the enemy lines. Iron scythes had been fastened to both sides of the chariot wheels. The scythes slashed at soldiers as at wheat. The king, usually safely in the rear and often on a hill, merely witnessed the action. Only Cyrus rode before his troops.

Battles did not take place often. Getting to the field where the enemy would stand and fight was half the problem of ancient warfare. When the Iranians invaded Europe, they had to cross the Hellespont between Asia Minor and Greece. Hundreds of thousands of men, horses, camels, and mules could hardly cross on ships. It would have taken too long, and there weren't enough ships. So the army engineers built a boat bridge. They placed hundreds of fifty-oared ships and triremes (warships with three banks of oars) alongside each other, leaving an opening in the line for ships to sail through. They stretched flax and papyrus cables across the boats from one shore to the other. Wooden planks, sawed to fit across the cables, were laid flat, tied at both ends, and covered with brushwood. Dirt was then heaped on top and stamped down. A fence was built on both sides of the bridge in case the horses shied.

The Iranian army reached the Danube but never conquered Europe. Iran was to be the last great Oriental power in the ancient world.

Bronze and iron pin used as votive offering.

CRETE
Island of the Labyrinth

Bull wall painting among the ruins of the royal palace at Knossos.

In the legends of ancient Crete, we hear of the world's first robot. This science-fiction monster was a bronze giant with a man's body and a bull's head. His name was Talos. Three times a day he patrolled the rocky coastline of Crete for King Minos. When enemy ships sailed into one of the island's ports, he hurled crushing boulders on them. If invaders managed to land, he heated his bronze body in a red-hot fire, grabbed them, and burned them to ashes in his fiery embrace.

Until 1900, Crete was an unimportant island, a land of ancient legends. The largest island in the eastern Mediterranean, it is now in good part a rocky waste. Its cities are small. Yet tradition said that ancient Greece inherited her art and her laws from Crete. Still, even in ancient days, people laughed this away with the proverb: "All Cretans are liars." It took the archeologist's shovel to prove

114

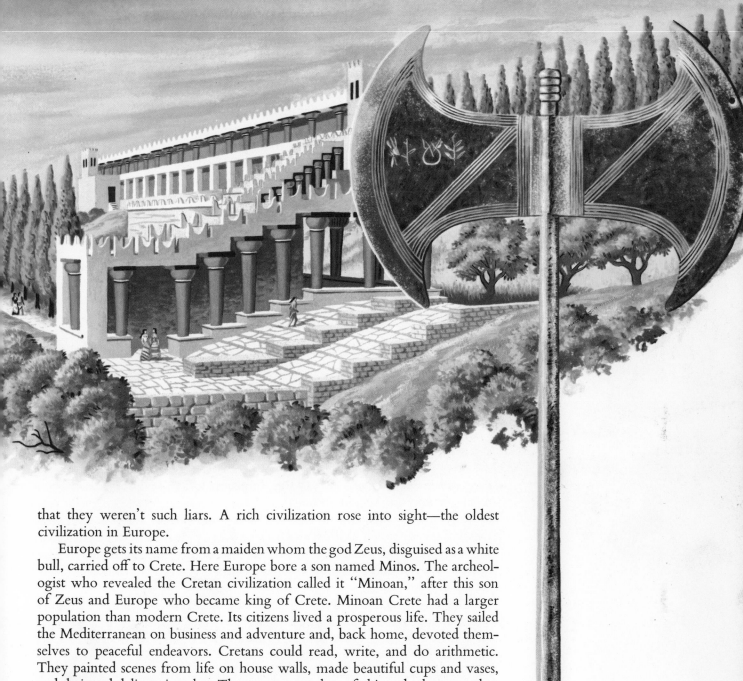

that they weren't such liars. A rich civilization rose into sight—the oldest civilization in Europe.

Europe gets its name from a maiden whom the god Zeus, disguised as a white bull, carried off to Crete. Here Europe bore a son named Minos. The archeologist who revealed the Cretan civilization called it "Minoan," after this son of Zeus and Europe who became king of Crete. Minoan Crete had a larger population than modern Crete. Its citizens lived a prosperous life. They sailed the Mediterranean on business and adventure and, back home, devoted themselves to peaceful endeavors. Cretans could read, write, and do arithmetic. They painted scenes from life on house walls, made beautiful cups and vases, and designed delicate jewelry. They may never have fashioned a bronze robot named Talos, but they won fame in ancient times for their skill as metalworkers. As a matter of fact, the Talos legend tells us how the Cretans cast bronze statuettes. Talos had a single vein in his bronze body running from neck to ankle. A magic fluid in this vein kept him operating. A bronze nail between his ankle and his heel acted as a stopper to hold in the fluid. When it was pulled out, the fluid drained from his body and he was a lifeless chunk of bronze.

Now, a Cretan smith casting a bronze statuette modeled it first in beeswax. He coated the wax with a layer of clay and baked it in an oven. While the figure was still hot, he drilled a hole near the base. If the statuette was of a human being, he pierced the baked clay between the ankle and the heel. The hot wax ran out, and a hollow pottery mold was left. (So it had happened to Talos.) The smith then poured molten bronze into the hole, filling the mold. After the metal had cooled, he broke the clay. He now had a bronze figure the size and shape of the original wax one.

Crete's royal palace, the House of the Double Ax. Its maze of passages and rooms made it a labyrinth, and its walls plastered with bulls probably gave rise to the legend of the man-bull, Minotaur.

115

THE LABYRINTH AND THE MINOTAUR

Crete's most famous legend told of a beast, also with a bull's head and a man's body, called the Minotaur. King Minos ordered a famous engineer named Daedalus to build a maze in which to keep this monster. Daedalus constructed the Labyrinth, a network of passages out of which no one could find his way.

A real "labyrinth" has been discovered on Crete. It isn't a maze to cage a man-bull, but a palace. A complicated group of rooms, halls, corridors, stairways, porticoes, altars, and courts covered six acres. The palace was five stories high, but the ground-floor level in one part was an upper floor in another part. Several entrances led into the palace, but none went a direct route. Every passage twisted and turned. To an outsider, it must have been a labyrinth.

It was a labyrinth for another reason. The word *labrys*, from which the Greek word for labyrinth comes, means "double ax." The double ax was carved on pillars and, modeled in bronze, stood on pedestals throughout the palace. For the double ax was the sacred symbol of ancient Crete—as the cross is the symbol of Christianity. "Labyrinth" really means, therefore, House of the Double Ax.

HOUSE OF THE DOUBLE AX

The House of the Double Ax was built in the hollows of a hill at Knossos, about three miles from the north coast of Crete. It was a half-hour's chariot ride to the sea. The House of the Double Ax was more than a palace where the king and his court lived. It was also a factory, where sculptors carved stone bowls, bronze workers made lances and armor, potters turned cups and vases on their wheels, and women wove cloth on their looms. It was a warehouse where the king stored chariots and arrows, huge pots of oil taller than a man, and valuable gold and silver objects. It was a government building, with offices for clerks and rooms for council meetings. It was a sacred building with shrines and altars.

Three palaces had stood at Knossos. The first had two wings of buildings off a central court. A second, grander palace was erected after the first had been leveled. A large rectangular court was surrounded by many rooms of state and the domestic quarters. Earthquake or attack destroyed the second palace, and the Cretans built a third palace on its ruins. The main wings were west and east of the central court. The west wing was the official side of the palace. It had a throne room with a stone throne where the king received callers. Twenty-two storage rooms held the wealth that poured into the palace as taxes. Jars able to hold 79,000 gallons of olive oil stood in this warehouse section. Stone-lined vaults had been dug in the floor, covered with stone slabs. They were safe-deposit boxes for the king's valuables.

The east wing hummed with activity. Smiths hammered and sawed metal, potters whirled their wheels, and painters mixed their pigments. Here, too, the king and queen lived, ate, and slept in private apartments. A grand staircase led from the central court to these apartments. Down its five flights of broad stone steps the queen and her ladies in waiting descended to her private rooms.

The queen of Crete had a separate bathroom and several latrines in her suite of rooms—novelties unknown to a queen like Elizabeth the Great of England, who reigned more than three thousand years later. The latrine was fitted with a seat and so arranged that rain water, led by pipes from the roof, flushed it. Her

A clay vase shaped like a bird.

116

bathroom had a terracotta tub that looked like a coffin, with handles on the outside. Appropriately, reeds were painted as decorations inside the tub. Servants filled the tub by hand from a cistern in a near-by room and emptied the bath water into the drain in the same room. Portable braziers or fireboxes could be carried where needed to heat the rooms. There is even evidence that the Cretan palace had a hot-water system.

Stone conduits, leading from the roof, carried away rain water. Waste water from the different floors flowed through drainpipes into a main channel that led to a near-by stream. Drains along the outer stairways trapped rain water and led it safely down, perhaps into the palace washtubs. Some of the stone drains are so large that a man can walk through them. The drainage system of the Knossos palace still works today when it rains. Tapered clay pipes, fitted with collars and stop ridges and cemented together, carried water from distant springs to the palace rooms.

The palace walls were built of stone, rubble, and sun-dried brick framed with wooden beams. They were then plastered and decorated with paintings—a bull charging, ladies dancing, and dolphins swimming. The walls glowed with color and glistened with bronze ornaments. Huge wooden pillars held up the flat roofs. The palace had terraces, colonnaded halls, and covered porches. In summer, hallway doors could be folded back into a recess behind the columns, to let in the summer breezes.

Cretan architects devised a novel way to light the palace rooms. They built light wells among the rooms. These were small, narrow courts or shafts open to the sky. The stucco wall of the light well was painted a dazzling white. Light was reflected into the rooms, air was let in, but dirt and wind were kept out. It was perhaps the earliest indirect lighting. Flowers growing in clay pots added a touch of the outdoors to the courts and light wells.

The northern entrance to the palace, facing the sea, had an inner and outer gate connected by a covered passageway. Towers and rooms manned by the king's guards protected this sea gate. Stone steps led up to a covered vestibule at the southern entrance. A paved road, with drains on both sides, ran from these steps to a port on the south coast. This was the first paved road in Europe.

Sea captains, merchants, and shipowners built houses around the palace. Beyond these, in what we would call suburbs, were the houses of the craftsmen—not the palace craftsmen, for they lived in the palace. Knossos covered about twenty-eight acres, six for the palace and twenty-two for the town. The

A sacred cave with a double ax, the symbol of Mother Earth, the great goddess of Crete. Pilgrims journeyed to the cave to toss down statuettes and other gifts to their goddess.

total population has been estimated at about 100,000. The largest city in Crete today has only a third as many inhabitants.

Knossos and Phaistos were the two main cities in Crete, but there were a hundred smaller cities or towns. A small seaport like Gournia contained about sixty houses on six and a half acres. Every city originally had its own palace and local ruler until the king at Knossos unified the country under his rule. Knossos then became the capital of Crete.

In early Crete, large houses were built for the whole family. When a man married, he built a new room onto the old house. Later, he built a new house for himself and his bride. Some of the early houses had no street entrance. To go in or out of his house, a man lowered a ladder over the side. He pulled it in at night for protection. As the towns grew—and grew safe, thanks to good government—doors and windows appeared in the houses.

The wooden doors weren't placed in the center of the house, but to right or left, with windows overhead. Sometimes the windows were divided into four panes. Glass hadn't yet been invented, so the windowpanes were made of oiled and tinted parchment. A house often boasted red windows.

The lower house walls were made of stone, the upper of sun-dried brick. Some were plastered outside and painted bright colors like stucco houses in the

118

United States or on the Riviera. Indoors, the walls were smoothly plastered and painted in bright colors, red being a favorite. The smallest houses had only a few rooms around a court. The larger houses, from two to four stories high, had twelve and more rooms, including a bathroom. An outside stairway led to the upper floors. The ground floor—and often the upper floors—were made of flagstone and cement or of cobblestones and earth. Since Cretans walked barefoot indoors, fleece rugs were scattered across the floors in winter.

Cretan towns were "modern" for the ancient world. Houses were built side by side. Paved streets divided them into city blocks. Drains on both sides of the streets carried off waste and rain water, and each house had its own cistern or well. The larger houses had piped-in running water.

Poor families slept on goatskins or fleeces laid on the floor. The better houses had stone benches for seats and stone platforms for sleeping. These were covered with pillows or skins. Setbacks in the walls served as cupboards, but there were also wooden chests for clothes and jewelry. Stone tables, like our marble-topped tables, may have been used for dinner parties. For light at night, Cretans had candlesticks and a variety of oil-burning lamps, from small bowls to giant stone lamps holding two quarts of oil.

There was no separate kitchen, and the smoke from the hearth or brazier

Splendor of the queen's suite in the royal palace. Here walls, ceiling, and even the bathtub were gaily painted.

119

Priestess of the snake goddess. Cretans believed snakes were the spirits of their ancestors, returned from the dead.

went out the door or the windows. Cretan housewives cooked meat stews in three-legged copper pots and scooped out the food with long ladles. They had a variety of pots and pans for preparing other dishes and made cheese from cow's and goat's milk, using earthenware strainers.

Women ground grain into flour in a mortar or a stone hand mill and baked bread in a clay oven. Peas, beans, squashes, and lentils were popular vegetables, and the housewife stored dried beans and peas in clay pots for use in winter. In a royal storage room, four hundred pounds of peas were found in one pot.

Fruit trees blossomed at the foot of the cypress forests, and Cretans ate plums and figs, quinces and dates. Large houses had indoor presses to squeeze oil out of the olives. Large town houses also had an indoor winepress, whereas in the country wine was made outdoors.

Since Crete is an island, fish and shellfish played a large part in the Cretan diet. A poor family could always fish for its dinner. All kinds of fish and shellfish were eaten—oysters, squid, octopus, mussels, crabs, and tritons. The triton is a sea snail that lives in a colored spiral shell. After the snails were eaten, the shells were pierced at the tip to make trumpets for shepherds to call in their flocks or for children to play with.

KING "MINOS" AND HIS "PARISIANS"

No walls surrounded Minoan towns, and the palaces weren't fortified. The king at Knossos didn't fear his neighboring princes or foreign invaders. His fleets of ships protected his island kingdom. The ancient Greeks credited King Minos with having the first navy in the world. The Greeks always spoke of King Minos as if he were a single ruler. Actually, Minos was probably a royal title, like pharaoh.

In myth, Minos was the god Zeus' son. In a way, this was true, for the Cretan king represented the gods on earth. He was a priest-king. At certain times, he journeyed up the slope of Mount Juktas to learn the will of the gods by a sign from the heavens. The townspeople anxiously awaited his return and the good word that the barley and the vine would ripen, the fishing fleets net great catches, and prosperity and peace be their lot.

The lily was the sacred flower of Crete. The priest-king wore a plumed crown of lilies and a lily necklace. He ruled with absolute power, every year sending out a messenger to proclaim his laws. These laws, engraved on bronze tablets, were read aloud to the inhabitants of the various towns.

The king lived most of the year in his Knossos palace. In summer, however, he moved to a smaller palace. A paved road connected the main and the summer palaces, and attendants carried the king in a kind of sedan chair or litter along this road. All who walked on it went barefoot, for it was a sacred road.

The king didn't keep himself hidden in the palace, segregated from his people. Since he was their high priest, he appeared before them to perform religious rites. He was also a merchant king—with far-flung business interests. Cretan cities were mainly seaports, bustling with activity.

Women in particular enjoyed a freedom known nowhere else in those days. They attended sporting events in arenas, went hunting in chariots, gossiped in front of the temples, and danced for the men in sacred groves. Of course, they had their duties. The mother strapped her baby to her back or to the back of her older child and went about her chores.

120

Men planted and reaped the crops; raised cattle, long-horned sheep, and goats; served in the king's guard and navy, and fished. They fished with lines from shore and trawled in deep waters, dove for sponges, and lured and trapped octopuses and squids. Cretans had the sea in their blood. Shells decorated their altars. Flying fish made of glazed pottery adorned their shrine walls.

Cretans were small, dark-haired people with bronzed skin and turned-up noses. They were about five feet four inches high, or two inches shorter than modern Cretans. A man let his hair grow long, but shaved his beard. He was muscular and slender, with a tiny waist tightly drawn in by a belt. Cretan boys may have been fitted while young with a tight metal belt padded underneath, to produce the incredibly narrow waist. Below the belt, men wore a striped loincloth. In religious ceremonies they sometimes wore long flower-embroidered robes, and there are pictures of them in "Turkish" trousers bagging at the knees. Outdoors, they wore all sorts of shoes—half boots, shoes with puttees wound round the leg, a kind of espadrille, and sandals. In winter, they threw a cloak around their shoulders. They loved jewelry and wore gold and silver necklaces, bracelets, armlets, anklets, and jeweled signet rings.

When a French scholar saw the first pictures of Minoan women, he exclaimed, "But they're Parisians!" And, in fact, the women seemed to be wearing their clothes and hair in styles then fashionable in Paris (in the early years of this century). The women were wasp-waisted, having adopted the male fashion of a tight belt. They wore short-sleeved jackets laced in front, with full skirts falling from the waist. Early skirts were bell-shaped like crinolines; later ones were flounced all the way down. Cretan women did their hair in ringlets across the forehead, with the rest of their long, wavy hair falling loosely in back. They wore ankle-strap shoes and sandals and sometimes sported high heels. Gold and copper hairpins kept their hair-dos in place, and sometimes gold or silver diadems or bands encircled their brows. Like the men, they wore earrings, necklaces, and bracelets.

BULL GRAPPLING, BOXING, AND TIDDLYWINKS

The first theater was probably built on Crete. It was an open-air theater, with two flights of stone steps at right angles forming the grandstands for the spectators. In the angle was a square royal box where the king sat on a canopied throne and with his royal party watched the sports events. Court ladies occupied the front seats in the grandstands, discussing the merits of the performers. The grandstands could hold about five hundred persons.

Cretan "bull fights" were acrobatic performances. The bull was never killed or even wounded. Probably, an oval fence was erected within the theater with entrances for the bull and the "matadors." The crowd thrilled to the sport, for it spelled danger. The bull could gore a performer who missed his timing.

Household snakes drinking milk from a low table designed especially for them. It was thought their presence protected the home.

A boy and a girl acted as a team, the girl wearing a man's loincloth. The bull came charging out. The boy grabbed the tips of the bull's horns. As the bull raised his head to toss the boy, the youth let go, getting enough spring to turn a somersault and land on his feet on the bull's back. He then performed a back flip, landing on the arena floor. His girl partner stood behind the bull to catch him as he landed or to break his fall if he slipped.

A steer wrestler was asked if any rodeo performer of today could do the Cretan bull-grappling somersaults. Impossible, he answered. Before the performer could get a grip on the horns, he said, the bull would gore him. Cretans, however, trained especially for the sport. Boy and girl cowpunchers ambushed wild young bulls in the country, catching the bull in a net stretched between two trees. Even girls leaped on the bull's horns and brought his head to the ground. The bull was then roped and led away.

Boxing was another favorite Cretan sport. Boxers sometimes wore gloves or a piece of leather wrapped around the fist and wrist, reaching to the elbow. The ancient Romans, who later used it and added metal weights under the leather to make it deadlier, called this a cestus. Older boxers wore helmets, but young boxers fought bareheaded and barefisted. Cretan boxers used a standard maneuver of today. They led with the right and guarded with the left.

For less strenuous sports, Cretans played games like checkers and backgammon on inlaid gaming boards. One board held small cups around the outer edges and a large cup in the middle. A game like tiddlywinks might have been played on it.

PILLAR AND AX, DOVES AND SNAKES

A pillar shrine stood in the middle of the grandstands. Therefore, bull grappling must have been a religious rite as well as a sport. The pillar was one of three objects sacred to the Cretans. The double ax and the horns of consecration were the other two. Cretans worshipped the Great Goddess, Mother Earth, the goddess who made plants grow and brought children into the world. Caves and hilltops were favorite places for her shrines, for the cave led to the underworld and the hilltop to the heavens. But there were also private shrines in palaces and houses.

A Cretan shrine was a small rectangular room with an altar or offering table in the center. Against the back wall, sometimes on a stone bench, stood the sacred horns, made of stucco-covered clay. A hole between the horns held the bronze double ax. Clay models of animals surrounded the horn. Worshipers pinned locks of hair to a shrine wall as offerings and gave what they could afford to the Goddess. The rich gave jewels and gold; the poor, fruit and flowers.

Blood, the precious life fluid, was given as a sacred offering to the Goddess. The worshipers brought in a bull and tied him on a table. While musicians played their lyres, women poured beer or milk before the double axes—a drink offering to the Goddess. The flute player struck up a holy tune, and the bull's throat was then cut, the blood flowing into a vase below.

The double ax had no practical use. It was a religious object, standing for the power of the Goddess and the authority of the priest-king. Cretan axmakers cast double axes in all sizes, from miniature models to axes with blades almost four feet broad. Sometimes several sacred objects were combined, and the double ax was set atop a sacred pillar, with a sacred dove perched on the ax. The pillars were made of solid stone or of several stone blocks. Pillar worship probably grew out of tree worship. To ensure good crops, Cretans hung small jointed dolls in their fruit trees. When the wind blew, the dolls moved their arms and legs and seemed to dance for the gods.

The dove was sacred because it flew to the heavens. Snakes were sacred because they came from the underworld. Some Cretans had a special room at home where they fed household snakes. Tubes like a combination of water pipes sheltered them, and tables with grooves led to a central cup. The snakes slithered in the grooves across the table and drank milk from the cup. Cretans believed

Bull grapplers. In a daring leap, the boy somersaults over the bull's back while his girl partner waits with outstretched arms.

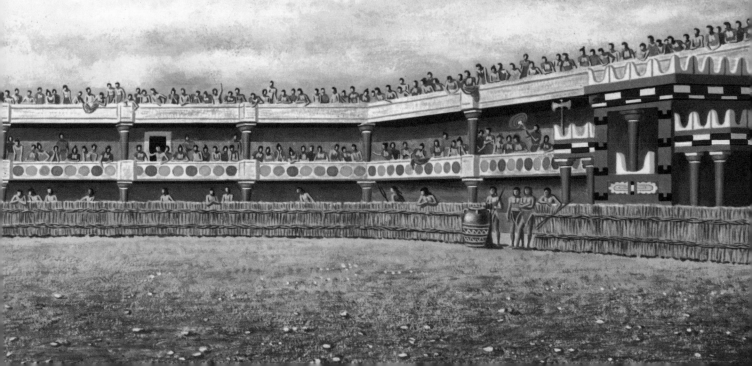

that the snakes were spirits of the underworld and protected the house. They also believed that snakes were ancestors—a grandfather or an aunt come back home from the grave. One Cretan belief—that the souls of the dead sometimes return as butterflies—is still current. Peasants call butterflies "little souls."

In early Crete, whole families were buried in the same house of the dead. Infants and young children were embalmed with honey, placed in pottery jars, and buried beneath the house so that their spirits would always be near home. Later, tombs were cut out of rock in the hillsides, and the dead buried there in clay coffins. In fact, a person's bathtub may have served later as his coffin.

SEALS TURN INTO WRITING

Cretans were buried with the possessions they thought they would need in the next world. A man had to have his identification bracelet. This was a stone or gem with a picture engraved on it—a personal seal. It was threaded and worn around the wrist or, sometimes, the neck. Early seals were shaped like beads. Eventually the hole for the thread grew wider, until the seal became a signet ring. Men used their seals to label their property.

The pictures on the seal gradually turned into signs that stood for words or syllables. This picture writing was scratched on clay tablets with a wooden or reed pen. Gradually, clerks simplified the pictures into strokes or lines. This linear writing was also incised on clay tablets and labels, but Cretans also wrote with black or sepia ink on clay and materials like parchment and papyrus.

In Crete, not only priests and the upper class could read and write. Craftsmen sometimes signed their work. And the outside walls of houses, excavated in modern times, were scribbled with words obviously intended for people passing by to read. Priests and noblemen don't scribble on house walls.

Perhaps this was the work of mischievous schoolboys. We know nothing about Cretan schools except that a student copied lines of his teacher's writing. School may have been held in the palace, for a business state like Crete needed many scribes to keep all the accounts. Most of the tablets found in the ruins of Crete are business records, like the tablets from early Mesopotamia.

The early picture writing of Crete cannot be read today. The first form of linear writing that grew out of it also cannot be read, but it may be a Semitic language like Akkadian. It was used all over Crete. The later form of linear writing was used only at Knossos, about the time the third palace was destroyed. This later form was deciphered only a few years ago. It turned out to be an early form of Greek.

KNOSSOS FALLS

If Greek was written in the House of the Double Ax, did Greeks then rule at Knossos when Crete fell? Cretan civilization began about 2800 B.C., when immigrants from the Egyptian Delta and Asia Minor joined the native fishermen and farmers. They brought techniques for working metals with them. Before long, Crete enjoyed an age of peace and plenty. The first Knossos palace grew into a splendid second one. Olive groves and vineyards yielded so much surplus that it could be shipped abroad in exchange for things that Crete needed. Fish-tailed boats made of cypress and cedar, with tall masts and high prows,

The Phaistos Disk. This clay tablet, the size of a dinner plate, has never had its picture writing deciphered. Scholars have guessed that it might be a treaty, a letter, or even a music score.

sailed south to Libya and Egypt, north to the Greek mainland, west to Sicily, and east to Syria. Cargoes of oil and wine, timber and purple dye, were stored in the holds. Cretans made dye from the murex long before the Phoenicians.

Robbery has been called the world's oldest labor-saving device. Piracy, or robbery on the high seas, must have been the second. To put an end to it, Cretans built slimmer, faster ships than before, with two and three masts. They decked over the oarsmen and installed a ram in the prow that could stave in an enemy ship and sink her. Cretan sailors cleared the sea lanes of pirates. Cretan manufactures found ready markets wherever they went. Egyptian noblemen thought so highly of Cretan cups—made as thin as eggshells—that they took them into the next world, via their tombs.

An earthquake or a foreign invasion leveled the second Knossos palace and temporarily ended Crete's prosperity. But the palace was rebuilt, and a strong government and powerful navy again gave the Cretans a golden age. The Greeks on the mainland bought Cretan wares and adopted Cretan artistic techniques, but they were unmoved by the peaceful Cretan spirit. The warlike Greeks invaded Crete about 1450 B.C. Crete was ripe for falling. So many of her cypress forests had been cut down to make ships that she had a wood shortage. When forests disappear, springs dry up and the earth yields less bountiful crops. Even flowers began to disappear, though the saffron crocus, which gave Cretans a favorite yellow dye, still grows on the island.

Greek soldiers landed in Cretan harbors and made their way to the palaces. They toppled the giant oil jars and set fire to the House of the Double Ax. An earthquake coming at the same time helped destroy Knossos and the other important cities. Soldiers looting the palaces of its treasures may have lost their way in the maze of corridors—and the labyrinth legend was born. On the corridor walls they saw paintings of charging bulls and men grappling with bulls. The earthquake shaking the palace foundations echoed through the halls like the roaring of an angry bull. Back home, the Greeks perhaps told their children tales of a mysterious man-bull hidden in a labyrinth.

As the strong south wind fanned the palace flames higher and the earth trembled, did the Cretans try to appease the anger of the Goddess? In early Crete, the people had sacrificed their king to the Goddess after he had ruled for seven years. Or did the Cretans join the Greeks in revolt against their king? If Greek was the language of the palace of Knossos at this time, Greeks may have been ruling the Cretans. Was the revolt, then, against their foreign masters? We shall never know what happened when the palace fell. But we know this: Crete was dying, and Greece was being born.

Cretan dance. Beneath branches hung with fluttering dolls, women dance in a sacred olive grove to ensure bountiful crops.

GREECE
Land of Heroes

Men traveled from market place to market place of the cities of ancient Greece, singing for their supper. Before crowds of eager listeners, they recited tales of heroes who had fought a ten-year war with Troy. To the audience, these tales from Homer were historical facts. The heroes were their ancestors.

As the centuries passed, Homer's *Iliad* and *Odyssey* were read only as great adventure stories. Troy had disappeared. Had it really existed, except in Homer's imagination? In 1870 Heinrich Schliemann, a German businessman, began digging for Troy in a mound near the Dardanelles. Like the ancient Greeks, he never doubted that Homer had written about real men and places. He used the *Iliad* and *Odyssey* as guidebooks—and found ancient Troy where Homer had located it. In the *Iliad*, the Greek hero Achilles chased the Trojan Hector three times around the city walls. These walls turned out to enclose a city, almost circular in shape, no wider than two hundred yards. Achilles had not performed an impossible feat.

Within twenty years, Schliemann unearthed not only Troy, but also cities in which the Greek heroes might have lived. "Mycenae," Homer had written, "a fortress rich in gold." In the graves of Mycenae, Schliemann found thirty pounds of precious metals, mainly gold. Its kings had been so rich that they had buried their children in wrappings of sheet gold.

The Mycenaean civilization of the early Greeks ended when invaders from the north destroyed their fortress cities. The invading Dorians belonged to the same race as the early Greeks and spoke a similar language. Many of the early Greek tribes, among them Ionians, fled to the Aegean Islands and the coast of Asia Minor. Six centuries later, Greeks would speak of their Doric or Ionic heritage. The Dorians, they said, were rugged, the Ionians soft. The Doric column that supported temple roofs was a solid, heavy-looking shaft. The Ionic column ended in a graceful spiral. Dorians strummed the manly lyre. Ionians puckered up their faces to play the flute.

Actually, the Dorian invaders had brought little more to Greece than the

Based on vase paintings, these illustrations show heroic warriors poised for combat.

iron sword used for slashing and a large metal clasp, like a safety pin, to fasten their cloaks. But the sea, the land, and the bracing climate stimulated all the Greek tribes. In the eighth century B.C. began that adventure in civilization which would be known as "classical" Greece. Soon, Greeks would contrast themselves with the rest of the world. Outside of Greece, they said, men went "bar-bar," or stammered. Anyone who didn't speak Greek was therefore a "bar-barian." Barbarians were uncivilized.

HOUSES—FROM MEGARON TO POTS

The Mycenaean Greeks built their fortress cities several miles inland, where they would be safe from pirate attack. To protect themselves from land attack, they built the cities on hilltops and surrounded them with huge stone walls. A dirt ramp led up the hill to the city gate. Anyone going up the ramp exposed his right side to the wall. Since ancient soldiers carried a shield in the left hand and a weapon in the right, they were at a disadvantage if they tried to storm the city. Soldiers defending the wall could shower down their arrows and javelins and hit the men and not the shields.

Herdsmen and farmers lived in villages of huts outside the city walls. When the enemy attacked, they abandoned their fields, piled their belongings into wagons, and drove their herds into the city. The city, small though it was, could hold the surrounding population.

The main building in the city was the chieftain's house, the megaron. This large rectangular building had originally been designed for a wintry climate, not for sunny Greece. The chieftain and his men ate, slept, and held council meetings in the megaron. They spitted and roasted joints of meat over a circular hearth in the center, which also heated the room in winter. Smoke drifted upward to a hole in the gabled roof. Behind the megaron, in an inner room or separate building, were the women's quarters. In front of the megaron was a vestibule opening onto a porch. Here along the vestibule walls servants laid beds for out-of-town visitors.

A manure heap stood in the courtyard outside the megaron. A flock of

geese or a herd of pigs roamed about loose. Sheds and storerooms surrounded the courtyard. Here the horses were stabled and the workmen and servants were quartered.

After the Dorian invasion, the towns outgrew their hilltops. They spread out below, where the farms had been. Walls now enclosed a large area of many houses and the original hilltop city became sacred ground. Where once the chieftain had offered sacrifices at an outdoor altar now stood the city altar with the temple of the city god or goddess. The Acropolis at Athens, with its Parthenon or temple of Athena, had originally been the town itself.

A common kind of house now consisted of a group of rooms around an open courtyard. Like the megaron, it was built of sun-dried brick set in a timber framework. Again, a columned porch for shade or sunning led into the main room. The main reception room, usually two stories high, faced south to catch the sun. The bedrooms were behind the main room or on the second floor. The outside walls facing the street were blank and windowless. Windows were built into the walls of rooms facing the courtyard. This arrangement guaranteed privacy and offered protection. In Greek, burglars were called "wall diggers" because to break into a house, a burglar dug a hole through the outer wall.

The house roof, pitched at a low angle, was thatched and covered with hardened mud or terracotta tiles imbedded in mud and straw. When a town was invaded, townspeople took to their roofs and showered down javelins and stones on the enemy. If they ran out of missiles, they pulled up the roof tiles and hurled those, too.

From the street, a long, covered entranceway led to the courtyard. Here stood an altar for sacrifice and a cistern to catch rainwater. The door of the entranceway was bolted, but many a lovesick lad bribed a servant to sneak him through under a bale of hay. The master of the house locked up his daughters, his supply storerooms, and his cupboard of valuables.

Tapestries decorated the walls. One Greek host was disgraced at a dinner party when a large tapestry fell down and showered his guests with dust. A couch was used for sleeping and dining. This was made of interlaced leather thongs attached to a polished wood frame. A mattress or coverlet went

Rolling wool fibers on her leg, a woman prepares them for spinning.

From right to left: The lady of the house directing clothmaking; weighing balls of wool; weaving at an upright loom; preparing wool fibers; spinning with distaff and spindle; folding finished cloth, and smoothing fibers.

over the thongs. A small three-legged table, like a cobbler's bench, was set before the couch at dinnertime and shoved underneath when not in use.

Clothes were stored in a wooden cupboard, but a man kept his cloak hanging on a nail in the wall, where it was handy. In fact, he hung all sorts of things on wall pegs and nails—his shield, spear, and sword; his lyre, bath scraper, and writing tablets. Decorative vases stood on the floor or on pedestals, and storage jars with pointed bottoms were set in the mud kitchen floor. If the master could afford it, he had a bust of himself in his reception room.

To help keep out winter winds, houses were built close to each other in narrow streets. Usually the streets were unpaved, but some were scattered with gravel and covered with lime mortar. With a shout of "Coming out!" a servant flung a pot of slops into the streets. A large city like Athens employed street cleaners to sweep the streets and unclog the drains. The drains, mere ditches around the houses, were covered with stone slabs where they crossed the street. Even the main road through Athens, which ran through the market place, was only fifteen feet wide. It was at best a three-chariot highway. Most cities didn't allow carts in the city streets, and cart owners had to park their vehicles outside the city gates.

Though some citizens boasted of owning hearth and home, many rented houses from landlords. After the Peloponnesian War, there was a serious housing shortage in fourth-century Athens. People slept where they could. Diogenes, the philosopher who went about with a lantern in daylight looking for an honest man, didn't live in a tub, as legend has it. Along with other residents of Athens, he lived in an old broken pithos, a large storage jar for oil, turned on its side. Some of these jars were ten feet high.

The Dorian chiton, a typical Greek dress, as worn by a woman and a man.

CHITONS, HIMATIONS, AND BEARDS

Diogenes went barefoot, wore rags, and let his hair grow long. Athenians nicknamed him "the dog" because he lived such a beggarly life, snarling at what they considered decent behavior. (Our word "cynic," a person who scoffs at current opinion, comes from the Greek for "dog.") The Greeks took pride in their appearance. Their clothes were simple but were worn with style.

Men and women wore similar clothes. The chiton, a kind of gown or tunic worn next to the skin, fell in folds to the knee or ankle. The woolen Doric chiton was pinned at both shoulders, whereas the linen Ionic chiton was sewn. The Ionic chiton had short sleeves, and the Doric could be pinned at the side to make sleeves. Long sleeves were the sign of a slave or a workman and so were never fashionable.

The woolen himation was especially suitable for outdoors. It could be worn next to the skin like the chiton, or over the chiton as a winter cloak. The Greeks considered it an art to drape the himation properly. A long square cloth, it was held from behind, thrown over the left shoulder, brought under the right arm, and then thrown back over the left shoulder. Men made fun of a man who wore his himation too short or so long that he tripped over it.

Men's clothes were usually bleached white or left a natural color, but women dyed their clothes or wove patterns or checks in the fabric. Himations were expensive and, for many trades, difficult to work in. Workmen wore a tunic that left one shoulder bare and was usually dyed brown so that it wouldn't show dirt.

130

In a typical agora or market place, men do the marketing, with slaves to carry their purchases. The market booths and awnings were taken down and cleared away for town meetings.

The fuller was an important man in a city. He softened and dyed woolen fabrics and cleaned the clothes. To remove stains, he rubbed the clothes in a whitish clay called fuller's earth, then brushed them with a wire-toothed comb to raise the nap. According to Athenians, fullers never returned clothes on time. If a man's only himation was at the fuller's, he might have to stay home until the fuller delivered it.

Cities had many clothes thieves. When men were busy bathing or exercising, thieves would make off with their cloaks. It wasn't uncommon at night, in the dark streets, for a thief to snatch the himation right off a man's back, leaving him stark naked.

Homer's heroes wore long hair and beards, but in the days of classical Greece short hair and a short beard were fashionable. A beard was the mark of a mature man, and shaving only became popular in the days of the youthful conqueror Alexander the Great. When boys reached the age of eighteen, they cut their hair short and dedicated the shorn locks to Apollo at his temple at Delphi, if they could afford the trip. Very close-cropped hair was a sign of mourning or stinginess. A stingy man had the barber cut his hair close to the head to save himself the expense of too many haircuts.

Indoors, men and women usually went barefoot. When a man called on

131

a friend, he removed his street footwear at the door. This was either a pair of leather sandals or a half shoe that covered the front of the foot and laced at the heel. Hunters, who pushed through sharp briars, wore high leather boots.

The shoemaker's and the barbershop were favorite lounging spots. They were right off the market place, and men could spy friends passing by the open shop front.

LIFE IN TOWN

A man went to the shoemaker's or the barber's before noon. He had been up many hours by then, however. Townspeople usually rose at dawn. From Persia they had imported an animal alarm clock—the rooster—which crowed and woke them. If he had a slave, a man washed out of a basin while the slave poured cold water over his head. To whiten his teeth, he rubbed them with powdered pumice (volcanic rock). He wrapped his himation about him—he may have slept with it as a blanket—and had a simple breakfast of barley or wheat bread dunked in wine.

Leaving his wife to look after the household, he went to the market place or to visit a friend in the early morning. Though most citizens had learned a trade, many of them looked down on business and left it in the hands of non-citizens. To the citizen of a city like Athens in the classical age, life was designed for leisure and for serving the state. All roads led to the market place, where the arts of leisure and politics were practiced.

The market place, or agora, was the nerve center of city life. It was an open-air market and meeting place, the main open place in town. Public buildings, law courts, the town hall, and columned porches surrounded it.

132

At the public fountain house women wait their turn to get the spring water pouring from metal spouts. After filling the jars, they carry them upright.

Merchants set up wicker and wooden booths and stands, with narrow lanes in between for customers to pass through.

The man of the house did the marketing, followed by a slave or servant carrying a basket. He enjoyed haggling with fish peddlers and wine merchants. The merchants stood behind their stands and shouted out their wares and prices. Some merchants were women—resident aliens or freedwomen. The only two market trades a woman couldn't ply in Athens were those of butcher and fish peddler.

The market was divided into sections. Here stood flowersellers with bunches of poppies and irises or garlands of myrtle leaves. There stood winesellers with pottery jars of wine. Fruit vendors buried rotten figs and olives at the bottom of their baskets and piled the beautiful fruit on top. Vendors watched out for hands that slipped into baskets to pinch free samples.

Butchers and fish peddlers kept their products under wicker mats. A fresh mullet was tossed onto the pan of a balance scale, and a sale was made. The peddler took the coin he received and put it in his cheek for safekeeping. He often kept as many as twelve coins in his mouth at a time.

Many of the shops—the barbershop, the shoemaker's, the doctor's clinic—were built in the back wall of a columned porch. Some were located off the agora, in a special street or neighborhood named after the trade. In such a street was the upholsterer's, where couches were made and sold. Here a man could buy a couch and everything that went with it—cushions, coverlets, and tapestries.

Professional cooks could be hired in the agora. Unemployed laborers congregated in a special place. Here a man could hire a house boy for the day, a charioteer to drive a rented chariot, or a field hand to help with the harvest. Horse breeders brought their animals into town to sell or swap. And the city

133

buyer was heard to complain that he had been sold a tail—from which a half-dead horse hung.

On fair days, the slave market did a flourishing business. Conjurors and magicians set up stands and charged admission or passed the hat. They swallowed swords, ate fire, and did tricks. They played the same "shell game" still practiced today: a pebble was slipped from one cup to another, and the on-looker guessed which cup held the pebble. The conjuror then produced it from the guesser's ear.

Men gathered under the porches to exchange news and to get out of the sun or a sudden rainstorm. In Athens, the philosopher Zeno lectured his disciples under one of these porches. His philosophy was called "stoic" because the word for "porch" in Greek is *stoa*. While a barber singed the hair off a customer's body or gave a haircut, old cronies sat around the barbershop, planning a dinner party or a night fishing trip by torchlight. In winter, the smith's forge, with its hot fire, was a favorite hangout.

At noon, some men went home for a siesta, but usually they bought lunch at the market place. A sausage from the sausage seller, who roamed about with his table of wares strapped in front of him or sizzling pancakes swimming in honey from the pancake maker, who cooked them in frypans over the coals of a brazier.

Business at the agora fell off in the afternoon. If the town magistrates had important news for the citizens, they sent a herald to the agora. He blew a trumpet and announced his news, like the town crier of later centuries.

In fifth- and fourth-century Athens, jurors would be leaving the law courts, hundreds at a time. Juries never numbered fewer than 201 citizens. When

A typical sandal.

citizens finished their public or private business, they spent the afternoon at a gymnasium or the baths. At the gymnasium they could exercise or watch others wrestle and box. Gymnasiums often had lecture halls, where some teachers taught for nothing and others for a fee. A "gentleman" philosopher wasn't supposed to charge, though he accepted gifts.

Street philosophers spent their days in the agora, the gymnasiums, and the baths, arguing with friend and foe. The most famous of them, Socrates, never ran a school or wrote a book. Of course, few citizens listened to their philosophers, then as now. The average citizen concerned himself with his property if he had any, his political duties, and his amusements.

Gymnasiums had open-air courtyards for wrestling, running, and broad-jumping. There was also a ball ground. Spectators could watch activities under the long porches that surrounded the court. The baths weren't elaborate. As late as the fifth century B.C. warm baths for men were thought effeminate. But by the next century, they had become a necessity. Women as well as men went to public bathhouses. Bathers brought their own oil flasks, sponges, and body scrapers. A large basin on a stand held the bath water. The bather could also crouch while an attendant poured water over him.

At sunset everyone headed for home or for dinner at a friend's house. Athenians were said to frown on men who walked fast and talked loud. On

In a shop just off the bustling market place, the shoemaker measures a customer for sandals.

the other hand, they fought for celery at the vegetable market as strenuously as athletes at the Isthmian games (the prize at the games was a celery wreath). Undoubtedly, they rushed and shouted with as much vigor as modern Mediterranean peoples.

Even their slaves weren't always timid. They talked often with freemen as equals and sometimes sassed their masters even though it meant a beating. If a slave spotted a coin in the street, he could keep it. If someone else saw it the same time he did, he shouted, "Shares in the luck!" and by custom took half. A stingy master wasn't above claiming "halves" with his slave.

After dinner at home, a man strolled about the market place, drank some wine with his friends, and went to bed early. In Athens, archers from southern Russia, who were slaves owned by the state, patrolled the city streets as police. But cloak snatchers and wall diggers lurked in the dark alleys.

A DINNER AND A SYMPOSIUM

When a man ate at home, his wife or servants prepared dinner. He reclined on a couch while his wife sat upright in a chair. Children, too, sat on chairs or stools. In Mycenaean days, the Greeks feasted on whole roasted sheep, oxen, and pigs. They ate fish only when they couldn't get meat. As the Greeks grew more civilized, their diet changed. Fish became a delicacy, especially eels. A Greek's mouth now watered at the mention of fried shrimp, baked turbot with mulberry sauce, and bass steamed in brine with vegetables.

Poor citizens and workmen ate simpler food—barley porridge sweetened with honey, cheese and onions, figs, bean or pea soup—and drank cheap wine. In Sparta, before the fourth century, the main course at dinner was an unappetizing black broth. A colonial Greek from Sybaris in Italy once dined with

Ancient Greeks reclined on couches as they dined, ate with their fingers, and drank wine from bowls. Afterward they played instruments, sang, and asked riddles.

some Spartans. "No wonder Spartans are the bravest men in the world," he remarked after eating. "Anyone in his right mind would rather die ten thousand times than eat such a meal." His home town of Sybaris, famous for its luxuries, gave the world its oldest known patent law. A cook who invented a new dish was allowed to patent the recipe for one year. A "sybarite" now means a person who loves luxury.

Today we use "symposium" to mean a group discussion. In ancient Greece, a symposium was a drinking party after dinner. The host invited his friends home for dinner. If he could afford it, he paid all the expenses. If not, he asked the guests to chip in for their share of the food, wine, and entertainment. If his dining room wasn't large enough, he gave his party at a friend's house. Uninvited guests often showed up. Friends were welcomed, for they gave parties in return. But a group of idle men hung about a rich man's house to feast at his dinners. They didn't repay with dinners of their own but with flattery. These men were nicknamed "parasites." A real parasite was a state official who dined with the priests after sacrifices. It was an honorable office.

The guests were greeted at the door by a slave who took off their sandals and washed their feet. They were escorted into the main room, where the dining couches were. A couch could seat two, and a dinner party might number six guests on three couches. They sat on the couches while a slave poured water over their hands. Separate little tables, with the food already on, were placed before the couches. The diner propped his left arm and shoulder on the couch pillows, stretched out, and ate with his right hand. It was finger food, such as baked fish, thrushes preserved in honey, or roast duck. The food had been cut into bite-size pieces in the kitchen, and bread was used as a sop. Sometimes the bread was cut into a finger shape with a hollow scooped out at the end. This made a sort of spoon. When he finished his first course, the guest wiped his hands on a piece of bread and threw it to the dogs which lay at the foot of the couches.

The first tables were then taken away, and the second tables brought in. These were laden with cheese, fruits, nuts, cakes, and perhaps a honeycomb. After the second course, a slave again poured water over the guests' hands, rubbed them with perfumed ointment, and put flower or leafy garlands on their heads. The floor was cleared and swept, and then the host and his guests spilled wine on it as an offering to the gods. It was the Greek way of saying grace.

The slaves now mixed the wine. Only barbarians, said the Greeks, drank straight wine. The Greeks always diluted it with water, usually two parts of wine to three parts of water. If possible, the wine was served chilled. It was chilled in a well; or a wine-cooler holding snow was lowered into the large wine jar on the floor. Greeks disliked beer—beer was for barbarians. Beer, they

said, made a man fall down and lie on his back like an animal. Too much wine made a man topple forward on his face—for wine, like ideas, swelled a man's head.

After dinner and with their wine, the guests played games. In one called cottabus, the player grasped his almost empty wine bowl, twisted his wrist, and tried to splash the dregs against a pottery figure balanced on a lampstand or at a pan hanging from the ceiling. A loud *ping!* guaranteed success in love. At other times, the target for these "love arrows" was the head of a slave.

The guests sang songs together and put riddles to each other. A guest who couldn't solve a riddle had to drink a bowl of wine mixed with brine. Probably the

138

most famous Greek riddle we know wasn't a dinner-party riddle but the one the Sphinx was said to have asked each traveler on the road to Thebes: "What creature walks on four legs in the morning, two at noon, and three in the evening?" Oedipus solved the riddle: "Man—he creeps in infancy, walks on his own legs in the prime of life, and as an old man walks with a staff." The Sphinx promptly committed suicide.

The only women at symposiums were courtesans and entertainers. A girl played a flute for the singing, or a girl acrobat somersaulted across the room. Sometimes the dinner party lasted till dawn. The guests went home through city streets alive with laborers on their way to work. If a man woke up with a hangover, he could eat acorns—said to be a sure remedy.

LIFE IN THE COUNTRY

Where states are only a few square miles in area, farms are necessarily small. In Attica, individual farms covered about fifty acres. Farmers grew three main crops in Greece—grain, grapes, and olives. The grain was harvested in April

Hunting the wild boar. Like many hunters today, the Greeks used dogs to flush game out of the thickets.

or May in the plains. In mountainous regions, harvesttime came a month later. After the harvest, the farmer often didn't plow his land until the following spring. Then he cut the ground with an ox-drawn plow and again before the summer drought hardened the soil. After the early autumn rains, he again plowed the earth and sowed his barley or wheat seeds. (Occasionally, in time of famine, he sowed spring seed.) In spring he hoed and weeded the rows between the sprouting grain. He therefore harvested his crop every two years, reaping about twelve bushels an acre.

The independent farmer was friendly with his neighbors. He lent them his plow, sickles, and winnowing baskets. He didn't stand on ceremony, and

Crouched on a rock above the sea, a boy fishes for his dinner, storing his catch in the basket under the water.

at a knock opened the farmhouse door himself. (His city cousin found it beneath his dignity to answer the door himself.) He ate his breakfast while putting down hay for his oxen or asses. (His city cousin never mixed food and work.)

If he needed money, the farmer could mortgage his farm. Stone slabs set up at intervals marked the boundary line between his farm and his neighbor's. When he mortgaged his land, the banker wrote down that fact on these stone markers. The farmer then couldn't mortgage the same farm twice.

The farmer's wife helped with the chores, ground the grain to make flour, and fed the family and the farm workers. If the farmer hired hands, he had to pay them wages and feed them, too. In early days, farmers wore leather clothes made from the hides of their farm animals or of game. Poor farmers even in later times couldn't afford woolen clothes unless they kept goats or sheep.

Greek farmers often raised bees. They needed the honey to sweeten their dishes. But, as a rule, they didn't keep herds as well as grow crops. Few Greek states had land rich enough to support cattle, especially through the winter. The Greeks considered cow's milk unwholesome and rarely drank it or used it for making cheese. Cheese was made from goat's and ewe's milk. Sheep farmers and goatherds lived where the soil was too barren to produce crops.

The farmer lucky enough to own a few sheep or goats had his clothing made by his wife. After the farmer had sheared and washed the fleece, his wife beat, combed, and carded it. She combed the long hairs and carded the short ones with a brush having bent wire teeth. She spun the natural-colored thread by hand, the distaff of wool under the left arm and the spindle in her right hand or in a disk on the ground. With the fingers of her left hand, she twisted the thread from the distaff, winding it round her spindle. Where the thread came out uneven, she bit off the extra piece with her teeth as she spun. When the spindle held enough thread, she put it into a basket and took it to her loom.

Like Penelope in the *Odyssey*, Greek women were famed as weavers. Early

140

looms were upright, the warp threads weighted to keep them in place. As the weaver wove, she rolled the top bar of her loom to wind up her weaving so that she would always be working at the same height.

The farmer loved to go hunting or night fishing. To make a torch, he bound strips of wood together and dipped the end into pitch. He lit the pitch, armed himself with a trident, or three-pronged spear, and went spear-fishing in a sea cove. When he went hunting, he put on boots, cloak, and broad-brimmed hat and whistled for his dogs. Greeks always hunted with dogs, a favorite hunting breed being a small reddish hound from Sparta. The dogs flushed boars out of the thickets, and when a boar came charging out the hunter hurled his spear.

In hilly country, the farmer could produce a larger crop worth more money per acre if he grew olive trees and grapevines rather than grain. Greek grapevines were dwarf plants that hugged the ground and needed no supports or trellises. Though fieldmice and foxes destroyed some of the vines, the strong summer winds couldn't tear them down. Farmers sometimes used the rows between the vines to grow vegetables.

Women worked in the vineyards, not only hoeing the ground and pruning the leaves in summer, but later picking the grapes. September was vintage time. The grapes were carried in baskets to the treading floor or wine-press. The treading floor, made of cement or acacia wood, had low walls that sloped to an outlet. Below this was a wine vat sunk into the ground. The workers trod the grapes, and the juice ran into the vat.

The wine was fermented in huge clay pottery vats. Often these vats were coated inside and out with pitch or resin, which gave them a peculiar flavor. The vats were buried in the ground or stored in cool cellars. After fermenting six months the wine was filtered into skins or pottery amphorae with pointed bottoms. The top of the amphora was stoppered and sealed, and both handle and stopper were marked to show the vintage year and where the wine came from.

A winetaster at work. After he has dipped his sponge into the wine he will smell it, squeeze some drops onto his hand, and taste it.

Greek winemakers used plaster, not cork, for stoppers. Therefore their wines had to be drunk within three or four years, or they spoiled. Often, lime, resin, or even seawater was added to cut down the wine's acidity. Some Greek wines today are still treated with resin.

CITIZENS, SLAVES, AND WOMEN

Except in Sparta and Thessaly, Greek farmers didn't depend on slave labor. The citizen class in Sparta, called Spartiates, owned the land but never farmed it. Helots, who were serfs rather than actual slaves, worked the land to support their Spartan masters. Helots may have been the original inhabitants of the state, for they outnumbered the Spartiates seven to one. Every year the government declared official war on the helots and made token raids on their farms. Young Spartans, organized into a secret police force, spied on the helots. At a sign of a helot plot, they butchered the leaders without trial or hearing.

Spartiates were not allowed to sell helots. Though they had no political rights, helots were forced to row in the navy and fight as light infantrymen. If a helot distinguished himself in battle, he might win his freedom. Then he belonged to the class that ran trade and industry for the Spartiates and worked their iron mines. This class also couldn't own property, had no political rights, and had to serve in the army and navy.

From the beginning of their history, all Greek states kept slaves. By the fifth century B.C., Greek industrialists depended on slave labor for their income. In mid-fifth-century Athens, there were 70,000 slaves out of a total population of about 155,000.

Slaves were usually, though not always, foreigners. Prisoners of war automatically became slaves. However, Greek states warring with each other often exchanged prisoners or allowed their families to ransom them. Slave traders bought slaves in Asia Minor, Mesopotamia, Thrace, and southern Russia (Scythia) and shipped them to Greek markets. Asiatic slaves, said the Greeks, were intelligent but not courageous, whereas the Russians (or Scythians) were courageous but not intelligent. Russian slaves made good policemen.

Female slaves were mainly used in housework and to weave in the cloth factories. Slaves were, however, usually men. In mid-fifth-century Athens, an average citizen's household had about three slaves. Not every citizen could afford a slave, for prices were high. An unskilled slave who could work in the mines was auctioned off for what would amount to about $30 in our money. However, in a city like Athens in the middle of the fifth century, an architect earned about twenty cents a day (in our money) and a farm hand about ten cents a day. Yet it cost about seven cents to pay for a public bath, and a fuller charged about ten cents to clean a himation. So even an unskilled slave cost a lot of money, in terms of purchasing power. The highest price paid for a slave—the overseer of a mine—was about $1200, but to buy a skilled slave—say, a swordsmith—ran to $120. States as well as private citizens owned slaves. These slaves worked as government clerks and policemen, musicians for the festivals, and state doctors.

Slaves in cities like Athens couldn't be distinguished from freemen or citizens. They wore the same clothes and worked alongside them in the trades. A master sometimes set up a clever slave in business for a share of the profits. Though, technically, the money a slave earned belonged to the master, the slave

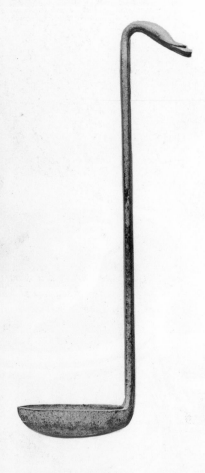

A bronze ladle.

was usually allowed to keep part of his earnings. With this money he could buy his freedom. One Athenian slave not only earned his freedom, but became the leading town banker. For his services to the state, the public assembly voted him citizenship.

Though slaves were treated better in ancient Greece than in ancient Rome or pre-Civil War America, they led a hard life. They could be bought and sold like a piece of furniture. In a lawsuit, they had to be tortured before giving evidence. Thousands of slaves ran away every year, and many a slave fled for his life to seek sanctuary in the temple precincts.

In the classical age, a Greek woman led a life almost as restricted as that of a slave. She spent most of her days in her dark and often dingy home. If her husband owned slaves, she managed them when he was away and supervised the weaving and the kitchen chores. She was allowed to visit a woman friend occasionally and to attend religious festivals. Sometimes she went to the women's bath and sometimes could sit in the back rows of the theater with the foreigners when a tragedy was playing. Women were never allowed at comedies and couldn't attend public games such as Olympic events, where men competed naked. When she did go out, she was always chaperoned by an elderly slave

Inside a forge. As customers look on, a smith hammers red-hot iron on his anvil.

143

or servant. A decent woman didn't go to the market place and never spoke to a man on the street. She never entertained her husband's friends and often met them for the first time at his funeral, when they called to pay their last respects.

Sparta, which so restricted male life, was the one Greek state where a woman had freedom. Athenian women were scandalized by the liberties their Spartan sisters enjoyed—and envious, too. Spartan girls, wearing a short chiton, wrestled, boxed, and raced with the young men. Wives mingled freely with their husbands' friends. Spartans wanted healthy women who would produce healthy, brave soldiers for the state. A Spartan mother seeing her son off to war advised him to return *with* his shield or *on* it. (Dead soldiers were carried from battle on their shields.)

In commercial cities like Corinth and Athens, women worked in the markets as food sellers, cloth weavers, and even shoemakers. But these freedwomen and resident aliens had few privileges and no political rights. Commerce, in fact, had originally lowered the position of Greek women. As the Greeks grew rich through trade, they adopted customs from the East, where women were kept in harems. In Mycenaean times and even later, women had held court with their husbands, had come and gone as they pleased, and in one state even had the right to vote in the public assembly.

In most Greek states, fathers arranged the marriages of their sons and daughters, sometimes with the help of a matchmaker. Brides brought their husbands a dowry, often a sizable one. A girl usually married at the age of fifteen, a man often as late as thirty. Before the wedding ceremony, the young girl took her dolls to a temple of the goddess Artemis. It was a coming-of-age rite and meant that she was putting away her childish life. After a ritual bath in a river or the sea, the bride was given a party by her father.

After the party, the best man drove the groom's chariot to the door, and the groom led his veiled bride into it. Sitting between the two men, the bride was driven off to her new home. In the country, the bridal couple rode in a mule-driven cart. Members of the wedding, carrying torches, serenaded the couple along the way. The bride's mother carried a torch lit from the family hearth to start the hearth burning in her daughter's home.

The wedding party showered the bride with grain, fruit, and candies when she entered her new home. Like our custom of throwing rice, this rite asked the gods to grant her many children. After bride and groom retired, bridesmaids stood outside their door to sing bridal songs. The day after the wedding, relatives gave housewarming gifts, and two days later the bride appeared for the first time unveiled.

A woman in labor called in a midwife, not a doctor. If the baby was unwanted, the father placed it outside a temple or exposed it in a mountain wood where wild animals would get it. Anyone finding an exposed baby could raise it as his own or to be his slave. When a boy was born, the father hung an olive wreath on the house door to tell the neighbors the good news. If the baby turned out to be a girl, a wooden circlet told the bad news. The newborn baby was put on the ground for Mother Earth to give him strength, then the father picked him up, accepting him as his child.

At mealtime, the baby sat in a wicker high chair with holes for his legs. Like today's babies, he played with a rattle. (A Greek philosopher is credited with inventing the rattle.) When he grew older, the child played in the courtyard or the city streets. He often had a pet dog, goose, or pig. Boys and

Vase paintings of a little boy pushing his toy cart and (below) of two boys playing with a ball.

A baby in a wicker high chair holds out his arms to his mother, and (below) a young boy plays a lyre.

girls floated toy boats in street puddles, teetered on seesaws, whirled through the air on swings, rolled hoops, spun tops with a whip, played catch with a stuffed leather ball, and flipped and caught astragals, or bone jackstones, on the back of the hand. Girls played "house" with dolls and pots, jumped on oiled wineskins to see how long they could stay on, practiced headstands, and juggled sticks on their fingertips.

SCHOOLDAYS

A boy went to school at the age of seven. Girls were usually educated at home, but vase paintings and terracotta figurines show reluctant girls, clutching their school tablets, being pulled or pushed to school. A slave walked the boy to school, waited for him during lesson time, and took him home afterward. He also taught the boy to dress, eat, and behave. The Greeks called this slave a "pedagogue." Today we use the word to mean "teacher."

Schools were large by ancient standards. When the roof of one collapsed, almost all of its 120 students were buried in the ruins. The student learned to write on a small framed wooden tablet coated with wax. He rested the tablet on his lap and held a pointed wooden pen, or stylus, in his hand. The teacher wrote a line of Greek at the top, and the student scratched a copy below with his stylus. If he made a mistake, he turned the stylus around and with the blunt end rubbed over the wax, erasing his mistakes. When the coat of wax wore down to the wood, his mother rewaxed the tablet at home.

When he had learned to write, he used a lesson book made of two or three tablets hinged together with rings, which could be folded flat. Later on, he wrote with pen and ink on papyrus paper.

The wax-covered tablets were used not only for school notebooks, but

145

also for business records and legal documents. Greek books, however, were rolls of papyrus. A book copyist wrote several narrow columns to a sheet, with wide spaces between. He used only one side of the sheet. The sheets were then pasted together and wound on a wooden roller. To read a book, you held the wooden roller in your right hand, opened it with your left, read the first page, and rolled it up with your left hand as you went on. Book rolls were either stored upright in baskets or pigeonholed. A label attached to the end of the roll gave the title and author.

A boy went to elementary school till the age of fourteen. He learned simple arithmetic with pebbles and an abacus or counting board, perhaps a little geometry, and drawing. Homer's epics were his main schoolbooks, and he learned many verses of the *Iliad* and *Odyssey* by heart. Boys who didn't behave were paddled by the teacher with a ferule—the long, hard stalk of a plant. At home, if a girl was naughty, her mother reached for a sandal to punish her.

At fourteen or fifteen, a boy studied mathematics, literature, and how to write and deliver speeches. Besides his scholastic studies, he learned the art of sports. This secondary education was given in a gymnasium, a word that meant a place for exercising naked. All school exercises and sports were played without clothes. In Sparta, the boys were lined up naked and examined every ten days to make sure they weren't getting fat.

A good gymnasium was often built beside a stream and had a wrestling ground, baths, lecture rooms, and a track for running. The wrestling ground was a walled, open-air room. A boy had to wrestle under the hot sun. He poured oil over his body from a small flask and grappled with his opponent. The best three throws won him the bout. Afterward, he scraped the dirt off his skin with his scraper and bathed from a washstand or dove into a stream.

The chariot race—high point of the Olympic games. The light open-backed chariots bounced dangerously and spills were frequent.

At Athens, a boy's schooldays lasted until he reached the age of eighteen. Then he underwent two years' military training, guarding his city's forts and patrolling its open countryside. After this service and if his family could afford it, he could have what amounted to a university education. Fourth-century Athens had two famous schools of this sort. Plato taught his disciples at a grove outside the city, the Academy. His pupil Aristotle lectured to his students in the shady walks of the Lyceum. Both words have come to mean schools of higher education.

There were no public schools. Schoolteachers were paid by the parents and usually earned small fees. At festival time it was customary for students to give their teacher a present, but stingy fathers kept their sons at home to save the expense.

THE OLYMPIC GAMES

Festival days were holidays for everyone. In Athens there were seventy festival days in the year. Every four years, Athenians honored their protecting goddess Athena with a festival that lasted from six to nine days. It opened with games and athletic contests featuring a boat race and a race with lighted torches. The torch race was a relay race between two teams, the torch being passed from runner to runner. The winners of the games received a decorated jar filled with oil from the sacred olive groves. We keep up this custom by awarding prize cups.

The most famous games in Greece were held in a little town called Olympia. Every four years, heralds left Olympia for all parts of the Greek world to announce the start of the games. The games were held in midsummer. A

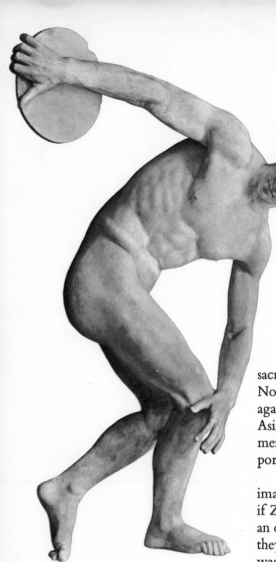

A famous sculpture, the discus thrower. Discus throwing was one of the five events in the pentathlon— an Olympic contest featuring broad jump, discus throw, javelin throw, running and wrestling.

sacred truce was declared; if Greeks were at war, they laid down their arms. Now men could get to the games and back home safely before the war began again. Thousands of Greeks from Greece and the colonies in Africa, Italy, and Asia Minor headed for Olympia. Slaves carried food supplies, cooking equipment, tents, and bedding. Most of the visitors slept on the floors of the town porches or beneath olive and poplar trees.

The Olympic games were held in honor of Zeus, whose gold and ivory image, forty feet high, sat enthroned in his Olympic temple. It was said that if Zeus happened to rise, he would lift the roof off the temple. Athletes took an oath on the sacred boar of Zeus to abide by the rules. Once they had sworn, they couldn't back out. If they broke the rules, they were fined. One boxer was fined because he arrived at Olympia after the boxing contest was over, put on his gloves anyway, and started pounding the winner.

The winners were crowned with an olive wreath, poets wrote odes about them, and cities held elaborate parades for their native sons. Athens gave money prizes to her Olympic champions and fed them at public expense in the town hall for the rest of their lives. At Sparta, Olympic winners had the honor of standing alongside the king in battle.

For the first event, the foot race, the spectators went to the Stadium, which could seat forty thousand. The grandstands, shaped like a horseshoe, curved around the finish line of the track. The hero Herakles is said to have measured off the track with his own big feet. In the double race, runners turned at the finish line and raced back to the starting line, a row of wooden posts set in stone slabs.

The most exiting event in the Olympic games was the chariot race, held in the hippodrome, an oval track surrounded by grandstands. Chariot racers cast lots for track positions. Each placed his marked pebble or wooden block in a jar. One of the ten judges of the games shook the jar and spilled the pebbles out one at a time. The athlete whose pebble came out first won the inside position.

The low-wheeled, open-backed chariots were pulled by four horses; in later times, by two. At the signal to start, the charioteers whipped their horses into action with long goads. The chariots bounced in the air and swirled up clouds of dust. Spectators watched breathlessly for the part of the course called

148

"the horse disturber." Here, at a turn, horses almost invariably shied, sometimes hurling out their drivers.

Whoever won the pentathlon was considered the finest all-round athlete. This contest featured five events—running, broad jump, discus throw, javelin throw, and wrestling. The broad jumper held weights like dumbbells in both hands to help push him forward. In the discus throw, the athlete tossed a metal disk that weighed up to nine pounds. In the javelin throw, he gripped a leather thong wound round the shaft, pulling the thong when hurling. This sent the javelin spinning in straight flight. The javelin's thong served the same function as the rifling in a gun barrel. In wrestling, the athlete had to throw his opponent three times, and he was allowed to trip him if he could.

The boxing event at the games wasn't judged on points or rounds. Boxers wound oxhide thongs around their hands and slapped each other with the flat of the hand rather than the fist, aiming mainly at the head. The fight went on, with the boxers getting bloodied eyes, knocked-out teeth, and bleeding mouths, until one boxer called it quits.

The pancratium was a free-for-all fight with no holds barred. Two opponents boxed, wrestled, strangled, kicked, and jumped on top of each other. The only thing they weren't allowed to do was gouge each other's eyes.

Between events, poets took the opportunity to recite their verses to the crowds in the grandstands. Herodotus, the father of history, even read his history of the Persian Wars aloud at the Olympic games. It must have taken him several days of steady reading.

Greek historians dated events by Olympiads, the four-year periods when the games were held. The first recorded date in Greek history is 776 B.C., the first Olympiad. The games were held every four years thereafter until A.D. 394, when a Christian Roman emperor forbade them as wicked pagan rites.

TRAGEDY AND COMEDY ARE BORN

Zeus had his Olympic games, but the god of wine and revelry, Dionysus, had drama contests performed in his honor. Greek theaters were sometimes large enough to hold a whole town—20,000 to 30,000 persons. In Athens, the spring and winter festivals ended with a three-day drama contest. Athenians arrived

The broad jumper (shown on a vase) held stone weights to give himself momentum in his leap.

at dawn to buy tickets to the open-air theater of Dionysus built below the Acropolis. Citizens who couldn't afford the price of admission—about seven cents in our money—were given ticket money by the state. They arrived with cheese, fruit, and wine and carried cushions to sit on. They had a long day ahead of them, for they would witness a quadruple feature. Each day a different playwright presented four plays—three tragedies and a short, often bawdy playlet. Judges chosen by lot decided which of the three playwrights should win the award for the best play.

The reward was only an ivy wreath, but sometimes a playwright won more than a wreath. After Sophocles had won a victory for a tragedy, he was elected a general. He made a better poet than general.

Greek audiences knew the plots of the tragedies before they saw them. The tragedies dealt with the heroes of Greek myths and how they met their destiny. But the audience followed the action of the plays with great excitement. Between plays they discussed the merits of the play, the actors' performances, and the dancing of the chorus. From their wooden or stone seats in the semi-

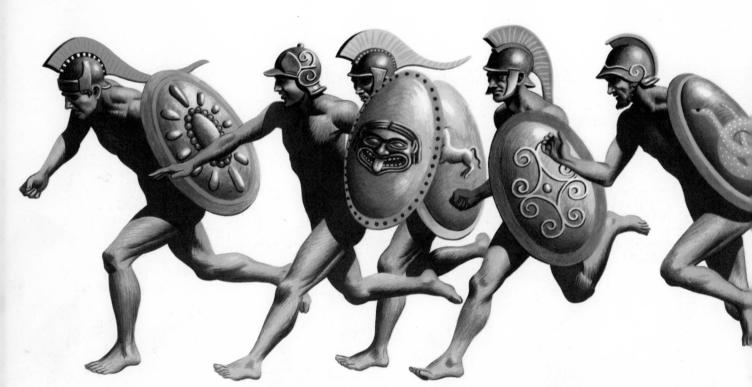

circle high above the performing area, they could hear every word, for the acoustics of Greek theaters were almost perfect. Even those perched on the rocks could hear. And to remind them that they were taking part in a religious ceremony, they could see the altar of Dionysus down below and his temple alongside the theater.

Before there was theater or drama, villagers paraded to the temple of Dionysus after the grape harvest, to thank him for his gift of wine. A group of them, dressed in goatskins or wearing horses' ears and tails, played the part of satyrs. Satyrs were supposed to be half-human, half-animal creatures of the

150

wood who accompanied the god. The players danced and sang, retelling the god's adventures. This performance was called a "goat song." Thus tragedy was born, for in Greek "tragedy" means "goat song."

In later goat songs or tragedies, the dancing and singing chorus sang of the exploits of heroes as well as gods. For in ancient Greece, heroes became gods. In the sixth century, Thespis wrote a dialogue for the grape festival. As part of the goat song, the leader of the chorus put questions to him and he answered as the hero. He became the world's first "answerer" or actor. (The Greek word for actor gives us our word "hypocrite," one who acts a part.) We call actors Thespians after this first actor.

Within fifty years, tragedy became more than a story told in song and dance with spoken interludes. It became drama.

There were never more than three actors and the chorus in Greek tragedy. However, there were many nonspeaking roles, like those of soldiers and attendants. And the three actors played several parts in the same play, simply changing costumes and masks.

To the Greeks, a mask helped to bring a god to life. They hung masks on trees in the country and on pillars in the city in the belief that Dionysus would spring alive from tree and pillar. In a similar way, an actor with a mask could, for an hour, bring a hero like Agamemnon back to life.

There were no actresses. Men played all the parts. The playwright Sophocles was especially skilled at playing women's parts. All Athens applauded when he acted the part of Nausicaa, the girl who, playing ball on the shore, found the shipwrecked Odysseus. What captivated the audience was the fast game of ball he played. Actors became public idols then as today. They traveled to

Usually heavily armed soldiers, these hoplites wore only helmets in Olympic races.

151

all the theaters of Greece and the colonies. A famous actor might receive as much as a talent (about $1000 in our money) for a single performance.

There was no stage in the Greek theater until Roman times. The playing area was the orchestra, which in Greek meant the place for the chorus to dance. It was a flat circular area with an altar in the center. Behind the orchestra, actors changed their costumes and stored their props in a tent or hut, the *skene*. This became our word "scene," for the hut was enlarged until it had three doors in it and served as a backdrop.

In early tragedies, gods stood on a high platform as though on Mount Olympus. The playwright Euripides had his gods appear from the top of the *skene*. A crane lowered them over the side, where they hung in mid-air. The Greeks accused Euripides of writing such complicated plots that often the only way he could solve them was to have a god appear unexpectedly to rescue the hero. They called this dramatic trick "the god from the machine."

Like tragedy, comedy was born from revels honoring the wine god. A band of masked jesters, like paraders in our carnivals or Mardi Gras festivals, sang and danced in processions, joking with the bystanders. Poets turned these impromptu performances into written comedies.

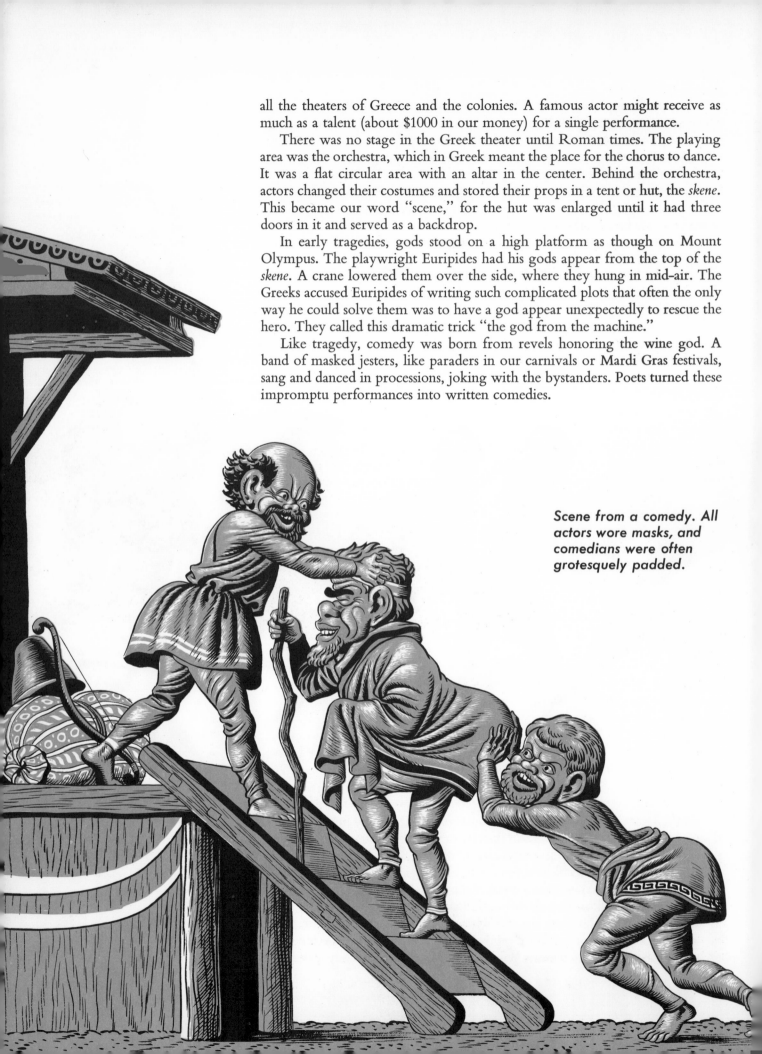

Scene from a comedy. All actors wore masks, and comedians were often grotesquely padded.

Comedies didn't deal with the past, as tragedies did. They poked fun at everyday life and politics. Men sitting in the audience heard their names mentioned by characters on the stage and even saw themselves lampooned. Comic actors wore grotesque masks with wide-open mouths. These masks were often caricatures of real persons. Actors also padded their legs and bellies, for a fat or deformed person was automatically funny to the Greeks. They also wore bizarre costumes, for they played characters such as wasps, birds, and even clouds as well as human beings.

Audiences at comedies hissed as well as applauded. Sometimes they pelted the actors with stones. In turn, the actors sometimes played tricks on the audience. If a fruit seller in a comedy threw a basket of figs at a fellow actor playing an average citizen, he might follow this up by tossing a basket of figs at the audience.

GODS AND TEMPLES

Religious festivals like the drama festival were regulated and run by the state. There was no one religion in Greece. Each state worshiped its own god and claimed that its citizens descended from some hero. Two states only twelve miles apart might worship different gods and heroes. The Greeks saw their gods as Homer pictured them. When the sculptor Pheidias was asked who was going to be the model for his statue of Zeus for Olympia, he answered by quoting Homer's description of Zeus.

The Greeks had no sacred book and no dominant priesthood. State officials were in charge of feasts and sacrifices. Every town hall had a hearth dedicated to the goddess Hestia, and when a city founded a colony it sent fire from this hearth to the new one. In the same way, fire from the household hearth, also sacred to the goddess, lit the new hearth of a bride's home.

A Greek didn't have to believe all the myths connected with the gods. Nevertheless, the state could punish anyone convicted of impiety. After he declared that the sun was a large lighted stone and not a god, a philosopher found it wise to move out of Athens.

A Greek didn't need a priest to perform any birth or death rites. Whenever he wanted to, the head of the family could pray to the gods and offer them a sacrifice in his own household. If he sacrificed an animal, he usually gave a dinner party afterward, the guests eating the meat that had not been burned for the god.

Greek religious fervor varied with time and place and depended on the individual. When the worship of Dionysus first came to Greece from Asia Minor, a kind of dancing madness seized his women followers. They swooped down on wild animals and children, tore them to pieces, and ate their flesh in the belief that they were thereby joined with their god. In remote country villages in Greece, human sacrifice continued until the second century A.D.

Several religions, called mysteries, promised life after death to those initiated in the secret rites. The most famous were the Eleusinian mysteries. The initiates walked in a torchlight procession on the sacred road from Athens to Eleusis, a town about ten miles away. They arrived after sunset and wandered about the sacred grounds in the dark except for the glow of an occasional torch in the moonless night. After purification ceremonies and fasting, they were led into a dazzlingly lighted initiation hall. Here they sat on eight tiers of steps to

A tragic and a comic mask. They fitted completely over the head.

153

Greek gods. (Above) Zeus, hurler
of thunderbolts, the supreme god;
(below) Hades, the terrible but just
god of the underworld, with his
three-headed watchdog Cerberus,
which prevented any of the dead
from leaving; (facing page) Hermes,
god of commerce, travel, and good
luck, carrying his herald's staff;
and Poseidon, god of the seas,
with his three-pronged spear.

witness sights they had sworn never to reveal. They kept the secret so well that no one knows exactly what went on during the four days at Eleusis.

The Eleusinian mysteries were rooted in the legend of the grain goddess Demeter, who followed her daughter into the underworld and brought her back to life. The initiates believed that, like the daughter, they would live again after going to the underworld. Like an ear of wheat, they would be cut down when ripe, disappear from the earth, then be reborn.

Though the Eleusinian mysteries became part of the state religion of Athens, most Greeks didn't believe in happiness beyond the grave. They pictured the dead as ghosts or bats fluttering in a dark cave.

When a man died, he was placed on a couch in the courtyard of his house, facing the door. A crown of vine leaves or flowers was placed on his head and an obol—a small silver coin—slipped into his mouth. The dead spirit might need the obol in the underworld. Athenians jested that the obol paid for the ferry ride across the river Styx, which was believed to separate the land of the living from the land of the dead.

Greeks didn't worship inside their temples, but at the threshold. The temple was the god's home. A statue of him stood inside on a pedestal with an altar before it. Sometimes the room of the temple housing the statue was open to the sky. The enclosed temple precincts were sacred ground. A runaway slave or a political refugee could seek asylum by entering the sacred grounds.

The statue within the temple might be made of ivory and gold over a wooden framework, like the statue of Athena that once stood in the Parthenon. The ivory was polished with oil to keep it from cracking. Athena was set back sixty feet from the main entrance, which faced east. When the sun rose, it made the ivory glisten like living flesh and cast a dazzling reflection from the beaten gold draperies. For the gold and ivory alone, the statue cost about 900 talents—$900,000 in our money.

The marble statues of Greek art weren't the white ghosts we see today. Sculptors tinted the skin a delicate flesh tone. The hair was painted, and the eyes were painted or made lifelike with colored stones. A goddess' robes were painted to imitate the gold damask or embroidered cloth of which they might have been made. Time has stripped the statues of their colors and temples of their red-tiled roofs, the paint on the limestone walls, and the blue and golden ornaments.

ORACLES—THE VOICE OF THE GODS

Before going to war, a state often asked a god's advice. A farmer worried about his crop might also seek the help of a god. Both state and individual appealed to an oracle. An oracle was a shrine where a god spoke through a priest. Greece had more than 250 oracles.

Scene from Homer's Odyssey *(vase painting). Odysseus stuffed the ears of his men with wax and had himself lashed to the mast to prevent being lured overboard by the song of the sirens, here shown as a human-headed kind of bird.*

At one oracle, a priest interpreted the movements of fish in a sacred pool. At another, in a sacred grove where snakes were kept, a priest could predict a fat or a lean harvest by the snakes' appetites. At Pherae, the god Hermes gave advice at his statue in the agora. The questioner lit the bronze lamps attached to the statue, threw a coin on the altar, and whispered his question in the statue's ear. Then he covered his ears with his hands and walked away. When he uncovered his ears, the first words he heard were the god's answers. A priest had to interpret their meaning.

The most famous oracle in the ancient world was the oracle of Delphi. The road to Delphi was steep and difficult. The setting of the oracle inspired terror and wonder among the thousands who reached the terraces at the foot of a gigantic cliff where the sacred buildings stood. On the temple of Apollo were inscribed such sayings as "Know yourself." A conical stone in or near the temple marked what the Greeks supposed to be the center of the earth.

Before consulting the oracle, the priests led a goat to the temple and sprinkled it with water. If the goat didn't budge, Apollo had given a sign that he wasn't in a talking mood. If it shivered and lowered its head, Apollo would speak. Whoever wanted to ask a question now wrote it down. The goat was sacrificed, and the priests entered the temple with the question.

Apollo sent his messages through a special priestess, a young girl. In later days, the priestess was a fifty-year-old woman dressed as a girl. In a secret room of the temple she chewed laurel leaves, drank sacred water, and sat on a golden tripod.

The priests sat below the tripod as the priestess went into fits of ecstasy or a trance. She uttered apparent gibberish and moaned, while the priests recorded her babbling. The priests were prophets who then interpreted Apollo's words coming through the medium of the priestess.

Many of the prophecies could be interpreted in a number of ways. Before attacking the Persians, Croesus of Lydia asked the oracle what would happen. The oracle answered that Croesus would destroy a great kingdom. The oracle didn't add—as matters turned out—"your own."

The oracle was often on the side of law and order. A Spartan who asked the oracle if he could lie under oath to gain property received a blistering reply. Before sending out a colony, a state usually asked the oracle's advice. Greeks from all over and foreigners from many countries made the trip to Delphi. The priests acquired a good deal of information from them about trade routes, unfriendly tribes, favorable locations for building a town, weather conditions, and so on. Delphi served as a kind of general information and travel bureau.

The Sphinx, a winged monster with a woman's head and a lion's body. In the legend of Oedipus, she asked people a riddle and killed everyone who couldn't answer it. Here (on a vase painting) Oedipus is about to solve it.

HOSPITALS AND THE FATHER OF MEDICINE

Greeks sometimes consulted the oracle of Delphi the way a businessman might consult a lawyer. Often they consulted priests the way we consult a doctor. At Epidaurus and on the island of Cos were famous temples to the god Asclepius. In Homer, Asclepius had been a physician whose two sons were doctors for the Greeks fighting the Trojans. Later Greeks made a god of this hero.

The temples of Asclepius and their grounds became a combination of hospital and health resort. They were built on high, open ground with nearby groves and an occasional mineral spring. Greeks from crowded, dirty cities could relax in a peaceful country setting and breathe fresh air. Sometimes these temples became merely fashionable resorts. Often the sick and maimed traveled to them as pilgrims do today to Lourdes, for miraculous cures.

The priests of Asclepius were also doctors, with a wide knowledge of surgery and how to treat disease. At Epidaurus men could exercise at a gymnasium, and a quarter-mile walk brought them to a huge theater. The priest-doctors prescribed exercise, rest, diet, and conversation as part of the god's treatment.

One of the most effective cures came from "temple sleep." After prayer and sacrifice, the patient went to a special building in the sacred grounds and slept beneath a colonnaded porch. The doctor suggested that the patient dream of a god—a suggestion the sick patient acted on to the best of his ability. One case recorded on a stone at Epidaurus tells of a man who dreamed that his slaves held him up for Asclepius to cut open his belly. When he awoke, he was magically cured of an abdominal abscess. What probably happened was that, after his temple sleep, he was held down by his slaves while a doctor operated on him to remove the abscess.

Hippocrates, the father of medicine, was descended from a long line of doctor-priests of Asclepius on the island of Cos. Like other doctors, this fifth-century doctor traveled throughout Greece, diagnosing and curing. He became the most famous doctor of his time, and his contemporaries considered him the perfect physician. Many medical works have come down to us as his, though some are older than Hippocrates and others were written by his disciples. His disciples, it is said, took an oath before they went out to practice medicine. They swore by the gods to honor their teacher and share their money with him when he was in need. "I will use treatment to help the sick according to my ability and judgment," the oath continued, "but never with a view to injury and wrongdoing. I will keep pure and holy both my life and my art. . . . And whatsoever I shall see or hear in the course of my profession . . . I will never divulge, holding such things to be holy secrets." Doctors have sworn the Hippocratic Oath down through the ages.

City doctors ran clinics where patients came to have bones set, swellings reduced, and cuts bandaged. Like other shops, the clinic was built onto the street wall of a house. Patients waited on stools or stood around while the seated doctor bled a patient's arm or bandaged a wound. Bleeding was as popular in ancient Greece as it was in eighteenth-century England.

POTTERS AND MONEY-CHANGERS

The doctor-priests of Asclepius handed down their secrets from father to son. In a similar way, fathers usually taught their trades to their sons. The philosopher Socrates was a stonecutter by trade—it had been the family business. In Athens, a man had to support his parents unless his father had failed to teach him a trade. At Sparta, heralds, cooks, and flutists had to train their sons in their trades. But in the other states a boy didn't have to follow in his father's footsteps.

A city boy had only to walk down the streets to decide what trade he wanted to learn. Each trade was usually in a separate street or part of town. Through the open shop fronts, a passer-by could watch the smith at his forge pounding out a tool on his anvil. In the furnituremakers' street, he could watch a carpenter steam wood to bend it, then turn it on a lathe to fashion a chair leg.

Physicians treating a fracture.

158

He could walk into a bronze foundry and watch the workmen pour molten metal into a mold or solder arms onto the headless torso of a statue.

In Athens, he could visit the Kerameikos. This was the part of town where the potters worked. Our word "ceramic" comes from this district. Some potters specialized in making dolls and animals for children. Others molded and baked roof tiles. For cheap, everyday bowls and dishes, there were pottery factories.

The potter who made decorative vases was an artist. To make a pot, he first washed and wedged his clay, slapping out the air bubbles. While his helper turned the potter's wheel, he placed a ball of clay on the wheelhead

In a clinic off the market place, a doctor bleeds a patient. From the left of the doorway a sculptured head of Asclepius, god of medicine and healing looks on.

A bronze foundry. On the left a man tends a furnace while others work on a bronze figure before attaching its head. Pictures, tools and casts hang on the wall. At right, two other workmen finish a giant warrior.

and shaped it as it spun. With a knife or a piece of string, he separated the bottom of the pot from the wheel, then let the pot dry until it felt leathery. He put it back on the wheel and smoothed it with metal tools. Using scrapers and damp sponges, he erased his tool marks. If the vase was to have handles, he shaped them by hand and then attached them.

While the vase was still leathery, the potter painted his design. In the early black-figure vases, he painted his design in black against the clay background, cut in the details, and added his other colors. In the red-figure vases, he sketched the design lightly with a blunt-pointed tool, then painted the outline of the figures with a narrow line. Next he silhouetted his figures by painting a broad stripe of black glaze around them. He painted the fine details within the silhouetted figure, filled in the black background, and added his other colors. After the vase was painted, he let the vase get bone-dry. Then he baked it in a kiln. The unpainted portions turned reddish under the heat because of the iron in the clay.

A city like Athens exported manufactured articles such as pots, and imported grain and timber, iron and ivory. Like many other Greek cities, it lay several miles inland but was connected with a port. Athenians built long walls the entire distance from Athens to its port, the Piraeus. These walls protected the Athenian supply line in time of war.

The Piraeus has several harbors. One had slips or sloping piers where about four hundred ships could be drawn up out of the water. Another was protected by a mole or breakwater built out from both shores, with heavy iron chains that could be pulled tight to prevent an enemy ship from entering.

Especially in spring and midsummer, the best sailing seasons, the harbors were choked with merchant ships. Ships were beached in winter, with tackle,

160

sail, and steering paddle stored indoors. Merchant ships depended on sailpower. Only the state and rich merchants could afford to hire oarsmen.

Greek ships that put into foreign ports usually bought a return cargo, for foreign money wasn't always accepted in Greek states. Athenian coins—with the head of Athena on one side and her sacred owl on the other—were, however, accepted everywhere.

Since each state could coin its own money, there was no standard Greek currency. A merchant with foreign coins had to exchange them for coins of the state where he was doing business. He went to the money-changer in the market place. The money-changer weighed each coin to see if it had the guaranteed weight. Then he rubbed the gold or silver coin with a black stone that looked like flint. If it was really gold or silver, the coin showed a black streak. The black stone was called a touchstone. We use the word to mean a test of something's quality. After testing the coins, the money-changer kept them and gave the merchant local coins in exchange.

MAN, THE "POLITICAL ANIMAL"

Athenian silver coin, about the 5th century B.C., stamped with the sacred owl of the goddess Athena. (Below) A merchant haggles with a money-changer.

If a storm blew up after a merchant ship had left port, she put into the nearest port. The captain now found himself in another state and had to pay new duties on his cargo and a new harbor toll. He might have sailed only as far, say, as from New York to Newark. Greek states were many and small. The islands of Ceos—thirty-nine square miles—had four independent states.

We call the states city-states because they were small and each was dominated by a capital city. The Greek called his state the *polis*. Polis was more than a geographical term. It meant the government as well—the citizens who ran the state. When danger threatened, the polis abandoned the land and fled to safety. Though the city might be destroyed, the polis was safe. Its citizens could pile aboard ships and sail to new territory. More than once, the leaders of Athens threatened to desert Greece forever and emigrate to Italy unless other states sent them military aid. Our words "police" and "politics" come from polis.

The usual polis rarely numbered more than 20,000 male citizens. Plato thought that the ideal state should have no more than 5000 citizens. Aristotle said that every citizen in a state ought to know everyone else at least by sight.

When the population of a state outgrew the food supply, citizens were shipped out to plant colonies. The colony became an independent state, though the citizens remembered the mother city, the *metropolis*. Naples and Syracuse, Monaco and Marseilles, were all Greek colonies. We use the very word "Greek" because of a colony. Chalcis, in Euboea, sent out a colony that settled about 100 miles south of Rome. The Romans called the colonists Graii because some of them came from a village called Graia. Graii became Graeci, the Latin word from which "Greek" is derived. The Greeks called themselves Hellenes, descendants of a hero named Hellen.

Of all the Greek states, Sparta had the most peculiar form of government, even to other Greeks. Spartan citizens couldn't own property or work at a trade. When a boy was born, he was brought before state officials. If they found him puny, they ordered his father to expose him in the mountains. Otherwise, he was assigned a helot farm and lived on its income.

A Spartan boy went barefoot and could own only one cloak. If he was hungry, he was allowed to steal, provided he was not caught. Spartans

Using scales suspended from the ship's yardarm, men load a merchant ship.

considered this good training in the tricks of war. If the boy was caught stealing, he was severely punished. Spartans even held a public whipping contest, the winner being the one who held out longest without crying out. Brave Spartan lads let themselves be whipped to death without whimpering.

From the age of seven to thirty, the Spartan drilled endlessly in military maneuvers. When he reached twenty, he was assigned to a soldiers' mess. Fifteen Spartans ate together, sharing food and expenses. Any rugged way of life has ever since been called "Spartan."

Two kings reigned jointly in Sparta long after the other Greek states had become republics. It was considered a healthy state of affairs if the two kings hated each other and disagreed—and usually they did.

Sparta's rival, Athens, in the days of her glory under the statesman Pericles, gave the world its first democratic government. Every citizen belonged to the assembly. Theoretically, all the thousands of citizens could attend the meetings, speak, and vote on issues. Actually, citizens living in or near the city, usually poor citizens, attended. Each was paid an obol—later it was raised to three obols—to attend. Meetings were usually held on a hill in the open air, where men sat on the ground or on folding stools they had brought along. The meeting opened with prayer and sacrifice, the issues were discussed, and the members voted by a show of hands.

A council of five hundred decided what issues the assembly would discuss. Every citizen over thirty was qualified to serve, but no one could serve more than twice. Members of the council weren't elected; they were chosen by lot. Athenian democracy wasn't representative democracy like ours. Nobody represented the Athenians. They made their own laws directly. That is why Aristotle said that man was a political animal—he lived through the polis.

Every year the assembly met to vote whether to exile a dangerous citizen. If it so decided, each citizen wrote on a piece of a broken pot the name of the man he thought should be thrown out of Athens. They placed the potsherds— or *ostraca*—in an urn. The man whose name was written on a majority of the *ostraca* was banished from Athens for ten years. He was "ostracized"—a word we use for someone banished from polite society.

Citizens wielded great power through the law courts. They could denounce a general in the assembly because he had lost a battle. He would then be arrested and held for trial. Athenians were also forever suing each other over property disputes.

Any citizen could serve on the juries. Prospective jurors gathered by the thousands to be picked for jury duty, especially the poor citizens, for the pay was three obols a day. A jury had to have at least 201 jurors. In important political trials, 1001 and more were sworn in.

Neither the defendant nor the accuser hired a lawyer. The charges were read out against the accused, and each side was allowed equal time to plead his case. A court clerk timed the speeches with a water clock. When documents had to be examined, he stopped the clock, then started it again when the speech continued. An accused man was always expected to say a few words in his own defense. If he had no gift for composing speeches he could buy one from a professional speech writer.

After both sides had testified, court clerks handed out voting pebbles or shells to the jurors. Comic writers accused some men of getting crippled hands from holding pebbles so many times on jury duty. If the jurors voted for acquittal in a criminal case and for the defendant in a civil case, they placed

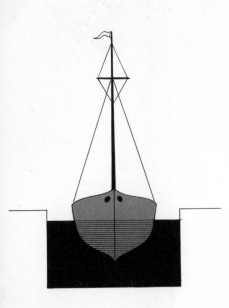

The Greeks made major advances in mathematics. Illustrated here is the principle, discovered by Archimedes, that a floating body displaces its own weight in water.

the pebbles in one pot. Another pot held the pebbles of jurors voting the other way. The pot holding the majority of pebbles decided the case.

Athens had a prison, popularly called "the House," but men weren't usually sent to jail when convicted. Instead they were deprived of their rights as citizens, stripped of their property, or sent into exile.

BY LAND AND BY SEA

Though they feared exile, Greeks were great travelers. They were the first tourists in the ancient world, traveling to Egypt to see the pyramids and up Mount Etna to look at the view.

Cross-country travel in Greece took a lot of stamina. A traveler had to climb and descend passes, many of them snowbound in winter. Greek roads weren't paved. Where the road went up a steep rock, steps were usually carved for a footing. Some roads had parallel grooves cut in them for wagon wheels, especially sacred roads for processions. Where one road joined another, the grooves veered off like sets of streetcar tracks. Road signs were merely piles of stones. A traveler reaching the stones offered a prayer to Hermes and tossed another stone onto the pile.

Sea travel was uncomfortable and dangerous. In winter, torrential rains or icy blasts from Russia kept the ships on the beaches. But in spring and summer the seas were alive with ships. Passengers sat on deck or in the open hold. They could crawl under canvas when a squall came up. Greek sailors preferred to sail within sight of their isles or mountains, but sometimes ventured into open waters. In the fourth century, a Greek sailed from Marseilles to Iceland and back. Greek ships reached the Azores, and it has even been suggested that they sailed to America. With a fair wind, Greek ships could make fifty nautical miles a day, a speed not bettered until the eighteenth century.

Greeks also went to sea to fight. The Phoenicians had invented a speedy warship, with pairs of rowers seated side by side. The Greeks improved on the model with the trireme. The trireme had a large square sail on a forward mast,

A mathematician using a geometer's compass.

Diagram of one of the most famous propositions in geometry: the sum of the squares of the sides of a right-angled triangle equals the square of the diagonal called the hypotenuse. Here 16 squares of one side plus 9 squares of the other side equal 25 squares of the hypotenuse.

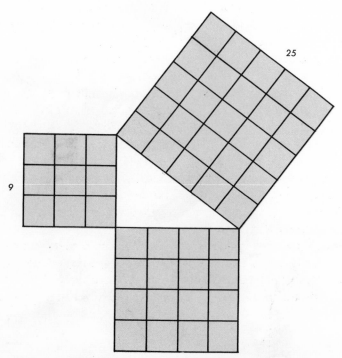

Cross section of an Athenian
trireme, showing how the
rowers may have sat. (At
right) With all oars pulling
at top speed, a warship,
equipped with a huge
battering ram, smashes into
a cruising trireme.

was steered by paddles at the stern, and was rowed by 174 oarsmen in three banks. About 125 feet long by twenty in the beam, it was the fastest ship afloat.

The trireme had a figurehead or a painted symbol on the prow. Below, just behind the hawseholes for the rope with the stone anchor, metal-tipped catheads stuck out. The stern curved into the air. In earlier days, when boats had been built to resemble sharks, boars, and birds, sailors had cut off the tailpieces of defeated ships as trophies.

When cruising, the trireme used its sail or the lowest bank rowed. In battle action, all the oarsmen rowed, the ship's flutist piping the stroke. Just above the waterline or just below, a triple-toothed ram projected ten feet in front of the ship. The trireme charged beak to broadside, ripping open the hull of the enemy ship and sinking her.

A favorite battle maneuver was to get up speed and head the ship to pass the enemy as close as possible. Just before she reached the enemy, the captain shouted, "Pull in oars!" Then she zoomed past the enemy ship, her catheads snapping off enemy oars like a bunch of long toothpicks. An oarless trireme was like a centipede without legs.

At the end of the day's battle, ships headed for shore. The crew waded onto the beach, carrying their fourteen-foot oars and seat cushions, then hauled their ship up the sands. Sailors slept ashore while lookouts perched on rocks watched for enemy movements. For food, sailors walked to the nearest market.

All citizens had to serve in the navy or the army. Admirals and generals were elected or chosen by lot. An admiral could become a general overnight—or an ordinary soldier.

If he could afford the armor, a citizen became a foot soldier called a hoplite. He had to buy his own bronze helmet, body armor made of bronze or metal plates sewn on leather, and bronze greaves that covered his legs from knee to

168

ankle. He wore a short iron sword at his side, held a bronze shield on his left arm, and carried an iron-tipped spear. His arms and armor weighed about seventy pounds, and on the march he brought his slave along to carry them.

The Greek cavalry was not very effective. Cavalrymen rode bareback or on felt blankets or animal skins tied over their horses. They wore boots with spurs, but their horses had no saddles or stirrups. Both horseman and horse wore protective armor made of small metal scales attached to leather or cloth. Attacking horsemen easily unseated each other. A thrust of the enemy's spear against his shield, and—whoosh!—he slid over the horse's tail and onto the ground, a helpless target.

Early Greek warriors had ridden into battle on horseback or in a chariot, dismounted, and then fought a duel. From the seventh century B.C., however, battles were clashes of hoplites. Grouped into phalanxes eight deep, with spears pointed forward, the hoplites looked like giant bronze hedgehogs heading for the enemy. A hedgehog can roll himself up so that his prickles protect him on all sides, but the right flank of the hoplite phalanx was extremely vulnerable. After hurling their spears, the hoplites closed in and fought elbow to elbow with their short swords.

The Greek wars of the fifth century drained the states of money and manpower. The Greek hoplite didn't relish being commanded. He could and did vote to oust his general.

In the fourth century Philip of Macedon swept down with his cavalry and his phalanxes and by 338 B.C. conquered all of Greece. His son, Alexander the Great, went on to conquer half the known world. He took Greek ideas out of Greece and scattered them as seeds across this world. Even when Rome ruled the world, a traveler who spoke Greek could be understood from Mesopotamia to Spain. Christianity was preached in Greek, and the New Testament written in it. This was a fitting tribute to the Greek philosophers who, centuries earlier, had declared that man had an immortal soul.

Greek potters were famous for the beauty of their vases. They decorated them with scenes from daily life and legend.

ROME
Ruler of the World

When we hail the return of a conquering hero down a main street with a parade and a paper snowfall of confetti, we're copying an old Roman custom.

Senators greeted a victorious Roman general outside the city walls and led him in a parade through the city. Musicians blew horns and trumpets, and townspeople lined the garlanded Sacred Way, shouting "Hurrah!" Soldiers carried the spoils of war—captured statues and battle standards—on their shoulders, on wooden trestles, and on carts. Bulls with gilded horns and chalk-coated bodies followed as sacrifices. The captives—princes and nobles—who hadn't been sold into slavery walked in chains or were dragged along. The general drove in a gilded chariot pulled by four horses. He wore a gold and purple toga and carried an ivory-headed scepter in his hand. A slave held a golden crown of laurel over his head. His legionaries, singing and joking, followed behind him.

A Roman triumph. Prisoners of war at the feet of the mounted emperor.

The Romans called such a parade a "triumph." Their real triumph consisted of turning a tiny city-state into the mightiest empire of the ancient world. In the eighth century B.C. Rome was a village on the banks of the Tiber, in the center of the Italian peninsula. The Etruscans from the north ruled Rome until the close of the sixth century B.C. Then the hard-working Roman farmers laid down their hoes, picked up their spears, and drove them out. Within 250 years, the soldier-farmers won the Italian peninsula from the Po Valley to the tip of the boot. They fought the Punic Wars with Carthage and won Sicily, Spain, and North Africa. ("Punic" meant Phoenician, for Carthage, in North Africa, had been settled by Phoenician colonists.) Rome then turned to the East and by the middle of the second century B.C. ruled the Mediterranean. For almost 500 years Rome was a republic, until civil war ended with Julius Caesar ruling as dictator. In 31 B.C. Caesar's grandnephew, Octavian, defeated Antony and the Egyptian queen Cleopatra. As Augustus, he was Rome's first emperor (27 B.C.). Thus there were three Romes—Rome the city, Rome the republic (510–27 B.C.), and Rome the empire (after 27 B.C.).

HOUSE INTO HOME

The Romans turned the house into a home. The early Roman included in his family not only his wife and children, but also his servants or "familiars." He conducted the family religious services, praying twice a day before the family hearth. The early Romans were farmers who worshiped the spirits of the land they had cleared. These spirits came indoors as household gods, called Lares. A statuette of a Lar stood in a wall niche. It was taken down and set on the table at mealtime, when family and servants ate together. The family also worshiped Penates, spirits of the cupboard. Romans burned candles or incense in front of images of the Penates, praying for full cupboards or prosperity. When a Roman spoke of his Lares and Penates, he meant "hearth and home."

As head of the family, the father had the power of life and death over his wife, children, and servants. As late as the statesman Cicero's time, the first century B.C., a man actually put his own son to death. Such a procedure was legal until the second century A.D. If a father didn't want his child, he abandoned it to die of cold or hunger or put it on a garbage dump. This custom continued till the third century A.D.

Boys and girls waited on table and listened to their elders' conversation without joining in. Their mother worked at her loom during the day and entertained at dinner with her husband. The old Romans of the early republic didn't believe in shows of affection. "Never kiss your wife unless it thunders," one advised. On many a tombstone, the most a loving husband would admit to the world were the letters SVQ—Latin shorthand for "never any complaint."

A BOY GROWS UP

Nine days after a boy was born, his father named him, then placed a small round amulet of gold, bronze, or leather around his neck. This was supposed

Pompeiian mosaic of a watchdog. Romans often used a sign warning: "Beware of the dog"

172

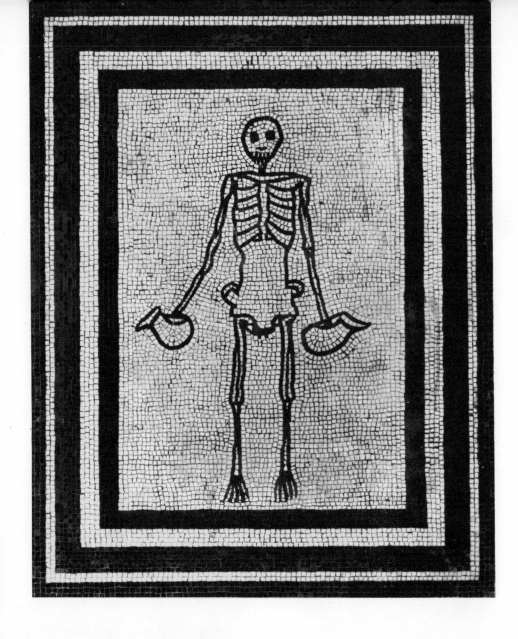

This mosaic, in his dining room, reminded a Roman that life was short and therefore to be enjoyed.

to keep away the "evil eye." A boy wore it until he reached manhood. In the early republic, his mother or an elderly woman relative took care of him while he grew up. Later, if his family could afford a Greek nurse, he learned to speak Greek as well as Latin. He played such games as blind man's buff, spun tops, rode a hobbyhorse, and walked on stilts.

Usually his father taught him to read and write, swim and ride. A well-to-do father bought a slave or hired a freedman to act as his son's tutor. Otherwise, when a boy reached the age of seven he went to school. There was no school building. The teacher rented a room in a ground-floor shop or held classes on a rooftop. Anyone could open a school if he could get paying students.

School began early. A boy left home before daybreak, carrying a lantern. A poor boy carried his own bag of writing tablets and bought a small loaf of bread for breakfast on his way to school. A rich boy was accompanied by a slave, who carried his books. Discipline was the teacher's main problem. If he held his classes in a shop, only an awning separated the classroom from the street and its noises. He was often a freedman who had learned to read and write while a slave in his master's service. He might have been a former prizefighter

Two girls play a game of knucklebones, similar to the modern game of jacks.

or a clown in a pantomime. Students who were sons of freeborn citizens didn't respect him.

The schoolday lasted six hours, with a noon recess for lunch. Boys sometimes sneaked into the circus to watch a chariot race instead of returning to classes. In the republic, there were a hundred holidays during which school was closed, and there was a long summer vacation. For five years, a boy learned the three R's. His arithmetic was "calculation"—how to add, subtract, multiply, and divide on an abacus. The simple abacus was a sandbox with movable metal disks. A more elaborate abacus had rods with beads that slid back and forth.

The teacher sat on a chair, while his students sat on benches, balancing waxed wooden writing tablets on their knees. They scratched their letters in the wax with a pointed iron pen called a stylus. (Our word "style" comes from this pen.) The Latin letters they wrote are the ones we adapted for writing English.

At twelve a boy studied literature at home or in school with a grammarian. Grammarians were mainly Greeks from Asia and Egypt. Students had to learn to speak, read, and write in Greek as well as Latin. Romans often made fun of these grammarians, who lectured their students on such subjects as "What Songs Did the Sirens Sing?"

In the early republic, a boy became a man at seventeen. He then took off his purple-banded childhood toga and the amulet around his neck and put on a plain white toga. Now he was a citizen and had to serve in the army.

A game of dice.

In the late republic and in the days of the empire, a boy sometimes put on his toga of manhood as early as fourteen. He no longer went into the army.

After he had put on his toga, a young man studied philosophy and the art of public speaking. At the end of the republic, he often went abroad for these studies—to Athens, Alexandria, and Rhodes. Caesar, Cicero, and the poet Horace all studied abroad. Later, in the empire period, he could get this "university" education at home, for the emperors endowed professorships, set up municipal schools, and awarded scholarships to poor students.

A GIRL GROWS UP

Roman fathers were devoted to their daughters and called them pet names like Birdie and Little Mother. In the early republic, they *were* little mothers, learning to cook, spin, and weave. In later days, especially in old-fashioned homes, girls continued to spin and weave. Papa proudly modeled for his friends the toga his daughter had woven for him.

The daughter of a well-to-do household had a Greek nurse who told her first fairy tales in Greek. She learned to paint because her mother believed that painting would help her to choose carpets and tapestries for her own home. She also learned to sing, dance, and play musical instruments. A young wife used to strum the lute and set her husband's poems to music.

If a girl didn't have a tutor at home, she went to school at about the age of six to learn to read and write. At about ten she became engaged to be married. Her father or guardian selected her future husband, often with the help of a marriage broker. The prospective groom gave the girl an iron or gold engagement ring with a pair of clasped hands carved on it, and they were married a few years later. At the end of the republic, when divorce was common, men and women married four or five times. Caesar married four times. Cicero divorced his wife of thirty years to marry an heiress younger than his own daughter. His wife was easily consoled; she herself married twice again.

If she was to be married in a religious ceremony, the bride wore a flame-colored bridal veil topped by a wreath of orange blossoms. After the marriage license was signed, a matron led the bride to the groom. The couple clasped

Three popular musical instruments: lyre, harp and double pipes.

Portrait of a girl from Pompeii.

hands, prayers were said, then bride and groom and guests attended a wedding feast. Like a modern bride, the Roman bride was carried over the threshold. Romans thought it an unlucky sign if she stumbled over her new doorstep.

Toward the end of the republic, a bride was usually married in a civil ceremony. Before witnesses, the groom asked his bride if she wanted to become "mother of the family"; she answered yes and then asked if he wished to become "father of the family." They were then legally married. Although she kept her own property and also managed her dowry, her husband was still supposed to be the head of the house. But as one Roman put it, "We rule the world, but our women rule us."

A twelve-year-old bride went from her father's house into her own—she stepped practically from the nursery into the world. A featherheaded creature spent her days at public entertainments and her nights at dinner parties. Other women went into politics, campaigning at election time and painting election signs on house walls. After the election, a coat of whitewash wiped out the signs. The Senate once passed a law limiting the jewels and clothing a woman might own. An angry matron made so good a speech against it in the Roman Forum, the public meeting place, that the men promptly repealed it. In the last years of the republic, women lawyers defended clients in the law courts.

During the empire, highborn ladies fought as gladiators in the arena, stripped for wrestling matches, and rode in chariots for a day's pig-sticking in the country. The buxom Roman matron became a thing of the past.

176

Girls wore corsets from childhood. Any girl who didn't have a delicate figure was called a "prizefighter." But Roman matrons never lost their courage. When the emperor Claudius ordered Caecina Paetus to kill himself and he was afraid to die, his wife Arria stabbed herself, pulled out the dagger, and handed it to him. "It doesn't hurt, Paetus," she said. On the tombs of their wives, Roman husbands paid them such tributes as this: "Short, traveler, is my message; stop and read it. The loathsome stone covers a lovely woman."

THE LIFE OF A SLAVE

A woman might, in a fit of temper, smash an expensive dish or order her hairdresser crucified because he had twisted her hair. Both dish and slave were her private property. When, in the second century B.C., Cato wrote a book on agriculture, he listed three kinds of farm tools: speaking ones (slaves), inarticulate ones (oxen and mules), and voiceless ones (wagons and plows).

To a man like Cato, a slave was a machine. When he was worn out from work and old age, he was thrown aside like a piece of junk. In the early republic, a slave doorkeeper was usually chained to his post like a dog.

During the ten years Caesar fought with the Gauls, he is said to have killed 400,000 of them and sold as many more into slavery. In the second and first centuries B.C., the Aegean island of Delos sold 10,000 slaves a day. Slaves were placed on a block, stripped, and branded. Slave traders and pirates raided towns and kidnaped men and women to sell into slavery. African and Asian chieftains also sold their unwanted children. Victorious generals rounded up soldier and civilian captives and exchanged them for gold and silver. In one deal, Caesar disposed of 53,000.

Slave marriages weren't recognized by law. Children born of slaves could be separated from their parents and sold elsewhere. Some slaves wore badges like the following: "Hold me if I escape, and return me to my master Viventius on the estate of Callistus." Runaway slaves who were caught spent their nights in chains or were put to death as a warning to other slaves.

In the second century B.C., a city household rarely had more than one slave. As Rome grew prosperous, even a lower-middle-class household had eight slaves. Not to have a slave meant absolute poverty. In imperial days, a rich man had so many household slaves—perhaps 1000—that he didn't know many of them by sight. The emperor might have 20,000 slaves— barbers and valets, cooks and bakers, porters and waiters, dwarfs and dancing girls, clerks and messengers.

In the country, the small farmer lost his land and drifted to the city. Rich landholders owned vast estates run by slave overseers and worked by slave labor. A master sometimes stationed a gang of his slaves along a road to kidnap travelers and work them as slaves. After the day's chores, the farm slaves were fed and locked up for the night in barracks.

Slaves sometimes rose in revolt and murdered their masters. The Thracian gladiator Spartacus escaped from a school for gladiators at Capua and with an army of fellow slaves held off the Roman legions for two years. Slaves who had revolted were crucified when caught.

In the cities, slaves worked for the state as street cleaners and aqueduct repairmen. Rich men hired out their craftsmen slaves or set them up in

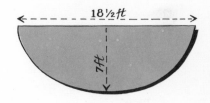

A pattern for a toga. The straight edge was often 18½ feet long. A purple stripe along this edge indicated that the wearer was a freeborn girl or boy, a priest or a magistrate.

A citizen wore a woolen toga with a tunic underneath. It was hot and heavy in summer.

business. The slave received a share of the money he earned. He could save up and buy his freedom. When he grew too old to work, his master sometimes freed him, registered him as a citizen, and had the government pay for his food.

Many well-known Romans began life as slaves. The playwright Terence had been a slave from Africa. His master educated him at Rome and then freed him. Epictetus, a crippled slave boy from Asia Minor, became a famous philosopher. Perhaps because he had been a slave, he advised Romans to keep two words always in their hearts: "endure" and "abstain."

In the empire, city slaves often lived a better life than poor freedmen. They lived in comfort, were treated as part of the family, and were mourned when they died. Sometimes a slave owned a slave of his own.

HOUSES AND "ISLANDS"

The early Roman lived in a quadrangular room, called the atrium, with an opening in the tiled roof to let out smoke from the hearth and to let in light and air. Here the family slept and ate, and the wife worked her loom. Side rooms were added, and the back of the atrium was decorated with wax portrait masks of family ancestors. Mourners wore these masks at funerals. The hole in the roof was enlarged and a tank sunk in the ground directly below to collect rain water. Under Greek influence, a garden with a colonnade was added back of the atrium. Dining rooms, living rooms, bedrooms, storerooms, and a kitchen were built around the garden, and the atrium became the reception room. Before the end of the republic, upper stories were added to the house. The house was called *domus*.

In some houses, the rooms on both sides of the entrance corridor were rented out as shops. The family used a private entrance from a side street

Street scene in a small town. Steppingstones in the street were useful in bad weather. Some were so high that they prevented wheeled traffic from using the street.

leading into the garden. Callers went through the corridor past a chained dog. Sometimes the dog wasn't real, but a mosaic or painting on wall or threshold with the warning *cave canem*, "Beware of the dog." In imperial days, the *domus* of the rich had colored mosaic floors, marbled walls, rooms heated by a furnace, windows made of small panes of glass, and pipes bringing water even to the upper floor.

Most Romans didn't have a *domus* and therefore didn't lead a "domestic" life. They lived in what were termed "islands." These were tenements, each of which covered an entire block. In the early empire, for every private house there were twenty-six blocks of these apartment houses in the city of Rome.

The islands were mainly four and five stories high, sometimes higher. Ground-floor shops opened onto the street from large arched doorways. The shops might be let to a grocer, a carpenter, or a tavernkeeper. Shopkeepers closed their shop fronts with wooden shutters at night and locked and bolted them. Inside each shop, a stairway or a ladder led to a room above. There in one room the shopkeeper and his family slept, cooked, and ate.

The ground-floor rooms were expensive, and only a well-to-do Roman could afford to rent them. The higher the apartment, the lower the rent. A poor man slept in the top attic, just below the roosting pigeons. He climbed two hundred steps to eat his bread, drink his sour wine, and sleep on a bundle of straw.

In the city of Rome, July 1 was moving day. If a man couldn't meet his rent, he and his family were evicted. They took their broken jugs and straw beds and went to sleep under the arch of a bridge or an amphitheater. Most of the tenements were built for a quick profit. When they began to sag and crack, the landlord patched them up. Sometimes they collapsed into the street, killing the tenants and burying passers-by. Fires broke out at night, trapping tenants in the higher floors. In one night, fires burned down the

Sacrificial offering to a god. An assistant gives the bull the fatal blow.

whole city of Lugdunum (Lyons, in France), called "the jewel of the provinces."

The city of Rome didn't have a fire-fighting brigade until the emperor Augustus created one. Firemen or tenants fought with buckets of water and rags soaked in vinegar. Roman "ambulance chasers" rushed to the scene of a fire and bought the burning building and land from the owner at a bargain price. Within a month or two, they had a new and equally inflammable tenement erected on the spot.

The windows in these flimsy tenements didn't have glass panes. The housewife screened them with curtains or wooden shutters to keep out rain and wind. In the city of Ostia on the Tiber, as well as in Rome, some apartment houses had windows with glass panes, balconies overlooking the street or a courtyard garden, and windowboxes planted with flowers. A furnace heated the ground-floor rooms and pipes led water to the first floor. Upper-floor tenants heated their rooms with braziers and filled their water jugs at a street fountain.

Some houses and the better apartment houses had latrines connected with street drains. But most tenants used chamber pots and emptied them into a special vat under the staircase or on a public dump heap outdoors. These were the dump heaps where parents also exposed unwanted children. Many a childless woman rescued a baby from such a place and raised it as her own. Lazy tenants on upper floors emptied their chamber pots out the windows, sometimes on the heads of passers-by. If caught, they could be sued for damages. Many towns had public latrines, where townspeople met, gossiped, and exchanged invitations.

THE ROMAN STREETS

The sewers of ancient cities were mainly for draining rain water and the overflow of rivers. The Etruscans had built Rome's earliest sewers. The Cloaca Maxima or Great Sewer, built about 500 B.C., drained the marshy ground below the Capitol, which became the Forum Romanum. About 14 feet high and 11 feet across, it empties into the Tiber. It still works today. An officer of the emperor Augustus once traveled the whole length of Rome's sewers by boat on a tour of inspection, ending up on the Tiber.

City streets were paved with stone slabs as early as 400 B.C. The streets were narrow and, in Rome before the great fire of A.D. 64, in Nero's reign, twisted and wound between the apartment houses and zigzagged up and down hills. City streets were rarely wider than sixteen feet, and on only a few could two carts pass each other.

Some streets had raised sidewalks, often built to prevent wheeled traffic from barging into shops and houses. To cross a street a person often had to wade through mud, though there were steppingstones at important corners. Driving in a carriage through city streets was considered bad manners. People walked, rode a mule, or were carried in a sedan chair or litter by porters or slaves. In the city of Rome, wheeled traffic was forbidden from dawn to dusk.

As soon as night fell, city dwellers went home. Shopkeepers boarded up their shop fronts, and housewives pulled in their potted plants and shuttered their windows. Even a city like Rome didn't have street lighting. Lamps

Coin showing Neptune, god of the sea, with a trident, his symbol.

181

on shop counters, on street-corner shrines, and over house entrances helped guide a man home on a dark or moonless night. Anyone venturing out after dark carried a tarred torch or a lantern with a burning candle or oil lamp inside. The first city in the ancient world to have street lighting was Antioch, in Syria—and that not until about A.D. 450.

City streets were dangerous at night. The city of Rome didn't have a police force until empire days, when Augustus created a patrol of night watchmen. Even then, bands of rich young rowdies would attack a lone traveler for a "prank." On a moonless night, thieves and housebreakers lurked in the dark, narrow streets, where a man could easily lose his way home. A person who caught a thief redhanded could kill him on the spot.

At night, drivers led in their mule carts and ox-drawn wagons laden with merchandise. All night long, hoofs and wheels clattered over the stone slabs, drivers swore at each other and their beasts, and crates banged on the stone curbs. Families in the front apartments of the "islands" rarely had an undisturbed night's sleep. At daybreak the wagons had to stop where they were. The animals were unhitched, and the merchandise in the wagons had to be carried on the porters' shoulders.

A DAY IN THE CITY

When the wagons stopped at dawn and people could finally doze off, they would be awakened by the sounds of the city coming to life. Bakers tethered their mules to turn the heavy millstones that ground the flour. A wine-seller

chained his pots together at a street corner, all ready for a day's business.

People rose at daybreak in the country and usually not later than seven in the city. House servants unshuttered the windows, scattered sawdust on the floors, and began sweeping with twig or palm-leaf brooms. In his bedroom, the waking master sat up in bed. He found the early-morning hours a good time to dash off a business letter or even a poem. He kept his window shutters closed and lit an oil lamp. Romans used clay and bronze lamps that hung from the ceiling or from a candelabrum or could be set on a stand. One cautious householder inscribed on his lamp: "Don't touch! I belong to Marcus, not to you." The lamps burned olive oil, which smoked and gave out unpleasant odors. If a writer's work lacked inspiration because he had worked too late or begun too early, Romans said that it "smelled of the lamp."

Men and women slept in their underclothes. A man threw his toga over a chair before he went to bed or used it as an extra blanket. He was out of bed, into his slippers or sandals, and dressed in a few minutes. If he was going out, he put on shoes that laced up the front. The tunic he had slept in went over his head, was tied at the waist, and reached to or a little below the knees. The emperor Augustus was so sensitive to cold that he wore four tunics. Indoors, a man wore only his tunic. When he went out, he draped his toga over the tunic. Only a citizen could wear a toga, a white woolen cloth six yards long by two at its greatest width. It was heavy, difficult to drape, and

A baker tends customers at the shop entrance while his workers take loaves from the kilns and weigh them.

in summer stifling. In the empire, citizens began leaving their togas at home. Eventually a man wore his toga only when he was laid out for his funeral.

Magistrates, priests, and freeborn children wore togas bordered with a purple stripe. The purple stripe was supposed to protect them from evil spirits. Men running for office wore a toga especially whitened with chalk, the *toga candida*, or "white toga"—and that is why we still call men who run for office "candidates." It was expensive to have a toga cleaned, so a poor citizen wore a dirty-gray toga.

Romans didn't bother to wash in the morning because they would go to the baths in the afternoon. In a well-to-do household, husband and wife slept in separate bedrooms. In the morning, she arranged her hair and put on her make-up. In the republic, a wife parted her hair in the center and tied it in a knot in back. In the empire, she wore an elaborate hairdo—curls and bangs, and hairpieces made of black hair imported from India. She chalked her face and arms or painted them with white lead, smoothed on black eye shadow, and rouged her cheeks and lips with red ocher or wine dregs. She removed her make-up only when she went to bed. A Roman maliciously said that a woman didn't sleep with her face—instead, she stored it in a hundred jars.

After she had made up, she put on her stola, a long loose gown that fell to the ankles. In the republic, the stola was made of wool, but in the empire it was sometimes made of Indian cotton or Chinese silk. But silk was expensive—a pound of silk was exchanged for a pound of gold. If she was going out, the Roman matron put on her jewels and threw a long shawl or cloak over her shoulders. She was fond of rings and wore as many as her fingers would hold. If the day was sunny, she picked up a peacock-feather fan before stepping into her sedan chair. Outdoors, a slave held a parasol over her head. If the wind was blowing, however, the parasol had to be left home, for it couldn't be shut.

In early days, men wore beards and long hair. The first barber came to Rome from Sicily in 300 B.C. Soon after, men wore short hair and were clean-shaven. The emperor Hadrian reintroduced the beard, supposedly to cover up a scar. Perhaps a barber had nicked his face. Everyone went to the barbershop. Not even slaves shaved themselves. When a boy came of age, the barber clipped off his "beard" with a pair of scissors. The boy then dedicated it to a god, pinning it in a temple to a "hair tree" where others pinned theirs.

Men went to the barber's early in the morning. As it is today, the barbershop was a gossip center. The customer sat in a chair in the middle of a mirror-lined shop. The barber covered the man's clothes with a cloth, wet the beard with water, and shaved him with an iron razor. (Romans didn't have soap.) He cut hair with iron scissors that worked like pruning shears. In imperial days, he wound his customer's hair around a hot curling iron, dyed it, perfumed him with fragrant oils, put make-up on his cheeks, glued bits of cloth on pimples, and stuck a crescent-shaped beauty patch on his brow. Customers sometimes opened a book and read in the chair, or wrote on a waxed tablet. A barber worked so slowly, Romans complained, that by the time he had finished the shave a second beard had grown.

Slaves and poor men went to a street-corner barber. A jab at the barber's elbow from the jostling crowds, and the customer had a cut cheek. If he was a free man, he could sue the barber for damages.

Shopkeepers and craftsmen left home at dawn to begin work. Even the

Hairdos of upper-class ladies.

Slaves holding parasols to shade young matrons from the sun.

unemployed left home early. Cities like Rome had a huge mob of poor citizens who did little if any work. The government gave them free grain once a month and their "patrons" gave them gifts of money and food. When a slave was freed, he still owed his master certain services. The master became his "patron," while he was a "client." His free-born descendants continued to place themselves under the protection of wealthy patrons.

A client called at the house of his patron early in the morning, waiting in an anteroom until the great man saw him or sent him away. He came to pay his respects, to perform errands, and to collect the food the patron distributed in little baskets to his clients. A tradesman client dashed to his patron's house for a handout before going to work. A widow often took her late husband's place in the group waiting in the anteroom.

After nine o'clock, the great man joined the street crowds, with his pack of clients following behind. In the center of every Roman city was a large open market and meeting place called the forum. Some cities had several forums. Colonnades, temples, and beautiful public buildings that were faced with marble and sometimes had roof gardens on top surrounded the forum. News in Roman cities was spread by word of mouth. Men met in the forum to hear the latest and to campaign for office. To get the crowd's attention, a man stepped up on the speaker's platform. In the Forum Romanum at Rome, this was decorated with the prows of ships taken in battle. (The Latin word for a ship's prow, *rostrum*, gives us the name of our speaker's platform.)

The basilicas, or law courts, were also located off the forum. Romans were the lawmakers of the ancient world—and had a passion for suing. Cases began before noon and sometimes lasted till sunset. The basilica was divided by screens or curtains into different courtrooms. A lawyer from one courtroom could often be heard by jurors sitting in another courtroom. Once, when a

185

Based on an Etruscan wall painting of the 5th century B.C., this illustration shows a race at the moment when the winning chariot reaches the finish post.

loud-voiced lawyer finished addressing the court, jurors and spectators in the court next to it applauded. A lawyer sometimes came to court with a hired audience to applaud his speeches and sway the jury. Lawyers' speeches were timed by water clocks, and both sides were given an equal opportunity. One lawyer talked so long, sipping water when his voice grew hoarse, that a critic suggested that he drink the water from the water clock. That way, he would end his thirst and the court's misery.

There were several kinds of water clocks. In one, a tank dripped water into a bowl, raising a float. A rod attached to the float turned cogs that moved an hour hand across a clock face marked with Roman numerals. In another, water pressure caused a small trumpet to blow every hour. A water clock in a dining room was a sign of wealth.

Romans also told time by sundial. Sundials weren't very accurate. The

Roman day was divided into twelve hours from sunrise to sunset. Hours were therefore longer in summer than in winter. An hour in midsummer would be seventy-five minutes long and an hour in midwinter only forty-four. Men sent their servants to look at a public sundial to find out what time it was. Eventually, craftsmen built sundials small enough to be carried by hand. If you had such a "pocket watch," you set it down in the sunlight to read the time. Sundials weren't dependable in cloudy or stormy weather.

PAPYRUS BOOKS AND PUBLIC LIBRARIES

Some Romans spent their mornings or early afternoons reading at the library or listening to an author read his latest book. Like Greek books, Roman books were rolls of papyrus, usually wound over wooden rollers. In the republic there were only home libraries. But a man who owned a library allowed scholars to use his books, provided they carefully rerolled each book so that the next person could read it.

Caesar had planned Rome's first public library, but Augustus actually built it. Roman libraries were modeled after the largest and most famous library in the ancient world, the Library of Alexandria, in Egypt. In the first century A.D. it had 700,000 books in its pigeonholed walls. The Ptolemies who had ruled Egypt collected some of its books by shady methods. Every ship entering the harbor of Alexandria had to give up any manuscripts on board. Ptolemy III had borrowed the official copies of the plays of Aeschylus, Sophocles, and Euripides from Athens, paying a deposit to guarantee their return. Instead, he put the manuscripts into the library and forfeited his deposit.

A rich Roman sometimes had a special room at home called an auditorium. Here his guests listened to authors read their latest books. There were also public auditoriums, but a writer could also read his latest effort in the forum or even in a public bath.

In the republic, publishers were usually wealthy friends of the writers. Cicero's friend Atticus, a rich businessman, had his staff of slaves copy Cicero's works. Atticus may have sold the books or given them away to friends. In the empire, after a writer had read his book aloud, he corrected his manuscript and took it to a professional publisher. Scribes acted as a "printing press." Sometimes they divided up the manuscript, each making several copies of the same chapter. At another publisher's, one scribe dictated while perhaps fifty others wrote down his words. There were women scribes as well as men.

When the books were ready for sale, the publisher listed titles, authors,

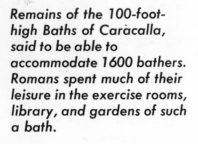

Remains of the 100-foot-high Baths of Caràcalla, said to be able to accommodate 1600 bathers. Romans spent much of their leisure in the exercise rooms, library, and gardens of such a bath.

and prices on a post outside his shop door. There was no such thing as a copyright—anyone could make his own copies of a book. A Roman writer earned fame, not royalties. Or he saw the sheets of his book end up as wrapping paper around a salt mackerel at the fish market.

Remains of the Claudian Aqueduct, the finest of the Roman aqueducts. Though they ran mainly underground, their arches span many valleys in Italy, Spain and France.

ROMAN BATHS

Seneca, Nero's tutor and adviser, once lived over a public bath. In his rooms, he could hear bathers below splash into the pool and grunt as they exercised with dumbbells. In late republican and in imperial times, Romans spent many of their afternoons in public baths. There were separate baths for men and women, or men used the baths at certain hours and women at others. Until the second century A.D. there were also mixed baths. The price of admission was low—the smallest Roman coin, about half a penny in our money.

After paying the entrance fee, the bather entered a dressing room, where he took off his street clothes. A bath attendant put them into a locker. If he wanted to exercise before bathing, he put on a short tunic and went to the exercise room. Here he played ball or wrestled. In one favorite ball game,

189

three players stood at the corners of a triangle. They threw a sand- or down-stuffed ball back and forth without warning or order. Players caught with the left hand and threw with the right. Romans were passionately fond of ball games. "I have the ball" came to mean winning at anything.

After his exercise, the bather removed his tunic and went into the warm-air room. This was a large room with a vaulted ceiling, heated by hot air coming through pipes from a basement or side furnace. After he was used to the heat, he went into the hot-air room. Here he sprinkled himself with hot water from a large tub and scraped the sweat from his body with a strigil. The next step took him back to the warm-air room to cool off. Finally he plunged into a pool of cold water in a room called the *frigidarium*. After that, he paid a masseur to rub him down with oil and perfume him. Men and women brought their slaves to the baths to wait on them.

A Roman bath had many rooms, such as those for warm air, hot air, and cold air. The frigidarium *had a pool of cold water.*

The large baths were faced inside and out with marble, the ceilings and walls were frescoed, and the floors were made of colorful mosaics. The Baths of Caracalla, a mile in circumference, could accommodate 1600 bathers. Such large baths contained an inside garden, a stadium, an art gallery, and even a library. Bathers could buy snacks like sausages and pastries from the vendors at the back of the garden colonnades. They met their friends at the fountains, strolled down the garden promenades, or read books in the library. Often they stayed in the baths till closing time.

Mains from the aqueducts fed water into the baths. Water was sometimes raised from the basement of a bath by a force pump. One water-lifting machine was worked by men inside a treadmill. Roman aqueducts are known today by the arches that span valleys in France, Spain, and Italy. Actually, the aqueducts ran most of the way underground. During the empire, the city of Rome was served by fourteen aqueducts and had an estimated daily water supply of 300,000,000 gallons—enough to supply a large modern city. Workmen quarried and transported 40,000 wagonloads of stone every year for sixteen years for one forty-six-mile aqueduct. The Romans were proud of their aqueducts; an engineer asked: "Will anyone compare the idle pyramids... with these indispensable aqueducts?"

The stone channels of the aqueducts branched off in the city into hundreds of distribution tanks or reservoirs. Water mains led from the bottom of the tanks to the public baths, fountains, and public buildings. From the top, pipes led to private consumers—houses and water mills. The aqueducts needed constant repairs because of leaks. But Roman aqueducts were so solidly built that some of them are still used today.

Baths and some houses were heated by a system that supplied warm air from a furnace through chambers under the floor and flues in the walls.

PORRIDGE AND PEACOCKS' TONGUES

After the bath, men and women went home to dinner. In the early republic, the main dish was a porridge made of spelt, a kind of wheat. The first professional cook came to Rome in 190 B.C., and the first bakery opened about twenty years later. The baker was also the miller, for poor people didn't have millstones with which to grind their wheat. A huge and profitable bakery

191

industry grew up because bread was the staple of the Roman diet. A baker at Pompeii had "Welcome profit!" written on his threshold.

Poor citizens were doled out grain by the government. They made porridge of it or took it to a miller, who ground it and baked their bread. A bakery turned out thousands of loaves at a time. Sometimes the baker stamped his name on the top of the dough.

Besides bread and porridge, the poor lived on vegetables, salt fish, and olive oil. Apart from a rare slab of bacon, they ate no meat. In fact, when Roman soldiers on the march ran out of grain and had to eat meat, they considered it a great hardship.

Romans usually didn't eat any breakfast. But when they did, they ate perhaps a piece of bread with some dried fruit. The cold remains of last night's dinner were served for lunch. Dinner was served before four in the afternoon. In well-to-do households it was a long meal. The elder Pliny, who wrote the *Natural History*, was considered a modest man because he spent only three hours at dinner. Banquets sometimes lasted ten hours.

A host giving a dinner party couldn't count on his guests arriving on time, what with cloudy days spoiling the sundial or water clocks dripping at different speeds. He sent his slaves to fetch them. Eight guests and the host made a good dinner party. Like the Greeks, the Romans reclined on cushioned couches. Three large couches were fitted together around a table, leaving one end open for serving. Three guests, who had slipped off their sandals, stretched out on each couch and leaned on their left elbows to eat. When a guest asked for his slippers, he was leaving. Guests wore loose dinner gowns when dining, in cold weather sending them in advance to their host's home.

In the early republic, envoys from Carthage dined at several Roman dinner parties on the same set of silverware. Only one citizen was rich enough to own silverware, and so lent his set to his neighbors. After Rome defeated Carthage, silver flowed into Rome from the Spanish mines Carthage had

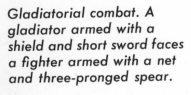

Gladiatorial combat. A gladiator armed with a shield and short sword faces a fighter armed with a net and three-pronged spear.

worked. Every well-to-do household soon had silver cups and platters. In the empire, Romans used knives, spoons, and toothpicks, but not forks. They ate with their fingers. Slaves poured perfumed water over the guests' hands between courses. Guests often brought their own napkins to tie around their necks. At the end of the dinner, they wrapped up some of the goodies in their napkins to take home with them.

Dinner was usually served in three courses. First came the appetizers—shellfish, lettuce, eggs; then the main dishes—chicken and ham; and finally dessert—apples and wine. Imperial Rome has become a byword for sumptuous meals—emperors gave twenty-two-course dinners. But even in the republic the menu for a feast included sea urchins, oysters, thrush on asparagus, roast hen, oyster and mussel stew, chestnuts, loins of doe and boar, game pie, sow's udders, pig's head, duck, hare, and bread pudding.

Roman poultry farmers raised more than chickens, ducks, and geese. They sewed the eyelids of swans and fattened them by force. They netted cranes and storks and raised peacocks. They force-fed geese with figs to enlarge their livers. They caged the squirrel-like dormice, raised snails, and penned wild boars.

It wasn't considered a banquet if peahen and wild boar weren't served. Mullets were often brought to the table in fish tanks and cooked before the guests. Hosts decorated their guests and tables with roses, and Nero had a dining room whose ivory roof tiles could be shifted to shower down a fortune in blossoms on the heads of the diners.

BREAD AND CIRCUSES

Poor citizens rarely ate at a feast. "The people," said the poet Juvenal, "anxiously want only two things—bread and circuses." They lined up every month for the wooden tickets that entitled them to free grain. In the early empire, over 300,000 Romans received these tickets. And public officials, rich men, and the emperors gave them their "circuses." The emperor Claudius called the public spectacles he gave the people *sportulae*. A *sportula* was the little basket of food a patron gave his poor client. (And so we get our word "sports.")

The circuses or public games began in the earliest days of Rome. They consisted mainly of chariot races, gladiatorial fights, and animal fights. Public games were held to celebrate the return of a victorious general and to pay homage to the gods who gave victories. Towns of all sizes held games, but so many people flocked into the city of Rome for the big games that they had to live in tents and shanties. Houses and tenements were deserted, and burglars had a field day with everyone at the games.

During the empire, the games lasted all day. Since they were originally religious in nature, citizens weren't supposed to eat in the stands. Still, some emperors shut their eyes to this rule. Slaves brought their masters hampers of food and jars of wine. The emperor's slaves even tossed fruit, nuts, and cheese to the poor citizens. The emperor also showered the spectators with raffle tickets. The lucky persons who caught them won everything from a jewel or a table to a ship or a farm.

Chariot races were held in a large stadium. More than 200,000 spectators could crowd into the Circus Maximus in the city of Rome. Originally a

A centurion, originally the officer in charge of a hundred soldiers. He carries a vine staff, the emblem of his office.

wooden structure, it collapsed so many times, crushing thousands to death, and caught fire so often that it was rebuilt in stone and decorated with marble.

The races began with a circus parade. With trumpets blaring, Romans carried statues of their gods on litters, or mules and elephants pulled them in wagons through the arch of the circus and paraded around the track. When the games official or emperor arrived, the crowds rose and cheered, waving handkerchiefs. Some emperors distributed free handkerchiefs beforehand.

At first there were ten races a day; later on, twenty-four, lasting the entire day. Like the jockeys of our day, the charioteers were great public favorites. The charioteer Diocles ran 4257 races, won 1462 first places, earned over a million dollars (in our money), and retired at the age of forty-two. Some charioteers were as young as thirteen when they competed.

In republican days, race horses were owned by private breeders. In imperial days, groups of capitalists invested in four different stables—called blues, whites, reds, and greens from the livery horse and charioteer wore. Spectators betted on their color. Supporters of the different colors fought bloody street battles with each other. One racehorse owner painted homing swallows with the winning color to let the folks back home know which stable had won. The emperor himself backed a particular color. To bet against an emperor's color was one way to show dissatisfaction with his government. Nero, who favored the greens, went to the circus in a green toga and had green copper dust sprinkled over the sand at the track.

The charioteers lined up their horses and chariots under arched stalls at one end of the track. A rope between the stall pillars held them in check until the games official tossed down a cloth to signal the start of the race.

A beast fight, before the imperial box at the arena. In some arenas the trained fighters could seek protection behind fences or inside cages.

Each charioteer's head was protected with a helmet that covered his forehead and cheeks in case of a fall. The horses' reins were fastened to his belt. If the chariot pole broke away from the horses or a wheel slipped off, he could be yanked out of the chariot and dragged along the ground. He therefore kept a knife in his belt with which to cut the reins. Charioteers had to race around the track seven times.

Horses as well as charioteers were idolized by the Roman public. The emperor Caligula saw to it that his favorite racehorse slept beneath a purple blanket in a marble stall, with a band of slaves to take care of his needs. The day before the races, Caligula sent his troops to keep the neighborhood quiet so as not to disturb the horse's rest. It was said that he even planned to make the horse consul—a high honorary office.

Gladiatorial fights began with the Etruscans, who had ruled over the early Romans. When an Etruscan chief died, his slaves, who had been war captives, were sacrificed at his funeral. At a later date, they were armed and fought each other to the death in hand-to-hand combat instead. The Romans adopted the custom, not only in honor of funerals, but for all public holidays. Captives, slaves, and criminals filled the ranks of the gladiators, but rich youths or ruined men sometimes joined them. In the republic, trainers kept schools of gladiators, especially at Rome and Capua. In Cicero's time, 5000 gladiators trained at Capua. Trainers exchanged and sold their gladiators, hired them out for games, and formed them into private armies. Under the empire, the government ran the gladiatorial schools.

At school, gladiators lived in tiny, windowless barrack rooms. Those who tried to escape were scourged, branded, and chained. Many committed suicide. When not training, gladiators were unarmed. When training, they were guarded by soldiers. Gladiators were fed mainly barley, which was supposed to make them strong. Each school had its own surgeon to care for the wounded.

A beginner practiced with a wooden sword, fencing at a post or a straw man. His trainer, who was often a former gladiator, called out the gladiatorial terms that were the Roman equivalents of our fencing terms like "parry" and "riposte." When the gladiator fought in the arena, his trainer and even excited spectators shouted out the terms. After he had mastered the strokes, he practiced with heavier weapons than those he would use in the arena.

196

Gladiators fought in amphitheaters—open-air, circular or elliptical buildings. The Flavian Amphitheater in Rome—known as the Colosseum—was an eighty-arched building three stories high, seating about 50,000 spectators. On hot sunny days, sailors from the fleet climbed to the top tier and strung strips of awning across the stands to shade the spectators.

Posters painted on house walls and on roadside tombs announced the dates when games would be held. The night before the games, the gladiators were given a free banquet. The public often came to stare, watching carefree men swill down wine and cautious men bid their families good-by. The games opened with a parade of gladiators, Then came an exhibition by the gladiators with blunt swords, to the music of horns, trumpets, and flutes. Finally, the fights began in earnest, with as many as 350 pairs of gladiators. One gladiatorial show lasted 117 days, with almost 5000 pairs of gladiators fighting.

There were several different kinds of gladiators. One fought with a net and a three-pronged spear or trident. If he failed to enmesh his opponent with the first throw of his net, he could draw it back with a string. His opponent, called a "pursuer", fought with a sword and protected himself with a shield and a visored helmet. When the net fighter fought with a Gaul, who wore a helmet with a fish on top, he sang out, "I'm not attacking you, I'm attacking the fish; why do you run from me, Gaul?" Other gladiators used lassos instead of nets; tattooed Britons fought from speeding chariots.

The inner ruins of the Colosseum show the underground rooms where animals and prisoners were caged and from which scenery could be raised.

Not all gladiators fought willingly. Armed with whips and red-hot pokers, their trainers goaded them into action. When a gladiator lay wounded on the ground, he put down his shield and lifted his left arm, asking for mercy. The games official or the emperor had the right to spare him, but usually left the decision to the spectators. If they thought he had put up a good fight, they waved their handkerchiefs or put their thumbs down, saving his life. If they put thumbs up toward the breast, they asked for his death. His opponent then finished him off and raised his right arm in a victory salute. (Because of a mistranslation, we now use the term "thumbs up" to mean approval, and "thumbs down" to mean disapproval. But the Romans meant just the opposite.) Attendants rushed out, hit the fallen gladiator on the head with a hammer to make sure he was dead, and then dragged him out of the arena.

The public worshiped victorious gladiators, despite the fact that most of them were slaves and criminals. Gladiators won bags of gold, had their portraits painted on vases and dishes, and had their deeds scratched on walls. Boys played at being gladiators, and women practiced fencing in gladiator outfits. Highborn ladies even entered the arena to fight. A gladiator who won many victories was finally awarded a wooden sword—the token of his freedom.

Gladiators fought in the afternoon, after business hours, so that everyone could watch the show. Animal fights took place in the morning. The Roman animal shows were said to have changed the habitats of many wild species. Leopards, ostriches, lions, rhinos, hippos, crocodiles, and panthers were hunted, caged, and shipped to Rome. Some of them were trained to do tricks. Monkeys drove chariot races. Lions chased hares, caught them in their teeth, brought them back to their trainers, then let them go.

Romans weren't satisfied with mere tricks. After Pompey, a general, paraded 500 lions and 17 elephants at the Circus, he let the lions loose in the arena. The spectators felt sorry for the trumpeting elephants, but that didn't stop the animal fights. In Augustus' reign, 3500 elephants were killed in the Circus at Rome. The animals fought not only each other, but also armed men. Like gladiators, animal fighters were usually slaves and criminals who trained at schools.

In the early republic, a criminal condemned to death might be thrown to a wild beast. This unusual punishment was later revived, and condemned criminals were tied to stakes or sent out unarmed into an arena of wild beasts. Below the amphitheaters were cellars where the animals were caged and the condemned men and women imprisoned. There was also machinery to raise scenery from cellar to arena. A criminal might rise from the cellar below the arena, dressed as Orpheus playing his lute and enchanting trees and stones. After the audience had fully appreciated the joke, a bear was released to tear "Orpheus" to pieces.

In the first century A.D. the beast shows were famous for two events. An African slave named Androcles was condemned to death and put into the arena with a lion. Instead of killing him—so the story goes—the lion recognized him as the man who had pulled a thorn from his foot in Africa and refused to attack him. Androcles was freed, and with his lion on a leash went from one Roman tavern to another, being treated to free drinks. The second event was the persecution of the Christians. In A.D. 64 a great fire swept for a week through the city of Rome. The homeless thousands suspected

the emperor Nero of deliberately setting the fire. Though innocent, he needed a scapegoat and ordered Christians rounded up. He had them fed to wild dogs, crucified, or dipped in pitch. Like torches, the tarred Christians were stuck into the ground of his palace gardens and set afire to illuminate night chariot races. Romans called this coat of pitch a *tunica molesta*, a "troublesome tunic." Whenever an emperor needed a scapegoat thereafter, the cry often went up, "Christians to the lions!"

Sometimes the amphitheaters were flooded for mock sea fights. Condemned criminals were dressed as Athenjans and Persians and had to row triremes on the artificial lake, refighting the battle of Salamis. It was a battle to the death. But the greatest mock sea battle was staged on a real lake by the emperor Claudius. Cavalrymen and soldiers with siege machines manned rafts to make certain that no criminal could escape. The spectators sat on the hillside or on stands erected on the banks. A silver Triton or water god, worked by machinery, rose from the lake and blew a trumpet to signal the attack. Two fleets of twelve triremes each, carrying 19,000 criminals, battled as Sicilians against Rhodians. Some of the men fought so bravely that the emperor spared their lives.

The Roman "circuses" continued well into Christian times. Gladiatorial fights lasted until the fifth century, the animal fights a century later.

SHOPPING IN TOWN

Despite free bread and games, craftsmen and shopkeepers worked hard at their trades. Shops were often located in streets named for a particular trade, such as the street of the glassmakers and the street of the harnessmakers. When Seneca lived in his apartment over a public bath, he could also hear the carpenter working next door and the blacksmith hammering away on the next block. Shops had signboards outside with trade names or easily recognized symbols—five hams, for example, indicated a butcher shop. Some tradesmen decorated their shop fronts and rooms with paintings. On the wall of a Pompeian inn, for example, the innkeeper had a painting of himself throwing out two customers, along with the words, "Do your brawling outside."

Some craftsmen worked in the back of the shop and sold in the front. A cutler, for example, had a case of knives and scissors on display in the front of his shop, while in the rear he had a forge where he made them. Wives often worked with their husbands, keeping the accounts.

Workmen in the different trades and crafts banded together into guilds. The guilds didn't try to better working conditions or raise wages. Members paid dues to hold feasts and celebrate birthdays and to save up for funeral expenses. A typical guild "feast" consisted of bread, sardines, and wine. There were guilds of furriers, ropemakers, sandalmakers, tanners, carpenters, house wreckers, paint sellers, perfumers, glassmakers, brickmakers, laundrymen, fullers, and porters. At ports like Ostia, even the shipping companies formed guilds. Mosaic pavements in front of their offices, with their guild names or emblems such as dolphins and anchors, can still be seen today.

Just as medieval guilds had patron saints, so each Roman guild had a patron god or goddess. On Vesta's day, which the bakers celebrated, they put wreaths on their donkeys, decorated their shops, and closed for a holiday.

Romans bargained with shopkeepers and craftsmen before buying anything, whether it was a cheap metal mirror or an expensive citronwood table. Even a schoolteacher expected the fathers of his students to knock down his fee. In the empire, things like statues, which had been luxuries under the republic, came within bargaining reach of many. If a man wanted an inexpensive statue of himself, he bought a secondhand one and had the head sliced off. He then had a sculptor model his head and fit it onto the old statue.

Roman vehicles. A cart carrying wine in a "tank" made of animal skins, and a passenger carriage of imperial times.

Facing page: A man-
"powered" crane.
The movement of the men
inside the treadmill operated
the wheels and pulleys that
did the hoisting.

Town criers walked through the streets and forums, announcing lost articles and runaway slaves and the dates of auctions. Men did most of the shopping, though women shopped for shoes, clothes, and cosmetics. Near the arenas, men and women could buy their horoscopes from fortunetellers. Hungry shoppers could stop for a bite or a drink at a kind of snack bar with a counter or at a small café with a back room and tables.

COUNTRY VILLAS

When they were tired of the games, the dinner parties, the shopping, and the city's heat and noise, rich Romans went to their country villas. A villa had once been a simple farmhouse. By the end of the republic, a villa usually meant a country retreat. If it had farmlands, the owner usually leased them to tenant farmers. Cicero owned seventeen country villas. If he wanted the mountain air, he went to his villa on a mountain slope with its terraced gardens and shady groves. For the sea air, he went to his villa at Pompeii, on the Bay of Naples.

In the first century A.D., Pompeii was a prosperous provincial town of perhaps 20,000—a town of bakers, fullers, wine merchants, innkeepers, bartenders, fishermen, shoemakers, gladiators, and soldiers. It wasn't a city of riotous living. But even towns the size of Pompeii had theaters, arenas, forums, and public baths. Rich Romans built villas on the beautiful coast of the Bay of Naples and took their holidays there. They were the "summer residents" of Pompeii.

In A.D. 63 an earthquake destroyed a good part of Pompeii. The government at first didn't even know whether the town was worth rebuilding. When Vesuvius began erupting in August of the year 79, Pompeii was almost a new town. Volcanic rocks and ash began cascading down the mountain and over the towns, villages, and farms that lay at its foot. Some Pompeians fled with all they could carry. Others waited in the hope that the eruption would stop.

Pliny the elder, the scientist, had watched the eruption from a distance. Being an admiral, he ordered a fleet of ships to make toward the coastal towns. He landed at a neighboring town of Pompeii to rescue an old friend, and there he stayed the night. When stones and ashes showered down on the house, he and his friend tied pillows on their heads with napkins and made for the water. Pliny died at the shore, choked by sulphurous fumes. A wave of darkness drifted over Pompeii, shutting up the townspeople as in a dark room. Then white volcanic ash covered the city like a layer of deep snow. Pompeii disappeared.

The villas that were buried at Pompeii were doll houses compared to the immense villa of the emperor Hadrian at Tibur (modern Tivoli, near Rome). Hadrian had traveled throughout his empire. Back home, he wanted to keep the memory of the finest buildings he had seen on his travels. On about 160 acres in the Sabine Hills he therefore built, though on a smaller scale, Aristotle's Lyceum, Plato's Academy, the Painted Porch of Athens, and a replica of an Egyptian canal and temple in a suburb of Alexandria. Among the other buildings belonging to Hadrian's villa were Greek and Latin libraries, theaters, baths, a stadium, palaces, slave quarters, army barracks, temples, and replicas of the Greek afterworld—the Elysian Fields (or Islands

Roman surveyors using an instrument called a groma to determine level ground for a camp or town site.

202

of the Blessed) and Tartarus (or hell). The last had underground rooms in imitation of the underworld where evildoers were supposedly punished for their crimes on earth.

TRAVELING ON THE ROMAN ROADS

A Roman traveled to his country villa by horse-drawn carriage or was carried in a litter by eight slaves. His son took short trips in a sports chariot. Towns had "taxi stands," where a traveler could hire a litter or a cart. Romans traveled by day, for even near the city of Rome it wasn't completely safe to travel by night. Soldiers who had deserted from the legions, runaway slaves, and escaped gladiators became highway robbers. A famous bandit roamed Italy with a band of 600 men and became almost a legendary hero before he was caught and sent to the arena.

For short trips, men drove in two-wheeled carts pulled by a horse or a mule. For longer trips, they rode in four-wheeled wagons pulled by teams of horses. The wagons were roofed over with cloth, leather, or even wood and were sometimes large enough to hold a bed and serve as a sleeper coach. Government officials and messengers often traveled on horseback. They received a *diploma*, or letter folded double, which guaranteed them fresh horses and lodging at government way stations.

The Romans, said a Greek of the first century A.D., "spanned the rivers with bridges, penetrated the mountains with carriage roads, peopled the deserts, and established order and discipline everywhere." They opened all the world's doors and gave each man "the opportunity to see everything with his own eyes." The Roman Empire had more and better roads than most countries of modern Europe before 1850. By A.D. 300 there were more than 50,000 miles of paved roads. The roads hadn't been built for tourists or trade, but to move the army and its supplies. After the army came a stream of administrators, colonists, and state messengers.

Where possible, Roman roads were built in straight lines, going up hills and over marshes rather than detouring. The Appian Way, built in 312 B.C. and connecting Rome with Capua, was Rome's oldest paved road. When it was extended to Brundisium (Brindisi) and had to cross marshland, Roman engineers had the roadbuilders erect a viaduct. Roman roads were built to last. They remained the commercial highways of the Middle Ages. Some Roman bridges are still used today. An example is the bridge over the Tagus, at Alcántara, in Spain.

Milestones, some over five feet high, were set up along each road every 1000 paces, or 1620 yards. These gave the distance from the nearest town and, sometimes, distances between towns. In the Forum at Rome, Augustus set up a Golden Milestone listing the distances from Rome to all the chief cities of the empire. Post stations and resthouses were also built at intervals along every road. Only government officials and messengers with diplomas could use them.

Towns grew up along the roads, with inns called by such names as the Camel and the Great Eagle. One advertised on its sign: "One word, traveler: enter." A famous stop along the Appian Way, thirty-three miles from Rome, was called the Three Taverns. Many Christians flocked to the Three Taverns to greet St. Paul when he arrived in Italy on his way to Rome.

Standard bearer. The movements of the standard helped direct the soldiers.

204

If they could, Romans stayed at a friend's villa on the road rather than take a chance on an inn. When Caesar was traveling to Puteoli (Pozzuoli), he once stopped over at Cicero's villa along the road. After he had left, Cicero dashed off a letter to his friend Atticus: "He wasn't a guest to whom you'd say, 'Do please come again on your way back.' Once is enough."

Romans buried their dead alongside their roads. The Appian Way was lined with tombs for nine miles outside the city of Rome. It was only wide enough for two carts to pass each other, and the tombs prevented the road from ever being widened. Some Roman tombs were community graves, with niches in the walls to accommodate the marble or clay urns holding the ashes of 3000 persons.

When the Christians buried their dead in Rome, they followed Roman custom. The underground rock tombs known as catacombs were usually excavated from private graveyards. They weren't secret passages—Etruscans and Romans had both built catacombs for their dead. In the Christian catacombs—corridors about three feet wide and six feet high, with small

Roman legionaries in military maneuvers (as pictured on a monument).

205

rooms between—the dead were buried in wall niches, row on row. Marble or tile slabs marked the graves. Christians went to the catacombs for funeral services. In times of persecution, some may have hidden in them.

THE ROMAN LEGIONS

The Roman roads were often built by soldiers called legionaries. The soldiers also worked on aqueducts and walls, harbors and bridges. They helped plant vineyards and wipe out plagues of locusts. In the early republic, every citizen served in the army. But by the end of the republic, only professional soldiers served in the legions. Besides his pay, the soldier received a *salarium*, money to buy salt. (His "salt money" became our "salary.")

Rome didn't have a standing army until the empire. It consisted of twenty-five legions, each legion numbering 6000 men. Men enlisted for

On the stern or poop of an incoming merchant ship, the captain offers a sacrifice to the gods as thanksgiving for a safe return. Statues of gods line the harbor.

sixteen (later twenty) years, weren't allowed to marry, and, if they were foreigners, became citizens when they were discharged.

A legionary carried an iron-rimmed shield that covered his body, wore a two-edged sword fastened to a leather belt on the right side, and hurled a seven-foot iron-headed javelin in battle. When the javelin struck, the shaft fell off or the head bent so that it couldn't be pulled out and thrown back. In one battle, enemy troops had to throw away their shields because they couldn't remove the heavy Roman javelins. The legionary wore a metal-plated leather coat of armor with a tunic underneath. When he was stationed in a cold country, he wore "barbarian" trousers.

Before a battle, the legionaries always built a camp. Under the empire, these camps were permanent buildings located on the frontiers. Surveyors chose a camp site that sloped downhill and marked off a quadrangle large enough to hold an army of two legions. The legionaries then dug a trench around the quadrangle and piled up the earth in a mound inside the trench. They drove tall wooden stakes into the mound to form a picket fence or palisade. Roads were marked out, crossing the camp at right angles, and where the roads reached the palisade, there were four guarded gates. The men built headquarters, a paymaster's office and a hospital, laid out a forum for a meeting place and camp market, and set up tents for themselves. In the camps of the empire, soldiers lived in permanent barracks rather than tents.

Legions were stationed at the same frontiers for hundreds of years. The

soldiers built clubrooms, warehouses, even baths. Towns grew up near the camps. Bonn, on the Rhine, today's capital of West Germany, was once a Roman camp. When a man reached the end of his enlistment, he received a lump sum of money, often married a local girl, and settled in the neighborhood of his old camp. Eventually the legionaries were recruited from the provinces where they served.

ROMAN GALLEYS AND MEDITERRANEAN PIRATES

The legions created the Roman peace. From the corners of the known world foreign goods poured into Italy. A rich Roman slept under an embroidered coverlet from Mesopotamia, hunted with dogs from Britain, ate mackerel caught off the coast of Spain, and spiced his food with pepper from the Malabar coast of India. Special pepper barns were built in the center of Rome to hold the spices from the Orient. Pepper became so important even to barbarians that Alaric the Goth demanded 3000 pounds of pepper as part of his price for not destroying Rome in the year 408.

The Roman woman cooked with Tunisian olive oil in Spanish copper pots, set her food on pottery dishes made in Gaul, and poured wine in Syrian glasses on her Moroccan citronwood table. She placed branches of Indian citron in her cupboards to keep the moths out of woolen togas. She combed her hair with an Indian tortoise shell and wore Iranian turquoises on her wrist and Indian pearls for earrings. Both men and women perfumed themselves with oil mixed with Arabian incense. After Nero kicked his wife Poppaea to death, he is said to have burned a year's supply of incense at her funeral.

It was expensive to ship by land. A Roman who bought an oil press at Pompeii discovered that it cost him more than his purchase price to transport it by oxcart the few miles to his farmhouse. It was cheaper to ship by water—by river barge or seagoing merchant vessel.

Roman sailing ships carried hundreds of thousands of tons of grain a year from Egypt, Sicily, and North Africa. It was cheaper to import grain than buy it locally. A fleet of grain clippers plied a steady route between Alexandria and Puteoli. Romans lined the shores when these giant ships reached Italy. Besides grain, the ships carried as many as 600 passengers. Even the emperor preferred to sail to Egypt by grain clipper rather than warship. When St. Paul sailed to Rome, he was almost drowned when one of these clippers was shipwrecked off Malta. Roman merchantmen sailed through the Red Sea and let themselves be swept by the monsoon to the Indian coast, to pick up cargoes of pearls, pepper, cotton, and cinnamon. A trade mission from the emperor Marcus Aurelius Antoninus reached the court of China in A.D. 166. The Chinese, who called the emperor An-tun in their *Annals*, recorded that the Romans "are honest in their dealings, and there are no double prices."

Throughout Roman history, the rich cargoes from Asia and Africa tempted Mediterranean pirates. Pirates in their swift ships found the slow-going merchantmen easy prey. But pirates attacked more than merchant ships. When Caesar was sailing to Rhodes to study at a famous school, his ship was boarded by pirates, who held him for ransom. After his family had paid the ransom, Caesar vowed to the pirates that he would return and wipe them out. He assembled a fleet at Miletus, in Asia Minor, sailed back to the

Coin with head of Caesar.

Head and tail of a coin. Above: Augustus. Below: Apollo, god of manly youth and beauty, poetry, music, and wisdom.

pirate lair, and made good his promise. Because they had treated him kindly, he had their throats cut before he crucified them.

Pirates raided coastal towns and sold their captives into slavery. Illyrian pirates off the coast of what is now Yugoslavia sent out fleets of hundreds of ships to board merchantmen. The southern coast of Asia Minor, with its many inlets and coves and mountain ridges beyond, was an infamous pirate stronghold. In the first century B.C., these Cilician pirates had a fleet of a thousand ships. They carried off whole towns and made treaties with others. They raided the Italian coast and held Roman women for ransom and even sailed into the Tiber and sank a fleet lying at anchor in the roadstead.

Rome finally put Pompey in charge of ridding the Mediterranean of these pirates. With a fleet of sixty ships, Pompey sailed from Gibraltar eastward, driving the pirate ships ahead or into his shore forces operating off the European and African coasts. The last ships surrendered off the pirates' rock fortress in Cilicia, a miniature Gibraltar five hundred feet above the sea. Pompey resettled the pirates as colonists, but that didn't stop piracy in the Mediterranean. More than a hundred years later, the emperor Vespasian had to send forces to destroy a pirate base attacking Egyptian and Red Sea trade. The base was the ancient city of Joppa, today's Jaffa, a seaport in Israel.

The battleship of the Roman fleet was the quinquereme, with 300 rowers. There were thirty oars on each side, with five men pulling each oar. The oars were so long that the handles had to be weighted with lead to help balance them. Though Roman citizens never rowed these ships, neither did slaves. If slaves were needed to man the oars, Rome took the precaution to free them first. Egyptian and Syrian lads left home to become sailors in the Roman fleet. They signed up for twenty-six years and became citizens when they were discharged.

Roman warships were larger than any wooden warship that fought in the Crimean War, in the 1850's. Antony's ships at the battle of Actium in 31 B.C., when Cleopatra's ships raised sail and fled, were as large as Nelson's at the battle of Trafalgar.

SACRED CHICKENS AND FOREIGN GODS

When the fleet sailed or the legions marched, a special officer went along with a coop of "sacred" chickens. Before battle, he fed the chickens. If they gobbled up their food, he interpreted that as a sign from the gods that the Roman forces would be successful. Once when an admiral was about to engage an enemy ship, the officer in charge of the sacred chickens tried to stop him, telling him that the chickens wouldn't eat. "Then let them drink," the admiral answered, tossing the coop overboard. He lost the battle—as a result, the Romans believed, of disobeying signs from heaven.

In Rome, elected officials called augurs looked for signs from the gods in the heavens or in the livers of sheep. Important decisions were never taken unless the augurs found the signs favorable. Augury became a political weapon. Toward the end of the republic, Roman Senators would postpone the vote on important issues by pretending to go outside to look for flashes of lightning. But even a hundred years earlier, Cato had already said that he didn't see how two augurs could pass each other without grinning. Still, the mass of the people remained superstitious, reporting showers of stones in the sky and

A coin struck by a money-maker named Carisius. On it are shown anvil, tongs, mallet and the cap of Vulcan, patron of smiths.

blood spurting from cut blades of wheat. Even the educated, who didn't believe in the signs, used to sacrifice a sheep just to play safe.

The early Romans had been "pious." Piety meant dutiful conduct to parents, relatives, public officials, and the gods. The Roman didn't pray to be made good. He asked the gods for health and wealth. By worshiping his household gods with the correct rites, he guaranteed himself prosperity at home. By taking part in the state festivals, he believed he was guaranteeing the welfare of Rome.

In his home a farmer never let the fire go out on the hearth. To let it go out meant disaster. For the same reason, the fire in the state hearth also was never allowed to go out. Vestal Virgins tended the fire in Rome. These were four (later six) girls from good families who had taken a vow of chastity. If a Vestal broke her vow, she was buried alive. After Vestals had served for thirty years, they returned to private life.

Public officials called pontiffs—"bridgebuilders"—had charge of the state religion. They were politicians as well as priests. Among their other duties, they kept track of the calendar, which until Caesar's time had 355 days in the year. They used to stretch out the length of a month to keep a friend in

The Romans were expert at besieging a city. Shown here are two kinds of artillery. Far left: an onager (the word means "wild ass"; its rear end kicked up when it was fired), and center: a catapult capable of hurling a six-pound javelin some five hundred yards.

Roman bridges were built to last. This ancient one at Rimini is still in use.

office, or cut short a month to hasten relieving a general of his command. Since they announced when the festivals would take place, a farmer sometimes found himself celebrating the harvest festival when it was time to sow. When Julius Caesar became chief pontiff, he reformed the calendar into a year of 365 days with a leap year every four years. The Julian calendar remained in use until the sixteenth century in most of Europe and until the eighteenth century in Great Britain and the American colonies.

The priest in charge of a Roman temple had to carry out the religious service exactly as it had always been done. If a mouse ran across the floor near the end of the service, the priest began the whole thing over again.

By the end of the republic, Roman temples had begun to crumble. Pilgrims visited them more to see the curiosities they housed than to honor the gods. Ancient temples were also museums, exhibiting famous relics and stuffed animal heads. Educated Romans had forgotten the names of some of their gods and the meaning of many of the festivals. A politician lost favor with Romans when he didn't go to the games, not when he didn't go to the temples.

But though the religious meaning might be lost, the old festivals were still celebrated. Country folk lit candles at shrines to woodland spirits and sacrificed a young goat at a country altar. After the sacrifice, the country girls hitched up their skirts and danced for joy. City folk still celebrated New Year's Day. In Rome, they went to the Field of Mars, to sing and carouse under the trees. They drank as much sour wine as they could hold. For they believed that they would live for as many more years as the number of cups of wine they could down. New Year's Day fell on March 15, the Ides of March. On such a day, in 44 B.C., Ceasar was murdered.

The emperors tried to bring back the old Roman religion. Every emperor made himself chief pontiff and was worshiped as a god. When Caligula became emperor, 160,000 animals were sacrificed at Rome. But why pray to Mercury to increase your herd, asked a Roman, and then decrease it by sacrificing the cows? Emperor worship was mainly an act of loyalty by the

212

emperor's subjects. Even the emperors didn't believe in their godhood. When the emperor Vespasian lay dying and was asked how he felt, he answered, "Alas! I fear I'm turning into a god."

Foreign gods as well as goods poured into Rome. Eastern religions took root in Rome as easily as the cherry tree first brought from Asia Minor in the first century B.C. They appealed to the people because they offered a personal relationship between worshiper and god. Women especially worshiped the Egyptian goddess Isis, who was usually depicted with the infant Horus in her arms, just like later statues of the Madonna and Child. From Persia, the Roman legions brought the worship of Mithras, a god of light. His worshipers observed the first day of the week as a holy day, were baptized and confirmed, and celebrated their god's birthday, December 25, with merrymaking.

Rome tolerated foreign gods as long as their worship didn't interfere with daily life or oppose the government. Christians were persecuted because they maintained that there were no gods but their one and only God. In Roman eyes they were therefore "irreligious." They wouldn't take part in the national festivals or go to the games. They were therefore considered unpatriotic. They wouldn't worship the emperor as a god—and so were dangerous political radicals.

According to legend, the emperor Constantine was converted to Christianity early in the fourth century after seeing a cross in the heavens with the words "By this sign you shall conquer." The political Roman empire was eventually conquered. But the empire of Christ with its center in Rome, the "eternal city," went on to conquer the Western world.

Roman roads can still be seen throughout Europe. Here is the Appian Way, called "the queen of roads," begun in 312 B.C.

Index

214

PHOTOGRAPHIC CREDITS

The publishers are grateful to the following museums and photographers for making photographs available: Alinari, pp. 136–7, 148, 157, 172, 173, 176, 188, 189, 197, 198, 199, 205, 212; American Numismatic Society, 181, 209 (top); British Museum, 20, 21, 28, 29, 44–5, 67, 96, 97, 100, 101; Chase Manhattan Museum of Moneys of the World, 208, 209 (center and bottom); Maurice Chuzeville (courtesy of the Louvre), 112; Ewing Galloway, 12, 73, 77; Gendreau, 76, 196; Giraudon, 25, 156; Madame Hassia, 64; Heraclion Archaeological Museum, 124; Friedrich Hewicker, 116, 120; Institut Royal du Patrimoine Artistique, copyright A.C.L., Brussels, 145 (top); Jewish Museum, 80 (top); Metropolitan Museum of Art, 36–7, 40, 43, 53, 60, 113, 128–9, 142, 144, 145 (bottom), 162, 168–9; Morgan Library, 22; Museum of Fine Arts, Boston, 140, 143, 149; William Rockhill Nelson Gallery, 24; Oriental Institute, University of Chicago, 58, 59, 80 (bottom), 90 (top), 108, 109; G. P. Putnam, Wonders of the Past, by J. A. Hammerton, 56–7; Thames and Hudson, Ltd., The Glory of Egypt, by Samivel, 72, and A Picture History of Archaeology, by C. W. Ceram, 61, 66; Stahley Thompson, 114; University of Chicago Press, The Code of Hammurabi edited by Robert F. Harper, 25, and The Culture of Ancient Egypt, by John A. Wilson (courtesy of Antiquity magazine), 68: University Museum, Philadelphia, 14, 16, 30.

BLACK SEA

Rome

Pompeii

ITALY

Carthage

MEDITERRANEAN

GREECE

Sparta

Athens

CRETE

SEA

EGYPT

Memphis

Mt. Sinai

NILE RIVER

Thebes

N

THE ANCIE